POLICING EGYPTIAN WOMEN

Gender and Globalization
Susan S. Wadley, *Series Editor*

Other titles in Gender and Globalization

POLICING
EGYPTIAN
WOMEN

Sex, Law, and Medicine in Khedival Egypt

LIAT KOZMA

SYRACUSE UNIVERSITY PRESS

For a listing of books published and distributed by Syracuse University Press, visit our Web site at SyracuseUniversityPress.syr.edu.

ISBN: 978-0-8156-3281-8

Library of Congress Cataloging-in-Publication Data

Kozma, Liat.

    Policing Egyptian women : sex, law, and medicine in Khedival Egypt / Liat Kozma. — 1st ed.

      p. cm. — (Gender and globalization)

    Includes bibliographical references and index.

    ISBN 978-0-8156-3281-8 (cloth : alk. paper)

 1. Women—Egypt—Social conditions—19th century.   2. Egypt—Social life and customs—19th century.   3. Honor killings—Egypt—History.   I. Title.

    HQ1793.K69 2011

    305.48'89276209034—dc23   2011025889

To my father, who should have been here to read this book.

Liat Kozma is a lecturer at the Department of Islamic and Middle Eastern Studies at the Hebrew University. She did her BA and MA in Tel Aviv University, and her PhD at New York University. Her first book, published in Hebrew by the Dayan Center in 2003, was titled *Women Write History: Feminism and Social Change in Morocco*. Her articles and research interests focus on women and sexuality in the modern Middle East.

Contents

Illustrations

Acknowledgments

This book began with what seemed to be a jewel from a treasure box: a copy of a police record from nineteenth-century Egypt, which my advisor, Khaled Fahmy, had us read in my first year in the graduate program at New York University. It was a story of a young girl who was found in a brothel and insisted that she was still a virgin. This case opened new questions that lured me to explore the Egyptian National Archives. The jewel box turned out to be more of a mine; relevant documents required some work to unearth among many fascinating murder mysteries and less fascinating land disputes and theft cases. They were also less polished than I expected them to be. But jewels they were all the same. This work therefore owes its existence first and foremost to Khaled Fahmy, who invited me into the archives, believed in my project and supported me all the way.

My committee members then helped me shape and develop this project. Linda Gordon's careful reading urged me to explore further questions that would interest scholars of gender in other societies and to clarify points that would not be clear to those who are not Middle East experts. Zachary Lockman offered useful comments and insights and continual encouragement to pursue this project. Molly Nolan raised important questions and urged me to frame my work to a doable scope. Eve Troutt Powell provided fruitful insights about slavery and served as a role model for pursuing research oversees while raising a family.

This work was undertaken mainly in the Egyptian National Archives, Bobst Library at New York University, Firestone Library at Princeton University, and the Social Sciences and History Library at the Institute of Advanced Study (IAS) in Princeton. I wish to thank here Nadia Mustafa and the other employees at the main reading room of the Egyptian National Archives for their assistance in

xi

locating and delivering the court registers. Peter Magierski, Middle East Studies Librarian at Bobst Library, helped me trace microfilms not listed in the catalogue, in both Bobst and in other libraries. Finally, the desk I was offered at the IAS's library during my husband's two years at the institute offered a refuge and a quiet spot for writing and editing my dissertation.

Mario Ruiz and Emad Hilal introduced me to the National Archives and helped me overcome the first obstacles facing a novice. They also helped me endure the loneliness of an Israeli scholar in the Egyptian archives, which was sometimes almost unbearable. The short tea breaks with Patricia Singleton in the archive's cafeteria were a welcome break throughout the spring and summer of 2004.

I am particularly grateful to my friends, Hanan Kholoussy, Hussein Fancy, Rebecca Johnson, Jessamine Price, Linda Kjosaas, Özlem Altan, and Muhammad Farag who helped me feel at home in Cairo, even in the most difficult moments. The apartment at Taha Hussein Street and Rebecca and Hussein's apartment in Muhammad Mazhar Street were like second homes for us and the kids. Muhammad Farag's cheerful visits and the tea we offered, which was never the right size, was a welcome friendship in the crowded city. During my frequent visits to Israel, Abigail Jacobson, Relli Schechter, Amy Singer, Iris Agmon, Yael Lerer, and Israel Gershoni offered encouragement and advice.

Several fellowships supported my research and writing. The Dean's Dissertation Award, awarded by the New York University's Graduate School of Arts and Sciences funded my last year of writing. The International Dissertation Field Research Fellowship, sponsored by Social Science Research Council (SSRC) funded my year of research in Egypt. The MacCracken Fellowship from New York University supported my years of studies and writing. The university's Andrew Sauter Fellowship for Predoctoral Students in the Humanities supported my first summer of predissertation research and the American Association of University Women (AAUW) International Fellowship supported my first year of study in the graduate program.

Earlier versions of chapters 1 and 2 were presented at the annual workshop of the department of Middle Eastern Studies at Ben-Gurion University. I am grateful to Aref Abu Rabi'a and Iris Agmon for inviting me to present my work to this very supportive and yet highly critical crowd, which pushed me to rethink my Ottoman context and be more critical of my archival sources. I am particularly thankful to Ron Shaham and Ursula Wokoeck for a close reading of chapter 1, which significantly contributed to its current form. Parts of chapter 3 were presented at the student conference in Tel Aviv University. Conversations that followed with Ella Keren and Ehud Toledano helped me develop a more nuanced understanding of race and life of slaves before bondage. Sections of chapter 3 were published as part of an article titled "Black, Kinless, and Hungry: Manumitted Female Slaves in Khedival Egypt" in *Race and Slavery in the Middle East: Histories of Trans-Saharan Africans in 19th-Century Egypt, Sudan, and the Ottoman Mediterranean,* edited by Terrence Walz and Kenneth Cuno, published by the American University in Cairo Press, and are reproduced here with the permission of the AUC Press, for which I am thankful.

In addition, I presented three of my chapters at the Middle Eastern and Islamic Studies' dissertation writing group and the history department's "History of Women and Gender" dissertation writing workshop. I found both forums excellent ones for openly discussing an initial draft and my thoughts in early stages of writing.

Many friends and teachers read and commented on chapters of this book or the entire work, and contributed to its present form. I do, however, take responsibility for all errors. In addition to my committee members, I wish to thank, in alphabetic order, Özlem Altan, On Barak, Indrani Chatterjee, Eyal Ginio, Alona Harness, Abigail Jacobson, Hanan Kholoussy, Everette Rowson, Sherene Seikaly, and Mitra Sharafi.

Turning a dissertation to a book is itself a challenge, and here I thank Mary Selden Evans of Syracuse University Press for believing in this project as it only was a rough outline for the manuscript it would become. Her encouraging words meant a lot to me even as I was about to give up. Peter Gran, On Barak, and the anonymous readers of my work urged me to push further my theoretical framework to frame the significant of my work. The year I spent revising my dissertation was supported by a generous postdoctoral fellowship of the Women Group of the Mexican Friends of the Hebrew University. I am thankful here to my colleagues at the Hebrew University, and particularly Ron Shaham, for their support throughout the process. I thank the Hebrew University's Authority for Research and Development for supporting the publication of this book.

Last but not least, I thank my family. Hanna and Ian Kozma kindly hosted us in Tel Aviv during our breaks from Cairo. My husband, Gady, who came to know nineteenth-century Egyptian women of ill repute on a first-name basis, challenged me with new questions and suggested new directions. Gady and our children, Noga and Ori, who followed me to Cairo, tolerated the frequent travels between Cairo and Tel Aviv, and then crossed the ocean with me for two years of writing in Princeton, New Jersey.

Introduction

In the winter of 1878, a man brought his daughter, Siddiqa, to Cairo's police headquarters after finding her away from home in the company of a prostitute. At first, Siddiqa told her father that she was still a virgin. He asked female neighbors to examine her, and they confirmed that her hymen was intact. He chose not to trust them, however, took his daughter to the police station, and demanded a medical examination. During her interrogation at the police station, Siddiqa insisted on her original version. The hakima (female medical practitioner) who examined her, however, claimed that her hymen had been damaged and that she had been deflowered "for some time now." Siddiqa then claimed that if her hymen was found to be damaged it was not due to premarital defloration. Her father had hit her back a few months earlier, she claimed. She bled as a result, but assumed it was menstrual blood. The police officers suspected she was lying, interrogated her further, and she then admitted that two prostitutes had seduced her into having sexual intercourse with men.[1]

This case, recorded in the police registers of precolonial Egypt, situates a female body at the center of competing narratives. In this story, a girl presented her own version as to the history of her body, while several authorities—her father, her neighbors, a police examiner, and police investigators—tried to confirm or challenge her versions, in search of the truth or maybe of yet another story that would reaffirm her culpability. This encounter is an instance of "state power" becoming part of familial control of a young woman's sexuality and as part of a woman's own experience of premarital defloration. It is one of multiple interactions that created and established a distinction between formal and informal medicine. It is also in these sites that the legitimacy of state power was established: where a young woman had to justify her injured hymen to a police officer and a father chose to use the police to discipline his daughter.

This book is about the formation of the state as a process that made a formal medical examination and a police investigation part of a commonsense understanding of social relations. It was such interactions between police officials and litigants that created what came to be known as the Khedival State and modern state power. I question here how formal police procedures and forensic examinations came to occupy such a crucial place not only in the official vision of order but also in Siddiqa's father's vision of objectivity and in Siddiqa's own experience of lost virginity.

~

Throughout the nineteenth century, the Egyptian province of the Ottoman Empire enjoyed increasing autonomy due to the efforts of Mehmed Ali Pasha, its governor from 1805 to 1849, and his heirs. Mehmed Ali created his own mass-conscripted army, waged independent military campaigns, and enacted a series of legal and medical reforms independently of Istanbul. In 1841 he forced the Empire to recognize Egypt's autonomy and his family as its rulers. His grandson ʿAbbas (1848–54), his son Saʿid (1854–63), his grandson Ismaʿil (1863–79), and Ismaʿil's son Tawfiq (1879–92) enacted further independent economic and legal policies, and created a localized Ottoman-Egyptian elite.

The governors' policies, alongside Egypt's integration into world economy, affected urban and rural landscapes. In Cairo, new neighborhoods featured new architectural styles modeled after Paris, and Egypt's rulers cleaned up the cities.[2] In the countryside, corvée workers dug irrigation canals and laid railroads and telegraph lines. Agricultural production was increasingly geared to meet the needs of European cotton markets. Public works projects and conscription to the army mobilized peasants, some of whom ended up in the cities.[3] As historian Judith Tucker demonstrates, these developments undermined the family as an economic unit and transformed power dynamics and gender relations. Economic and social transformations affected women most powerfully, as they deprived many of family- and community-based social protection. Migration to the cities, conscription to the army, and the corvée disrupted rural communities and deprived women of their protective networks.[4]

The growing power of the Egyptian state over communities, families, and individuals during the nineteenth century has been the focus of much scholarship in recent years. An increasingly powerful state required more and more non-elite labor, taxes, and agricultural production. Public security and health increasingly became the state's concern, creating new power relations that disciplined and colonized the bodies of Egyptian men and women, their homes and families, their social organizations, and their control over their lands.

Timothy Mitchell's 1988 *Colonising Egypt* is part of this scholarly tradition. Beginning from the early nineteenth century, he argues, the Egyptian state acquired new ways of infiltrating, rearranging, and colonizing the lives of individual subjects. This new state order created a modern individual, constructed as an isolated, disciplined, receptive, and industrious subject. Disorder (or the appearance of disorder) was therein constructed as a constant threat.[5] Following Mitchell, historians of modern Egypt studied Egyptian state-building efforts in terms of growing state control. State control over rural production, a strong police force, a conscript army, and the corvée all serve as examples. In particular, this power manifested itself in the state's treatment of social margins—the vagrant, prisoner, and prostitute. The policeman, the forensic expert, and the hygiene inspector, among others, enforced new regulatory measures.[6]

One alternative to this Foucauldian understanding of power is the argument that state control did not work because non-elite men and women resisted state encroachment on their everyday life. The state, this argument goes, represented an alien political force, which enforced itself through unjust impositions such as taxation, corvée, and conscription. It also represented an alien, Turkish-speaking culture differentiated in speech, conduct, dress, food, manners of transportation, and allocation of space. Peasants did not sympathize with or even understand the rulers' political agenda and never cared to. They felt no loyalty to the state and were reluctant to cooperate with its officials.[7] Such attempt to reconstruct subaltern agency situates non-elite men and women at the margins, if not totally outside power relations. It represents the counterautonomy of agents facing a similarly autonomous and coherent state, which also exists externally of and prior to historically constituted power relations.

My starting point here is different. I see modern state power as an outcome of multiple interactions between institutions and individuals, or between policemen and individual litigants. Similarly, I argue that Siddiqa's narration of lost virginity is not merely a reflection of naïve understanding of her body or an autonomous rebellion against oppression. Her understanding of her body is also a product of social relations, constructed through familial, communal, and institutional interactions. As I see the modern state and modern subjectivities as mutually constitutive, neither the "resisting agent" nor Mitchell's "disciplined self" are conceptually sufficient to explain what happened in Siddiqa and her father's interaction with the police, nor to explain the significance of such interactions in creating both modern state power and individual subjectivities.

Historian John Chalcraft criticizes Mitchell for paying little attention to the practices and discourses of the poor and subordinate, and I agree. Such discourses, once integrated into historical analysis, enable a better understanding of complex processes such as modernity, colonialism, and state formation.[8] In searching for the discourse of the poor, I do not assume its autonomous, a priori existence. I argue that our understanding of the modern state must incorporate the ways in which the disempowered learned to inhabit new norms, practices, and relationships. In this kind of relationship, agency cannot be reduced to resistance, and resistance does not exclude power and does not exist independently of it.

Such debates rely in part on the works of the subaltern studies group, historians of colonial India who since the 1980s affected research agendas of historians of precolonial and colonial societies. The works of Ranajit Guha, Shahid Amin, and others rewrote colonial and national histories to incorporate the experiences and voices of non-elite men and women. National historiography, they argued, ascribed independence to elite struggle and erased class- and caste-based conflicts within the nationalist movement, as well as subaltern struggles against colonial and indigenous oppression. Their own scholarship thus strove to reconstruct subaltern beliefs, practices, and struggles that were autonomous from elite dictates or leadership, which can be extracted by reading elite and colonial sources against the grain. Instead of a master narrative of modernization or transition to national independence, they offered multiple moments of confrontation and change, noting particularly functional, sometimes violent, changes of sign systems.[9]

Rosalind O'Hanlon's 1988 critique of the subaltern studies project is relevant to my own project. In a nutshell, she argues that human agency is never autonomous from power and that it is through multiple power relations that human subjectivity is constituted. Subaltern studies scholars, she further argues, failed to acknowledge that subaltern subjectivity did not simply oppose power but was also constituted by it. Because hegemony (or power) sets terms of resistance, analyzing the latter without the former renders our understanding of non-elite subjectivity incomplete. She offers, instead, a way to see power relations as a productive process in which power, resistance, and agency are constituted, which often yields unexpected outcomes. Power relations, she moreover emphasized, can be traced within subaltern groups and not merely between the subaltern and the elite—thus rendering power more diffuse and complex. In the early 1990s, the subaltern studies group abandoned its original emphasis on social history and focused instead on analyzing colonial and elite discourse—a move shared by some historians of the Middle East as well.[10]

My discussion of agency also relies on Saba Mahmood's reading of Michel Foucault and Judith Butler. Power, Mahmood argues, is a productive force and not merely an oppressive one. It creates new subjectivities—new forms of desires, objects, relations, and discourse. Social norms therefore are not merely an outside imposition, but rather come to constitute the very substance of one's intimate, valorized self. The subject here does not precede power relations in the form of individual consciousness, but is produced through these relations. Agency, to Mahmood, is the capacity of action that specific relations of subordination create and enable. It is bound up with historically and culturally specific disciplines through which a subject is formed.[11]

My ambitious aim in this book is to explore those historical processes that transformed ways in which women and men in precolonial Egypt came to think of themselves and the world around them. The challenge posed by the subaltern studies school, I believe, is still relevant. Social historians, including myself, are striving to recovering subaltern discourses while translating the previous critique to guidelines for empirical research. Recovering subaltern discourses, as I see it, entails reconstructing the ways in which modern subjectivities were constituted in specific times and places. Because I do not take a universal human subject as my point of departure, what I seek is a fragmented picture, a kind of mosaic, in which women's perceptions of their bodies and their experiences are constituted through specific positions and power relations in which they were situated. As I am looking for change over time, Egypt's nineteenth-century transformations (legal, medical, political, economic) are necessary for demonstrating how individual subjectivities and self-perceptions were transformed.

Subaltern studies scholars were criticized for leaving the state out of their analysis. As I demonstrate in chapter 1, this can be said of Egyptian historiography as well. When historians did acknowledge the presence of the state, they often presented it as a monolithic instrument of oppression and exploitation, whose institutions are closed to negotiation and conflict. Writing subaltern history in which individual subjects are products of power relations should also see the state as a process, in which dominant and subaltern forces are interdependent, in which interactions and dialogue transform both the state and non-elite men and women. As I demonstrate in the following text, this is also a methodological observation. The documents we read, namely, police and court records, do not reflect merely the perspective of state functionaries who wrote them and, similarly, cannot be read for autonomous voices of those illiterate litigants who resorted to the legal system. The documents, such as the actors presented in them, are necessarily a product of a dialogue.

One important starting point is looking at the changing roles of local communities in defining individual identity, providing protection, and controlling conduct. Individual life in Ottoman societies, including Egypt, was organized around several social institutions or networks that served as social anchors: the neighborhood, the guild, the Sufi order, or the village community. They took upon themselves certain tasks of economic and social regulation. In the nineteenth century, centralizing state power entailed transformation of community and family-based solidarities and modes of control. A newly formed bureaucracy was taking upon itself roles that had been previously relegated to relatively autonomous social networks.

As the guilds were dissolving, for example, guild members, both craftsmen and workers, had to adapt creatively to survive unequal world economic integration and Isma'il's state-building efforts. They compromised for subsistence-level prices, which at the very least could keep them working. Some evaded taxation or hired workers without reporting them. At the same time, new institutions and procedures enabled new forms of mobilization and new modes of agency. Guild members wrote petitions protesting unfair contract, guild dues, wages, and work conditions. They formed informal networks, below or above guild level, to protect their interests. Alongside an intermittent struggle for autonomy against the state, guild members also struggled to attain those benefits that this state could bestow.[12]

Similarly, Mine Ener demonstrates how the poor actively sought and received assistance from the new institutions, such as state-run shelters that were originally designed to punish and confine them: it was therefore the poor, rather than bureaucrats, that came to define the actual functions of these shelters.[13] Mario Ruiz further argues that families utilized the newly founded judiciary councils to initiate complicated lawsuits, bolstering the state's legitimacy to establish legal parameters for individual negotiation of family power. Families contested, undermined, or simply ignored state's elaborate mechanisms of control.[14] State institutions, such analysis suggests, enabled new modes of operation and created new ways of thinking of social relations.

These transformations also coincided with transformations in social meanings of the normative family. First, following European pressure, the slave trade was abolished, and later the institute of slavery itself dissolved; slaves could gain their freedom regardless of their enslavers' wishes. Slavery had long been a part of the Egyptian household, and it was now increasingly delegitimized. These changes transformed not only Egypt's political and economic status but also power relations within families and life choices of individual women.

Second, during the later decades of the century, the Victorian bourgeois family came to symbolize modernity and political maturity and became a model for an emerging *effendiyya* class. In this process, "superstitious" non-elite Egyptian women were commonly evoked as symbolic of Egypt's "backwardness": their poverty, sometimes their dark skin, and their "deviant" sexual conduct interfered with elite vision of the clean, Europeanized parks and boulevards. They were interfering with an emerging elite vision of the family, which was based on the conjugal, free, bourgeois couple; refined, competent wives and mothers heralded the new era.[15]

In the 1860s, new income from the cotton boom, caused by the American Civil War, allowed further growth of state bureaucracy and substantial infrastructure expansion. When income from cotton export decreased later in the decade, Egypt turned to large-scale foreign borrowing, which eventually led to bankruptcy and increased European control. In the 1870s, the Egyptian government could no longer pay its own employees. In 1876, Egypt declared insolvency. Britain and France subsequently set up a debt commission to oversee Egypt's budget and ensure it met its financial obligations. These measures affected many parts of Egyptian society: peasants felt a renewed tax burden, state employees were not paid, and the army was substantially reduced. The last measure brought much relief to the countryside, but it created much resentment among the substantially reduced officer corps. These developments ultimately led to the 'Urabi Revolt and the British occupation of Egypt in 1882.

Women, Sex, and Social Marginality

This book focuses on women who were positioned both on the margins of social networks and on the margins of gendered normative notions of respectability. Nineteenth-century Egyptian respectability was gendered, sexualized, and, to some extent, class-specific. Women's respectability depended on their family status as well as on their sexual conduct. For upper-class families, respectability meant seclusion and minimal contact with men. The upper-class ideal of female seclusion was supposed to prevent any casual interaction between the sexes. Similar norms affected lower-class women. However, because they could not be secluded in the home like their upper-class counterparts, their surveillance was entrusted to the entire community.[16]

Social historians have recently begun studying society's approach to women who transgressed social and normative boundaries. Most works on nonmarital sex in the Middle East, however, continue to rely on prescriptive texts such as the Qur'an, *fiqh* literature, and Ottoman and twentieth-century legislation.[17] The discrepancy between law and practice remains a pertinent question. Treating social relations, rather than illicit sex, as a unit of analysis shifts our focus from laws to social practices, allowing us to examine illicit sex as embedded in historically specific trajectories.[18]

To understand the social norms that determined the boundaries of respectability and family, this book studies instances of violation and transgression that attracted state intervention as they posed a threat to the existing social order, moments in which social order was destabilized and then restored, disturbing the boundaries separating respectable from unrespectable in the process. Those were moments of transition that transformed women's status and relation to the family: manumission turned slaves into free women; marital defloration turned girls into wives and mothers, whereas premarital defloration could marginalize them; and finally, "respectable" women who turned to prostitution threatened to destabilize accepted normative boundaries.

Relying on Foucault's *History of Sexuality* and her own research on the Dutch Indies, anthropologist Ann Stoler demonstrates how colonial power forms, produces, and navigates desire to consolidate and reproduce racial differences.[19] Like

Stoler, I am interested in patriarchal control of women as a domain in which state power was consolidated. It is here—in the familial domain and on the individual body—that reorganization of power is felt most powerfully. Whereas Stoler focuses on colonial discourses, I am more interested in particular power relations within families and communities, which new practices and discourses were creating.

Historians of colonial and precolonial India explore similar questions and demonstrate how patriarchal control of women's sexuality was vital for state formation, as well as for class- or caste-based identities. It was the relationship between central authorities and local communities that affected how widows, adulterers, or the child bride would be handled. In a 1995 issue of *Contributions to Indian Sociology*, Uma Chakravarti examined how a centralizing Peshwa state helped consolidate patriarchal control of women to reimpose caste distinctions within the Brahman elite in eighteenth-century Maharashtra; Veena Poonacha demonstrates how the colonial state affected marriage patterns and social handling of nonmarital sex among the Coorg caste, making sharper distinctions between male and female sexual transgressions; and Pren Chowdhry studied how widows in colonial Punjab could use new laws to make new claim for controlling their own sexuality and property.[20] Lata Mani's work on sati in colonial India and, more recently, Veena Das's work on women's memories of violence during the partition similarly demonstrate how state power created new modes of control of women, and how instances of violence and control created women's own subjectivities.[21]

The focus on the social margins, and here on those who were somehow relegated to the margins of the normative family, highlights some of the power relations that constitute modern societies. Like the scholars previously noted, I am interested in the social margins because conflicts over who controls women's sexuality and their conduct in public space was essential for the everyday of state formation. Who married whom and where, who would be a legitimate child and who would not, how a girl would have to narrate sexual assault and to whom— all of these edicts were changing and, with them, people's perceptions of their familial and communal roles. It is through the margins that the normative is defined, and anxiety over the boundary between the normative and the deviant reveals that transient and dynamic nature of those boundaries, often assumed to be rigid and well defined. Focusing on communal and official control of women on the margins allows me to question changing relations between center and periphery, between communities and state officials, and between "society" and "the state."

The present discussion bears on contemporary debates on women's involvement in illicit sex in Islamic societies, particularly on the disputed issues of honor killing in Turkey, Jordan, Palestine, and Israel[22] and on the Huddud Ordinance in Pakistan, which stipulates the death penalty for illicit sex.[23] In both debates, it is argued that death used to be the customary and/or Islamic punishment for illicit sex. Other reactions to such violations are normally silenced or ignored. This work argues, instead, that at least in one historical setting—late nineteenth-century Egypt—women who transgressed customary notions of honor could lose their social standing but very rarely lose their lives. Moreover, families, communities, and state authorities punished them in some cases but sought to reincorporate them in others.

The ability to use indigenous sources and to focus on social history allows as to "provincialize Europe," to use Dipesh Chakrabarty's book title. Chakrabarty urges historians of non-European societies to do so by producing narratives in which Europe would not be the main agent of historical change.[24] The focus on colonial discourse characteristic of recent historiography and anthropology is important for unraveling modes of knowledge that inform our understanding of world history to this very day. Without diminishing the significance of such scholarship, it does produce narratives critical of European hegemony but still leaves Europe at the center. My own narrative, by contrast, uses indigenous sources and makes non-elite Egyptians historical agents by describing how global and local changes were lived through their communities and life choices. Global economy, abolition of the slave trade, and legal reform are narrated through the locales in which they took place: the neighborhood community, families, and individual bodies.

A Note on Sources and Methods

Some of the sources used here are familiar to historians of Ottoman societies: European travel accounts, legal jurisprudence (fatwa), and shari'a court records. These records are far from transparent. They involve multiple layers of translation and mediation, representation and self-representation. Scribes have translated testimonies from colloquial Arabic to formal Arabic; from fragmented stories they weaved a coherent narrative, which sometimes includes legal reasoning and framework lacking in the original testimony. Sometimes they have also summarized cases from written notes, which might have been written hours, days, or even weeks after actual court deliberations. In addition, these sources represent only cases heard in court, omitting crimes and conflicts settled extrajudicially or concealed from the state.[25]

The formation of a new state and modern bureaucracy also entailed new kinds of registration. The new documents narrated events in ways that could be reviewed by higher authorities as well as by litigants themselves, who had the right of appeal. They had to include legal reasoning, relevant proof, cause and effect, relevant testimonies, dead ends and false leads. The new legal system entailed a new organization of power that required minute attention to detail, registration of facts, cross-referencing, and the ability to compare across different institutions within the same hierarchy. This period therefore witnessed the formation of a new kind of documents – narratives that state officials learned to compose and litigants learned to relate.

New state institutions produced an unprecedented plethora of records, which only few historians have hitherto explored. The rich police and court records stored in the Egyptian National Archives, moreover, have no match in other pre-colonial societies and make the Egyptian case a fascinating case study. Police files include detailed summaries of investigations and recommendations for conviction, but not actual verdicts. These summaries include testimonies, interrogations of witnesses and suspects, forensic findings, and shari'a court rulings, as well as correspondences with administrative units and individuals related to the investigation. Furthermore, Supreme Council records include, alongside the verdict, a detailed summary of the police investigation including the forensic medical report, rulings of lower councils, a summary of shari'a court proceedings, and sometimes the parties' appeals as well. They include police recommendations for conviction and/or the rulings of three legal instances, along with the relevant article of law. Such records provide some of the ruling's rationale and, sometimes, conflicting views within the system itself as to how certain cases should be treated. Third, appeal records expose some of the tensions involved in the state's interaction with its subjects as well as within and between state institutions. Finally, the rich archival sources allow comparison with shari'a court, council, and police records—sometimes of the same cases—to gain a broader perspective on the system as a whole.

My research program had a threefold challenge, as I set out to explore the officials' perspectives, non-elite perspectives, and change over time. The first was apparently the easiest, as it was state officials who authored these documents and whose point of view was dominant. However, even this perspective proved incomplete, as the state was not a coherent entity and archival sources could only allude to the complexity of power relations and struggles within its institutions. The role of subaltern administrative ranks, moreover, was left mostly undocumented.

Studying the objects of police investigations and court discussions proved a more daunting task. In studying non-elite in the archives, I found Carlo Ginzburg's methodological insights most helpful. Ginzburg reads medieval inquisition texts as dialogical, using Mikhail Bakhtin's terminology. Inside a text written by and for the elite, he argues, the historian can trace a dialogue between the author and the objects of his writing. In the space between the policeman and the men and the women he interrogates, argues Ginzburg, the historian can trace non-elite perspectives. Rather than represent a mere reflection of the elite perspective, these echo the voice of the interrogated.[26] Ranajit Guha and the subaltern studies project likewise saw documents written by colonial or indigenous elite whose content necessarily embody, not merely the will of their authors, but also the will of subaltern insurgent.[27] Similarly, Egyptian nineteenth-century records encapsulate dialogue between policemen and witnesses, crime victims or suspects. What I sought in these records were therefore patterns and tropes, and then cases diverging from them. At the same time, a comparison with many other similar cases mapped at least part of the options available to women and men in given situations.

Although I find microhistory and Ginzburg's notion of a "dialogic text" most helpful in recovering subaltern narratives, my purpose is different: I am less interested in preexisting beliefs and more interested in tropes and narratives played out in court. I do not use microhistory to trace subaltern autonomy, but rather to reconstruct the ways in which the intimate domain was touched by processes associated with Egypt's integration into the world economy and imperial interests. I am interested in the dialogue itself, as it is through this dialogue both the state and individual subjects are constituted.

Finally, it is the historian's task to trace change over time. Police and court records usually are fragmentary, relating an individual story rather than a comprehensive narrative. To trace historical change, I compared earlier and later verdicts to identify new procedures, new reasoning, and changing perspectives. I also looked for traces of economic and political influence on the social treatment of marginal women, such as the abolition of slave trade or the transformation of Cairo's urban landscape.

Chapter Outline

Chapters 1 and 2 focus on two institutions that gained importance in community and family life during the decades under review—the legal and medical systems, respectively. In both chapters I examine specific interactions between state personnel and individual litigants and question how such encounters created notions of formal and informal justice and medicine.

The next three chapters focus on three categories of women: slaves, prostitutes, and girls who were involved in premarital sex. All were touched by changing definitions of the normative family, affected by changing modes of control, and constructed as a threat to the normative family and the respectable neighborhood. Chapter 3 focuses on slaves and manumitted slaves; it questions how these women coped with new realities of abolition and of freedom as they lost the kinds of protection their enslavers' family could offer but also had state institutions as their protectors. The following chapter discusses the urban neighborhood and the role of police and *shaykh*s in regulating urban order. The struggle for neighborhood respectability, the capability to choose one's place of work and residence and the power to restrict it, were yet other sites in which modern state power was formed. Finally, the last chapter returns to Siddiqa and similar girls who were brought to the police station following premarital defloration. Here I question how new notions of body and of justice permeated both official discourse and people's narration of sexual assault and intimacy. My conclusion then questions how these institutions and processes constitute a social history of modern state formation.

POLICING EGYPTIAN WOMEN

1

Egyptian Legal Reform

On 27 November 1865, 'Abdallah 'Ali Sulayman from Abu al-Waqf village in al-Minya Province in Upper Egypt approached the village *qadi* and informed him that his maternal cousin Sariyya had been murdered by her maternal and paternal uncles for alleged involvement in extramarital sex. The *qadi* hastened to contact the district police with only his word and reputation to support his claim, as his informant, once interrogated, denied their conversation. After years of deliberation, two of Sariyya's uncles were convicted of the murder, their sentences reduced from five and three years to three years and eighteen months, respectively, due to the weakness of evidence. Relying on circumstantial evidence alone, as even the young woman's body was not found, al-Minya's district police and three legal instances were convinced that she had indeed been murdered and that the killers had indeed been her uncles.[1]

This murder case is interesting for two main reasons. First, it provides documented evidence of "honor killing." Second, it portrays a short-lived legal system that came to see honor killing as a crime. The existence of a handful of honor-killing cases in the archives of precolonial Egypt is related to the emergence of a new relationship between the central authorities and other sources of power and authority. The authority to discipline girls for alleged sexual misconduct was contested here. Different social actors—council members, lower-rank *qadi*s, local policemen and village headmen, neighbors, cousins, brothers, fathers and mothers of murder victims—played their part in the drama of Egypt's transformation in pre-colonial decades. I use "honor killing" as a case study of multiple competing and complementing power relations. More than any other case discussed in this book, it confuses notions of "subaltern resistance" and "state oppression." In a close analysis of one case study, the positioning of each

1

actor is carefully analyzed to demonstrate how particular choices and strategies are produced.

Sariyya's murder case does not indicate that "honor killing" was a prevalent, or even common, way of controlling and regulating young women's conduct. Patriarchal control of women involved multiple sites and practices that women sometimes lived with, sometimes resisted, and sometimes helped enforce. Honor killing was one endpoint in the patriarchal control of women's sexuality—one that was not omnipresent but, at the same time, cannot be dismissed or ignored. Historians of Ottoman societies found no explicit evidence of honor killing in earlier periods. One of the questions this chapter will address is why such murder cases figure in the records of Khedival Egypt.

I use honor killing as a starting point for discussing the social history of Egyptian legal reform. Rather than concentrating on official decrees, regulations, and institutions, such a history would explore a new organization of social relations within and between communities. This case is an example of new kinds of social relations that came to create a modern state in the Egyptian province of the Ottoman Empire. Legal reform entailed new roles for *shaykh*s and law enforcement personnel; it offered families and communities new ways of addressing justice. State power, in this stage, was a process in which litigants and defendants had an active role to play: state intervention, in many cases, was not forced on resisting peasants; it was often invited in, and at an increasing rate. Each actor's behavior in Sariyya's murder case was related to new ways of understanding how law can be used and how law works. Individual choices by Sariyya's maternal cousin, Abu al-Waqf's *qadi,* local police officials, and, later, council members made Sariyya's murder trial one of the multiple sites in which a modern state was established.

Histories of Law and Society

The dominant paradigm in both Ottoman and Egyptian historiographies presents mid–nineteenth century reforms as having taken place above and apart from society. It is a story of an elite initiative, Western-inspired reforms, and an extension of the state into hitherto autonomous domains. These reforms, articulated in this narrative, met popular indifference or resistance. Historians Rudolph Peters, Nathan Brown, and Latifa Salim, for example, argue that non-elite Egyptians did not share the elite culture and value system and had their own perceptions of justice. The state, to them, was an exploitative entity, which constantly demanded labor and taxes and gave very little in return.[2]

The counterargument sets to vindicate the Tanzimat state and to prove that laypersons were well aware of the new legal institutions and could use them freely. They saw it as "an ultimate refuge against injustice committed by their superiors, and they were willing and capable of presenting their cases there in an attempt to redress this injustice."[3] Judith Tucker's argument regarding nineteenth-century shari'a courts is similar: the legal procedure and substance of court deliberations were familiar and convenient enough to encourage non-elite women to view the court as an institution of their own.[4]

Both arguments, though seemingly contradictory, share similar assumptions regarding the relationships among law, society, and state: legal reform is an elite initiative, which the people may then accept or reject; "state" and "society," moreover, are represented as preexisting and coherent entities—during a period in which the very notion of "state power" was taking new forms, exactly when the "state" as separate from the person of the ruler was created through the formation of a new bureaucracy and came to rely on new social elements outside the small Ottoman elite.

Understanding what legal reform meant for nineteenth-century Egyptians thus entails breaking down these dichotomies. Indeed, more recently, social historians have been looking at the Tanzimat state not in terms of what "it" was trying to achieve but rather in terms of how the very notion of statehood came to be perceived and practiced, and what role legal institutions and practices came to play in creating, to use Timothy Mitchell's term, an effect of the state.[5] What we are looking for, therefore, is not a preexisting, self-conscious coherent entity that masterminds and implements a set of reforms. It is rather the formation of a discursive construction that we seek: a process that forms a modern state and turns it into a meaningful entity in people's lives. It is a process that creates both elite and non-elite notions of justice and law. The legal arena is one forum in which this consolidation of power took place.[6]

Avi Rubin, Iris Agmon, and Milen Petrov have raised such questions about the formation of the Tanzimat state over the second half of the nineteenth century. Agmon's research of Haifa and Jaffa's courts portrayed nineteenth-century Ottoman centralization as a process that took place in multiple locales, adopting and adapting their version of reform. The Tanzimat, to Agmon, was therefore a combination of selective implementation, amalgamation of local practices and instructions from the center.[7] Rubin focuses on the Ottoman center in the late nineteenth century and demonstrates how a continuous process of standardization, generalization, and systemization of the judicial sphere created a new notion of the state as a separate entity from the person of the ruler, a new concept that had to be displayed and enacted. Centralization, growth of the bureaucracy, and struggle against groups that previously gained their power as mediators—all these were part of a process that created the effect of the state.[8] Historian Milen Petrov studies the impact of the Tanzimat on the cognitive and epistemological worlds of non-elite Ottoman subjects, and he presented the court as an arena for practical negotiations and ironing out of differences between the official vision of the Tanzimat and its many subaltern understandings. Conceptualizing legal reform as a dialogue, Petrov argues that litigants deployed key elements of Tanzimat discourse in making their claims in court.[9]

In the specific Egyptian case, the changing nature of the state entailed, first, a changing composition of the elite. Already in the seventeenth century, Ottoman elites became localized in the empire's provinces, while local elites integrated in the Ottoman administration. These elites enjoyed a large measure of autonomy in exchange for revenues and recognition of Ottoman sovereignty. Until the late eighteenth century, no specific household managed to achieve hegemony. During the first half of the nineteenth century, it was the family of Mehmed Ali, an Albanian-born Ottoman official, who achieved hegemony within the Ottoman-Egyptian elite and took over the governorate. In 1841, Mehmed Ali achieved an Ottoman recognition of his family's hereditary rule in the Egyptian province. During the first decades of the nineteenth century, Mehmet Ali's administration, as in other parts of the Ottoman Empire, was composed of his loyal in-laws, kinfolk, and freed white slaves.[10]

Mid–nineteenth century Egypt became a state ruled by an expanding bureaucracy, whose power derived from its positions within the system itself rather than from personal relationship with the khedive, a process that brought about the formation of what Ehud Toledano terms "an Ottoman-Egyptian elite." Mehmed Ali and his heirs, he argues, strove to form an autonomous Egypt within the Ottoman Empire. The creation of an elite committed to long-term service in the province and having a distinct Ottoman-Egyptian identity was a crucial part of this project. Mehmed Ali and his family offered Ottoman officials significant benefits and encouraged them to stay in Egypt, while at the same time integrating new social elements from the local population.[11]

This new elite shared a common cultural heritage, loyalty to the royal family, and commitment to lifelong service in Ottoman Egypt, which separated them from the larger pool of officeholders and created a localized elite. The new administrative elite was composed of Turkish-speaking bureaucrats who had already lived in Egypt for most of their lives—a new Arabic-speaking, educated elite, a product of new state schools and students' missions to Europe and, finally, wealthy rural notables who were incorporated into state administration. According to historian F. Robert Hunter, between 1848 and 1879, 983 pashas and beys occupied high-level appointments, and the elite itself numbered several thousand individuals.[12]

This elite was not the sole maker of state. The institutions they formed and operated would not have acquired importance if people had chosen to ignore them. It is important to understand the changing composition of the Egyptian elite, however, if we want to start arguing that what the concept of state meant in 1800 was not at all what this would come to signify only fifty years later. The formation of bureaucratic institutions manned by interchangeable officials created an effect of the impersonal power of a state, in previously unknown dimensions and scope.

The neighborhood and the village, hitherto autonomous from the central administration but for taxation purposes, became part of the bureaucracy: rural nobility was integrated in the expanding bureaucracy, and bureaucrats and policemen from other parts of Egypt were employed in the countryside. The state came to incorporate new social elements, such as notables' sons, rural *shaykh*s, and local policemen. The state came to include much more than a handful of officials; it was a social entity that provided justice, regulation, employment, and telegraph and postal services. It was embodied not only in the person of the tax collector coming from Cairo or the provincial center, but in the village *shaykh* who was now answerable to Cairo and in the notable's son who studied at Qasr al-'Aini Medical School and was later appointed district medical inspector.

Reform of the Legal System

Tanzimat legislation, beginning from the 1839 Gülhane Edict, was inspired by Enlightenment principles as articulated in the French Declaration of the Rights of Man and of the Citizen and in the American Bill of Rights. Most notably, the

Gülhane and the Codes that followed decreed the nominal equality of all sub-jects regardless of their religious affiliation and the obligation to protect the "life, honor and property" of its subjects. These were couched in the rhetoric of Islamic political philosophy and law, and some of these legal principles were deeply rooted in Islamic legal philosophy and Ottoman legal tradition. At the same time, the Tanzimat were a broad social process, which made the central state's influence in everyday life felt more keenly than ever before in Ottoman history.[13]

A series of legal reforms reflected Egypt's governors' efforts to assert their autonomy from Istanbul. In 1855, following prolonged negotiations between Cairo and Istanbul, Egypt adopted the 1851 Ottoman Penal Code but adapted it to Egypt's specific legal and economic realities. The Egyptian Sultanic Code included entire chapters and references applicable specifically to Egypt. Its final structure reflected both Egypt's subordination to and its autonomy from the Ottoman Empire. The legal system developed over the following decades was one whose verdicts were ratified in Cairo rather than in Istanbul. Its personnel, more-over, was appointed in Cairo, and they were not promoted to other parts of the empire but rather remained in Egypt for their entire career.[14]

At the same time as establishing Egypt's autonomy, the reform was also designed to assert the authority of Egypt's governors over competing sources of power, such as previously independent local governors, the shari'a courts, and finally, unofficial judicial or normative authorities such as muftis and *shaykhs*. Between 1849 and 1883, the Egyptian administration subordinated both shari'a courts and local governors to a hierarchy of judiciary councils that applied the Sultanic Code. This judicial hierarchy was headed by the Supreme Council of Adjudication *(majlis al-ahkam)*, which also served as the highest court of appeal. By 1871 this system encompassed no less than five legal instances, from the small village level to the Supreme Council in Cairo, in addition to the shari'a courts.[15]

The division of labor between council and shari'a courts deserves some clari-fication. Historian Rudolph Peters, who conducted the most comprehensive and detailed study of the Khedival legal system, describes the councils as a secular judiciary, independent from the "religious" court system.[16] Peters's work is very helpful in understanding Khedival legal institutions and procedures in many respects, but his distinction between secular and religious, in this context and for this time period, is somewhat misleading. I noted earlier that many aspects of the Tanzimat reform were embedded in Islamic and Ottoman legal principles, albeit concurrently embracing Enlightenment principles and terminology. As in the Ottoman center, moreover, legal reform involved rationalization and standardization of shari'a courts—the introduction of registration standards, a hierarchy of courts and supervision measures. Legal reform concerned, as previously noted, with proper implementation of the shari'a did not have secularization as its purpose; this meant virtually nothing to most nineteenth-century reformers.

The existence of an administrative judiciary, moreover, conformed more with the Islamic principle of *siyasa* than with any notion of "separation of powers," as Peters implies. Historically, the principle of *siyasa* allowed the ruler and his officials to pursue justice when Islamic rules of evidence did not allow conviction. Before the nineteenth century, both local governors and shari'a courts applied *siyasa,* which in the Ottoman Empire was embodied in the *qanun*. In Khedival Egypt, shari'a courts remained part of the criminal procedure: shari'a courts adjudicated criminal cases when a shari'a punishment was in order, and cases were forwarded to the council only when it was not applicable. The innovation here was the unraveling of the *qanun* from both the shari'a courts and local governors, and its bureaucratization and systemization in the form of administrative councils of adjudication.

The difference between the councils and the courts, moreover, was more *procedural* than *religious:* shari'a court accepted only evidence based on actual presence in the crime scene, namely, eyewitness reports or confessions. The *siyasa* process, on the other hand, also admitted circumstantial and forensic evidence. Shari'a court procedure required the presence of all parties or their representatives, whereas the councils handled mainly documents, authored by police, medical experts, shari'a courts or petition writers. The councils adjudicated penal cases, moreover, only after receiving a shari'a court verdict, which indicated whether or not a shari'a offense has been committed. These differences are important in understanding the kinds of documents available to the historian and in stressing the inadequacy of the religious/secular dichotomy. It is important to keep in mind that these institutions were deeply rooted in the Ottoman legal tradition more than a manifestation of a Europeanizing judiciary.

Several aspects of the reform reflected the rulers' concern with public security and maintenance of order. The acceptance of circumstantial and forensic medical evidence meant that new modes of proof and legal evidence were allowed in adjudicating criminal cases, and the shari'a principle of leaving the right to initiate legal action in murder cases to the discretion of the victim's heirs was no longer considered adequate for maintaining public security.

Beginning in the 1830s, Egypt's police stations started investigating criminal cases alongside their role of maintaining order. By the 1850s, each of Cairo's and Alexandria's quarters, as well as many of Egypt's villages, had their own police station. The larger cities also had their own police headquarters. People turned to them to resolve private disputes or to initiate criminal investigations.[17] Policemen were ordered to investigate crime scenes thoroughly and to send all relevant evidence along with all suspects and witnesses to the police legal claims department. This department served as a public attorney: it specialized in legal procedures and was responsible for compiling of cases for submission to the councils.[18]

Neighborhood and village *shaykh*s were incorporated into this system of regulation and control. They were instructed to make frequent rounds in the streets and alleys under their jurisdiction and deal with minor disputes or occasional problems that they noticed themselves or that were brought to their attention. Both policemen and *shaykh*s were authorized to resolve disputes, to detain individuals for a few hours, or to enforce small fines without informing their superiors. They were expected to be familiar with all the inhabitants in their neighborhood or village and therefore had to report the arrival of outsiders, as well as all births and deaths. This information was used to confirm reputations and histories, particularly of those without criminal records. In the nineteenth century, village *shaykh*s were gradually incorporated into high ranks of state bureaucracy.[19]

Litigants' right to appeal within thirty days of their verdict was designed to serve justice and at the same time allowed for a more rigid control over low-ranking councils. The significance of the appeal procedure cannot be overstated. First, it constituted a break with the finality of shari'a judgment. Second, it gave the central administration more control over the provinces, as crimes carrying heavier prison sentences had to be forwarded to a higher court for approval, even without an appeal. Finally, it enabled litigants to appeal their verdict and have their voices and concerns heard at different stages of the legal procedure. As I demonstrate in the following text, official decrees ordering the foundation of new councils indicate that people's extensive use of the appeal procedure was one of the motivations for the system's expansion and growth. Already, one notices that "resistance" is not an adequate category for explaining how and why people used the system; it is an indication that this system was very much in use.

One may also observe a particular concern with monopolizing legal arbitration and streamlining legal arbitration to officially sanctioned institutions. Historically, shari'a courts were not interested in central registration or in monopolizing arbitration and enabled a wide range of forum shopping. In Ottoman Egypt, shari'a courts employed *qadis* of four schools of Islamic jurisprudence and allowed litigants to choose between them. Similarly, muftis' opinion was a pluralistic practice. Acting in private capacity, muftis advised *qadis* and also provided specific advice to Muslims facing real-life conflicts and dilemmas. Local communities had their own mufti whom they could consult and later submit his fatwa to court.[20] In Khedival Egypt, this plurality was no longer tolerated.

A January 1855 decree, for example, noted that people did not trust the rulings of the *'ulama* assembly and turned to the shari'a courts instead. People complained, the decree stated, that the assembly did not rule their cases properly according to the shari'a. The failure of *'ulama* to properly observe the shari'a was seen as obstructing state-defined justice: "If the provisions of the shari'a, which are the most significant basis of our Islamic *millet* are not kept in utmost accuracy and further attention to the truthfulness of the basic elements of each case—the result would be the loss of people's rights and the implementation of the court's ruling would lead to nothing but harm."[21] Another decree from the same month indicates concern with people's choice to resolve disputes in different courts and to use one court for a case that another had not adjudicated to their satisfaction, yet another indication of a plurality the central authorities were trying to eradicate.[22]

Taken together, these decrees imply that the designs of policy makers were only part of the picture. Monopolizing legal arbitration had been an official design, but many Egyptians continued to use other courts or legal authorities, to the discontent of the central administrations. These decrees also demonstrate the inadequacy of "secularization" as an analytical tool here. This was not a secularizing project but, rather, one set to rationalize and standardize both shari'a courts and administrative councils of adjudication.

At Midpoint: 1863 to 1865

Taking place in 1865, Abu al-Waqf's murder case marks a midpoint in the formation of the Khedival legal system, which by then had been effective for more than a decade. A couple years earlier, in January 1863, Isma'il Pasha replaced his father, Sa'id, as Egypt's governor, and within weeks he obtained Ottoman recognition of his title as khedive. In the months and years to come, Isma'il took it upon himself to "modernize" Egypt and make it into a recognizable part of Europe. One of his projects was the expansion of bureaucracy, including the legal system. Isma'il utilized the income from taxes and the cotton boom to finance and later enlarge his administration. Within days of his accession, Isma'il ordered the formation of five new provincial councils, and the following year, the foundation of a new hierarchy of councils—the appellate councils *(majlis isti'naf).*[23]

During the months and years following his ascendance to power, an increased interest in order was apparent—the efficient and smooth functioning of the legal system, a manifestation of state power that had to be publicly displayed and recognized. A 1863 decree instructed scribes to mark and number clearly each case adjudicated and each petition received. The chair of each council was instructed to review the notebooks on a weekly basis and to make sure that cases were indeed being adjudicated in the order in which they were received. Lower court instances were to submit biweekly reports to the Supreme Council of Adjudication enumerating cases treated, impending, and delayed, and the reason for delay. Scribes could be punished for failing to maintain this order.[24]

The council hierarchy expanded during Isma'il's period in response to the extensive use that low-ranking officials, as well as individual litigants, were making of it. In January 1863, on the eve of Isma'il's rise to power, the legal system was composed of a two-tiered hierarchy of councils of adjudication, which reviewed criminal cases forwarded to them from urban police headquarters and from the provinces. By 1864 the existing councils were jammed with cases, especially at Supreme Council level, and defendants sometimes waited years for their sentence—at least part of this period spent in prison. A new level of courts was created between the Supreme Council and the local councils: first two appellate councils were founded in Alexandria and Cairo, then three in the provinces. These adjudicated cases forwarded to them by local councils, and their decision could then be appealed to Supreme Council.[25]

Decrees and regulations from the mid-1860s onward serve as some indication, from officials' perspectives, of the kind of roles that low-ranking personnel came to play in village and neighborhood life. Several decrees, for example, instructed local policemen, *shaykh*s, and rural officials how to deal with disputes brought to their attention. One such decree ordered police officials not to register

minor offenses or disputes unless one of the parties wished to have the settlement in writing. The same decree, moreover, instructed village *shaykhs* to resolve
minor disputes on the spot, without troubling the district's administrator unless
absolutely necessary. When disputes did reach the district administrator, he too
was encouraged to reach a mutually agreed-upon settlement, rather than forward
the case to his superiors.[26] In a similar vein, an 1880 Police Act ordered policemen to settle fights independently that did not result in injury, verbal abuse, or
any offense punishable by one-day detainment. These were also encouraged to
broker disputes and settle minor cases in reconciliation.[27]

These detailed instructions imply that people chose to turn to the authorities
and involve them in their disputes often enough to burden existing legal institutions and personnel. In tracing the effect of the state, moreover, these decrees
portray a picture of state formation within communities, rather than one ema-
nating from above. A modern state was thus articulated not by the police station
in urban neighborhoods and rural districts but, rather, by these communal disputes in which central authorities were clearly not interested, yet which people
kept bringing to the offices of lower-ranking officials. Official decrees clearly state
that no registration is necessary as no higher-ranking official would be likely
to review minor cases, yet registration was a meaningful tool in people's lives
and life choices. People's reliance on official registration is not new. Historians
of shari'a courts have demonstrated that people often used the courts for the
sole purpose of having an accident or change of ownership officially recorded for
future reference. What interests me here is what is often called "the penetrating
gaze of the state," which seems to be far from top-down imposition. If we are
to view these decrees as responses to actual practices, what we see here is both
bottom-up and top-down processes, which turned the state into a meaningful
presence in everyday life.

I discussed previously the attempts by the central authorities to impose the
monopoly of newly formed legal institutions over pluralistic social-legal fields.
These efforts persisted through the mid-1860s as litigants continued to see the
legal field as pluralistic and resorted, for example, to both official and unofficial
muftis in seeking legal opinion. At midcentury, muftis were appointed in different levels of the judiciary and administration and were consulted by litigants,
administrators, and *qadis*. The grand mufti in Cairo was placed at the top of that
hierarchy and supervised the uniform application of the Hanafi school of Islamic

jurisprudence. At the same time, the central administration refused to recognize opinions by unofficial muftis.[28] An 1865 decree stated the following:

> It has been brought to our attention that some Jon Does issue fatwas related to shari'a cases dealt with in the shari'a courts, in the *awqaf* ministry and particularly in the Supreme Council of Adjudication. It also transpires that the parties who obtain such fatwas believe them to be valid and see them as an authoritative source that would enable them to achieve their goal—ignorant and unaware of the fact that these fatwas have neither value nor significance whatsoever. They therefore travel to the different courts and government departments, leaving behind their work and livelihood, basically for nothing. This phenomenon causes grave problems and great dispute between the parties, and these John Does assume the honorable position of muftis for their own personal profit.[29]

From litigants' perspectives, a mufti's opinion gained legitimacy from a person's knowledge and status, not from official recognition. From the center's perspective, unofficial muftis were harder to standardize and control. Peters sees this decree and the ones that followed as a measure against those individuals whose knowledge of the shari'a was defective.[30] State deliberations about unofficial fatwas, however, demonstrate once again a process of monopolization and systemization. These decrees mention neither the quality of unofficial fatwas nor their adherence to the shari'a. It was the notion of regularization itself with which the central authorities were concerned. At first intending to license muftis whose fatwas would be accepted by government authorities, a 1873 decree stated that the *'ulama* decided to ban any outside fatwas. Such a decision, the decree stated, "would save the government and the people a lot of unnecessary trouble and prevent all sorts of mischief and evil."[31] From the state's perspective, then, the muftiship, or at least fatwas recognized by official councils and courts, could be legitimized only by their official status and recognition—that "effect of the state" once again: not by the power to regulate muftiship, as the initial decree had suggested, but rather by monopolizing it completely.

Finally, another process that affected Egyptian legal system in this midpoint of its operation was Egypt's financial situation. During the mid-1860s, a process began that would culminate in Egypt's bankruptcy in 1876. The cotton boom caused by the American Civil War burst in the mid-1860s, and Isma'il resorted to his first public loans, which financed his urban and agricultural development plans as well as indemnity to the Suez Canal Company for return of rights to land and labor conceded by Sa'id. Isma'il used these funds to build new factories, government schools, and railways and expand the irrigation infrastructure. Extremely high interest rates and the burst of the cotton boom, among other processes, led to Egypt's bankruptcy the following decade.[32]

Already in 1865, a series of decrees ordered budget cuts and dismissal of some of the workers in all councils and police stations as the expanding bureaucracy began to burden the Egyptian budget. In the case of Alexandria's police station, for example, "some of the employees were found to be redundant, and their work can be relegated to other departments or individuals." A budget cut of 46 percent was therefore ordered.[33] A similar procedure took place in the councils. Some council scribes were dismissed, and mufti positions were unifed.[34] Six years later, budgetary considerations also dictated new council and court fees. The poor could still apply for exemption, but these fees probably succeeded in restricting court access.[35]

So far, this chapter focused on the legal system itself, on the Khedival state that produced the sources I have consulted. Ann Stoler recently argued that before we read our sources *against* the grain, we must first read *along* the archival grain, that "we need to look for regularities, logic of recall, densities and distributions, consistencies and misinformation, omission and mistake. Assuming we know these scripts diminishes our analytic possibilities. It rests too comfortably on predictable stories with familiar plots."[36] Iris Agmor's work on Haifa and Jaffa courts, noted earlier, is exemplary in deciphering the logic of the archive and of documents themselves. To me, it is but a tool, a step before searching for aberrations and inconsistencies: it is the subaltern that I am after, not merely the state that recorded her. Because I claim here that the state and the subaltern were mutually constitutive, understanding honor-killing cases is only possible within the legal system that adjudicated it and within the state that recorded it.

Honor Killing and Khedival Justice

Beginning in the mid–nineteenth century, Hunter argues, the administrative and legal transformations outlined previously affected communal and official handling of crime. The central administration thrust itself into areas previously regulated by customary law. In murder cases, for example, customary and Islamic law allowed for mediation and reconciliation between the murderer and the victim's heirs through payment of blood money. In the Egyptian reformed legal system, by contrast, formal trial replaced the community in murder cases, even if the parties agreed to reconciliation. By so doing, the state tried to substitute itself for the customary authority of family and community. The Khedival state thus strove to monopolize not only means of violence but also means of arbitration.[37] "Honor killing" brings us even closer to home: not only to the communal or tribal level, but to the very heart of the patriarchal family. The question that Hunter does not ask and that I would like to explore now, is how families and communities chose to handle this new intervention into this realm.

Historians have not found evidence of "honor killing" before the twentieth century. The reasons for this silence are related to its place in customary law and to the nature of the Ottoman legal system. Honor killing was sanctioned by customary law and hence neither a victim's relatives nor her community were likely to report it. Dror Ze'evi cites the disproportional number of fatal accidents involving women and girls as evidence of honor killing in seventeenth-century Jerusalem. Local *qadi*s and state functionaries, he argues, helped conceal such killings from the state (and hence, from the historian) by recording them as accidents. State authorities, in turn, were not too interested in such cases, which they considered part of the so-called "private" realm of family and community.[38] Beth Baron notes that in British-colonized Egypt, the press publicized cases of honor killing of prostitutes and highlighted officials' sympathy toward the killers and public support of their act. Her discussion relies on press representations and on recorded popular ballads, but it does not rely on contemporary archival sources.[39]

In what follows, I use some of the honor-killing cases found in the archives to demonstrate how new notions of state power changed the ways in which both state authorities and non-elite Egyptians chose to handle such murders. First, new legal institutions and procedures made it possible to adjudicate crimes even when a woman's heirs were not interested in prosecution. Second, in Khedival Egypt it was the *shaykhs*' legal duty to report unnatural death, and they could be punished for failing to do so. Third, these processes also affected family and community dynamics.[40] It is impossible to know whether state interest in honor crimes managed to deter potential murderers. It did inevitably affect the choice to commit such murder and the choice to report it. Finally, council verdicts did reduce the sentence of "honor killers" and explicitly acknowledged the role of this practice in Egyptian society. Official handling of honor killing, then, reflects a complex interplay between family, community, and central authorities.

I opened this chapter with the story of 'Abdallah 'Ali Sulayman from Aba al-Waqf village, who approached the village *qadi* and informed him that his maternal cousin Sariyya had been murdered for an alleged violation of her family's honor. The *qadi* informed the police, who then started an investigation. When questioned, the cousin denied his conversation with the *qadi*. All parties involved denied the accusations and even the woman's death, but none could explain her disappearance. Sariyya's husband claimed she had left him because he was too poor for her and could not maintain a standard of living to which she aspired. He later claimed they got divorced, but he could not prove it; nor could he tell the police where she was. The *shaykhs* of the village, when questioned, claimed they knew nothing of Sariyya's disappearance or of her alleged misconduct. Inquiring of a woman's whereabouts, the *shaykhs* further claimed, was the responsibility of her family, not theirs. Sariyya's neighbors then claimed her paternal uncle told them she had run away.

When confronted with the suspects' denial and the lack of evidence, the *qadi* insisted on his account, claiming that as *qadi* he was committed to the truth. "If I am wrong," he said, "let the suspects bring the woman as proof that she is still alive." Shortly afterward, Sariyya's mother-in-law paid the *qadi* a night visit and confirmed the allegations, adding that her son, the victim's husband, was not involved in the murder. In the police station, however, she denied her conversation with the *qadi*. Moreover, while awaiting trial, one of the defendants fled from prison. Another suspect, Sariyya's maternal uncle, was given permission to look for her and spent several years doing so, to no avail. Al-Minya's Council of Adjudication convicted the uncles and sentenced them to two-to-five years in prison. The Supreme Council of Adjudication then reduced their sentences due to the weakness of evidence.[41]

In Egyptian historiography, Upper Egypt is often noted for its rebelliousness and its refusal to accept central authority. Upper Egyptians were the first to be conscripted to Mehmed Ali's army, and in the 1860s and 1870s, they were the first to suffer from Isma'il's harsh overtaxation. During the reign of Mehmed Ali and his heirs, many peasants' revolts were recorded in Upper Egypt against the corvée, conscription, taxes, expropriation of land and animals, and the decline of wages and rise of rents that led them to the verge of starvation. Some of these revolts were only subdued using substantial military efforts on the part of the government.[42]

Sariyya's murder case should be understood in this context—of a struggle between Cairo and Upper Egypt to enforce new standards of intervention, as well as a new relationship between center and periphery. This case, moreover, is one example of how the state as a process was formed not only in the Khedival office in Cairo but in multiple localities that endowed an abstract "state power" its legitimacy and substantiality. The penetrating gaze of the state was, if anything, invited in, as initiative lay in the hands of local actors; their individual actions played a significant role not only in the lives of Abu al-Waqf village and in the lives of Sariyya's family, but also in negotiating and defining the role of the state—or the effect of the state—in rural life and in the lives of local actors. Their agency, the choices they made in resisting custom or family pressure and in informing the authorities is contingent upon their location within familial, communal, and institutional context.

One such actor is 'Abdallah 'Ali Sulayman, whose motivation for turning to the *qadi* is not specified, but without whom this case would not have reached the authorities. He may have had some personal grievance against his cousin's paternal cousins; he may have been appalled by the murder, of which other members of his family or community clearly approved. He probably wished to assert his objection to the murder and even have the killers punished, but he wanted to do so without antagonizing his community. A direct testimony in the police station would have resulted in community or family sanctions that he may have wished to avoid. An indirect testimony at the *qadi*'s court or private residence could be easily denied but at the same time carried the weight of the *qadi*'s reputation, which made it credible in the police station and therefore initiated a serious investigation.

The *qadi*'s identity is unknown because the particulars of rural judges were not registered. He might have been an outsider to the community as *qadi*s were often educated in Cairo and appointed in the provinces. As an outsider, if indeed he was one, he might have been seen as representing state authorities; as an outsider he might have been less likely to sympathize with local customs. As a Cairo-educated appointee, he might have seen "honor killing" as a backward and unruly Upper-Egyptian practice, and he might also have seen himself as a personification of a *mission civilatrice*. As *qadi,* he might have seen "honor killing" as an un-Islamic practice that he did not wish to condone.

He could not adjudicate Sariyya's case in his court for procedural reasons. Without formal complaint by the victim's immediate heirs, no legal proceedings were possible; neither did he have any shari'a evidence—an eyewitness testimony or a confession. Sariyya's relatives, moreover, provided him with no shari'a proof and could not even produce a body that would prove Sariyya's death. Further, ethical standards of Islamic jurisprudence forbade a *qadi* to use knowledge that had reached him outside official court deliberations. Acting as a private person or as a state official, he could use his knowledge to bring a case to the police. He thus chose to inform the state authorities whose tools of investigation and legal procedures could enable conviction.

He was not the one expected to report this crime, however. The village *shaykhs* were the ones officially obliged to report any births and deaths that took place under their jurisdiction, and they were held accountable for failing to do so. Police and council records throughout the period include cases of *shaykhs*—of both neighborhoods and villages—who were questioned and sometimes punished for failing to report an out-of-wedlock birth or unnatural death. The case of Abu al-Waqf village is therefore not an exception. The response of the *shaykhs* is interesting: women's disappearance was not their responsibility to detect and report but rather was that of the women's families. They resorted here to gender segregation norms and related notions of honor: women did not "roam about the marketplace," as *shaykhs* claimed in a similar case that also took place in Upper Egypt, and therefore their disappearance could easily go unnoticed.[43]

Sariyya's murder case is also a good example of how the legal procedure at the councils enabled conviction when the shari'a court could not obtain it. The adjudication of Sariyya's murder was made possible because of new legal practices and procedures the councils had created and perpetuated. The councils' rules of evidence enabled the persecution of cases that the shari'a's strict rules of evidence could not enforce. More important, they replaced the arbitrary justice of local governors with a systematic bureaucratic process in which decisions by lower-ranking levels of the administration were regularly reviewed by higher ones. A cross-examination in the police station, police investigation and questioning, also supplemented the shari'a procedure.

In Sariyya's case, her minor brother's guardian pressed charges against the killers in the shari'a court, but he failed to prove his claim according to shari'a rules of evidence. Al-Minya's Council of Adjudication, however, chose to convict the defendants on the following grounds: the *qadi*'s consistent testimony that two of her family members informed him of the crime, the defendants' failure to produce the woman whom they claimed to be still alive, the defendants' lies and frequent changes of testimony, and one of the defendants' choice to escape from prison.[44] The reasoning, then, is highly circumstantial. Taken together, however, the circumstantial evidence convinced the council that Sariyya was no longer alive and that her uncles were indeed responsible for her murder. Finally, the Supreme Council decided to reduce the killers' sentences due to weakness of evidence. This self-corrective measure was yet another characteristic of the Khedival legal system and its standardization project.

Initiative from below thus met with a centralizing drive from above. Sariyya's case illustrates what scholars have seen mainly as a top-down process: a centralizing bureaucracy could not tolerate murder. Taken slightly differently, my argument is that there was no preexisting "state" that assumed new roles; such new roles and practices were forming the modern state. Where the centralizing drive met with communal crimes and litigation, a modern state was formed. The adjudication of a murder case through a three-tier judicial administration created one linkage between Cairo and Abu al-Waqf village, initiated by local actors as much as by decision makers in Cairo, and created new notions of state and justice.

≈

I wish to finish here with another example that took place in the mid-1860s and that highlights other aspects of those troubled interactions that came to be known as state power. Village *shaykh*s informed local police of the disappearance of a certain girl named Qanawiyya. In her interrogation, her mother told the police that her daughter was rumored to be "prostituting herself," and her paternal uncles then plotted to murder her, but her father tried to dissuade them. One of these uncles' wife further confirmed that her husband and his brother planned to kill Qanawiyya after they had heard of her out-of-wedlock pregnancy. Qanawiyya's brother then confessed that after hearing of his father's refusal, he murdered his sister together with one of his cousins.

The police referred the victim's parents to the shari'a court, where their son and the husband's nephew were accused of murder. The parents had no claims against their son but wished to press charges against the nephew. In response, both claimed they had conspired to kill the girl together, but it was her brother who gave her the final blow and was therefore the only killer. Because the parents had sued only the other man, however, the shariʿa court acquitted both. Isna's Council of Adjudication then sentenced them to nine years' imprisonment. The Appellate Council reduced their prison term to five years, and the Supreme Council of Adjudication then reduced it even further.[45]

One interesting aspect of this case is the role of the shariʿa court. As noted, honor-killing cases did not reach shariʿa courts before the nineteenth century because the victim's heirs had no interest in legal procedure. In Khedival Egypt, the police forwarded murder cases to the shariʿa court as a matter of procedure, and the victims' closest heirs faced the difficult choice of suing their own kin for an act they themselves may have supported. Even when they did not support the murder, however, they were still reluctant to press charges against their sons. In another murder case of a girl named Tarkiya, for example, seven of the relatives were involved in the crime, but in the shariʿa court the only one liable was the one who dealt the final, fatal blow. Tarkiya's parents then chose to put the blame on a man named Hawwash, who died in prison while awaiting his trial. This choice, in practice, absolved all parties of liability, at least in the shariʿa court.[46] In Qanawi-yya's case, the son confessed that he was the one who murdered his sister; because the parents had accused only his cousin of the murder, both got off the hook. In both cases, it seems the parents knew exactly what they were doing. In the council, which relied on circumstantial evidence, the murderers were convicted.

Qanawiyya's case also reveals a complex dynamics behind the choice to murder a family member. When the girl heard of her uncles' intentions, she managed to escape twice before getting caught; and her father tried to make the killers change their minds. One can only speculate about the victim's father's status within the extended family, and the status of the family in the village, which must have played some role in these negotiations. The younger generation then chose to commit a murder that the elders chose to avoid, which again reflects familial and communal dynamics on which we can only speculate. In Tarkiya's case, her paternal cousins murdered her after having failed to convince her brother to do so himself. The brother did agree, however, to leave her alone with his cousins, knowing the fatal outcome.[47]

Another interesting aspect of such cases is that the councils, which did seriously investigate and prosecute such murders, found them to be of lesser magnitude than other murders. In Qanawiyya's case, as in most honor-killing cases I found in the archives, the Supreme Council of Adjudication commuted the sentence pronounced by lower instances. In three out of five cases I examined, lower-instance councils imposed prison terms of three to five years, and the Supreme Council of Adjudication commuted them to two years, or even a few months. The Supreme Council's verdict explicitly stated that the motive for the crime, the preservation of family honor, was a noble one, which partly absolved an individual from responsibility for a grave crime such as murder.[48] In one case, the Supreme Council verdict explicitly stated that because the defendants were "the closest ones to her, some of them being her shari'a heirs, it would not have been easy for them to commit any act against her unless she had done some terrible deed that led them to do what they have done in order to protect their honor."[49] In another case, the killers' sentences were commuted from eight and six years in Jirja's Council of Adjudication to eighteen and twelve months, respectively, in the Supreme Council of Adjudication, as they had killed their relative because "they were infuriated by her neglect of her honor and feared scandal and shame."[50] Such verdicts might imply state incorporation of a non-elite normative approach to honor crimes. Murder was still condemnable, but "honor killing" was an honorable act, the motivation for which should be acknowledged and the perpetrator pardoned, at least partially.

The interaction between state authorities and people's normative understanding of justice will be further explored in the following chapters. The diversity of people's responses to honor killing in the handful of cases discussed in this chapter demonstrates that people's understanding of justice was far from uniform. Some chose to conceal the murder; others chose to inform the authorities; and still others chose to do so indirectly, without being implicated. At the same time, as reflected in council verdicts, state authorities were clearly attuned to popular notions of justice.

The victims are absent from these narratives. Research on honor killing in contemporary societies demonstrates that such murders often have little to do with actual sexual intercourse and more to do with either a perceived personal autonomy of a female family member and the challenge she posed to male control or to power relations within the extended family or community. In reaction, certain male family members use violence inside their families to assert power within the larger social network.[51] Council records never question the perpetrators' motives. Only one case mentions that the girl had tried to escape prior to the murder. Of the others we know nothing.

Conclusion

Scholarship on "honor killing" has long tended to focus on its primordial nature and to ignore the modern state as an explanatory factor. More recently, feminist scholarship has sought to explain the persistence of femicide within complex interactions between nation-states and local communities. Legislators and law enforcement personnel often turn a blind eye to or even sanction "honor killing" to preserve the authority of local and tribal leaders, and thus their loyalty to the state.[52] The honor-killing cases discussed here are different, but here as well, it was not women's well-being that was at stake in the councils' choices to persecute murderers. This choice was related instead to the authority and autonomy of local leaders and to emerging power relations between the central authorities in Cairo and Upper Egypt.

One way to study legal reform is to examine new legal institutions: police stations, councils of adjudication, and shari'a courts. Beginning in the 1840s and 1850s, Egypt's police regularly conducted criminal investigations, interrogated witnesses, and examined forensic evidence. Newly formed councils of adjudication reviewed police reports and issued their verdicts in accordance with the *qanun*. The structure of these institutions and their development does not concern me here, as recent works have dealt with such details at length. Instead, I am interested in asking how this system worked and what were some of the practices and processes that rendered it meaningful in people's lives. A social history of legal reform, then, means questioning what kinds of power relations police stations, councils of adjudication, and courts effected in urban and rural communities, and what kinds of roles *qadis*, muftis, policemen, and *shaykhs* came to play in communal life.

A social history of law and of legal reform maintains that although legal principles and regulations were formulated in Cairo by the elite, their actual meanings were transformed through such interactions between litigants and policemen. Such interactions created new notions of state power and role. The social history of state formation entails writing it not as a process that was simply masterminded by Mehmed Ali Pasha or his heirs but, rather, as a multiplicity of sites and interactions involving many social actors and creating new power relations. From this standpoint, the role of central authorities in monitoring communal life was an outcome of social interactions that legitimized newly created institutions. Questioning how a modern state was formed, then, involves exploring these sites and the specificities of communal relations. The "modern state," involving new power relations within and between communities and individuals, was the making of communities themselves. Without the meanings people ascribed to them, without the many actual uses they came to serve in their community, state institutions are virtually meaningless historical entities.

2

Medicine, Law, and the Female Body

A Jewish woman named Rahil Fisha was convicted for causing the death of her neighbor, Sarah Cohen, at childbirth in Alexandria. When labor was near and Sarah was agonizing in pain, her sister-in-law asked for Rahil's help. Rahil advised her to apply some alcohol on the laboring woman's thighs to intensify her contractions and facilitate birth. The alcohol caught fire and caused the death of both woman and child. Rahil was convicted for causing Sarah's death and sentenced to six months' imprisonment. Important for our purpose here, she was convicted because she overstepped professional boundaries and meddled in business in which she had neither training nor knowledge. She was neither a hakima nor a midwife, only a neighbor, read the Alexandria Appellate Council's verdict.[1]

In 1827 Mehmed Ali Pasha hired French surgeon Antoine Barthélémy Clot, who later became known as Clot Bey, to oversee a thorough reform of the Egyptian medical system. A few years later, Clot Bey opened a school for hakimas (female medical practitioners)[2] with the purposes of replacing Egyptian midwives, whom he dubbed "the most ignorant and superstitious in the world," and introducing modern medical standards to labor and birth.[3] The school never managed to recruit enough students to be able to replace midwives at childbirth. Based at police stations, the hakimas intervened mainly in complicated births and served as forensic experts in criminal investigations. Due to the shortage in trained personnel, midwives were conscripted to participate in state-sponsored vaccination campaigns. Because they delivered most of the babies, they were charged with reporting every birth and could be held accountable for failing to do so. In some cases, they served as forensic experts as well. As Hibba Abugideiri argues, this division of labor complicates any clear categorization of "modern" and "traditional," "state agents" and nonstate actors.[4]

Consistent with my argument in the previous chapter, I demonstrate here how the police station and more specifically, the hakima's office, became a site of state formation. It was also a site in which new notions of body and knowledge were articulated. In these particular sites, women's narration of their own bodies was already a product of the encounter with state officials. In other words, women's narration of their bodies in the police station and their intimate experience of their bodies were inevitably mediated through power relations, as well as through language. Particularly here, agency was enabled and articulated with the newly formulated legal and medical language encountered in the police station, which made bodily experiences intelligible.[5]

In late nineteenth-century Egypt, the emergence of new examinations and procedures created new experiences of the female body. These sometimes replaced, and more often supplemented, existing idioms and practices that similarly existed in specific power relations and medicated bodily experiences (and were thus no less "authentic" or "real"). The new subjectivities created through these interactions create the capacity for action—challenging, going to court, reclaiming control over their bodies, asking for a hakima's assistance.

In this chapter, I am interested in discourses and practices that made female bodies legible and question what kinds of abstractions and categories women used for understanding their bodies, based on police and court records as well as writings of elite critics of folk medicine. At the same time, I question how hakimas gained an authority that led women to consult them and parents to bring daughters in for investigation, and rendered other women— both midwives and laywomen—insufficiently equipped to handle complicated birth or to read evidence on women's bodies. I argue that interactions between the hakimas and individual women established boundaries between the knowledgeable hakima and the "ignorant" midwife. Women who turned to the police station and had their bodies examined for traces of crime were the ones who reaffirmed the authority of police personnel, and most notably the hakima, over their bodies. Such interactions, moreover, simultaneously created new categories of self-knowledge and new ways of narrating and of making sense of their bodies.

"The Most Superstitious Midwives in the World"

> So the day is coming, we hope, when the dangerous "remedies" of
> the modern Nile Dwellers will be no longer practiced, but will be rel-
> egated to the archives of human error.[6]

Many nineteenth-century women made sense of their bodies through norms
and practices that followed them throughout their life cycle, in sickness and
in health. During the last decade of the century, male reformers and foreign
observers recorded these practices as traces of a disappearing world. These did
not disappear—quite the contrary. Anthropologies of present-day Egypt note
the persistence of popular practices that supplement, and sometimes replace,
unaffordable medical procedures, or such that have failed to yield a desirable
outcome.[7] It was at this point in time, however, in mid–nineteenth century, that
a new discourse emerged that singled out certain understandings of the human
body as "superstition," "ignorance," and "health hazards" while giving promi-
nence to scientific medicine, which had not yet acquired much of an advantage
in healing and life saving.

Part of the normative understanding of the human body, if we are to believe
the written accounts by foreign or elite observers, was related to the jinn. These
are invisible beings, either harmful or helpful, that interfere with the lives of
mortals. They were held responsible for physical and mental well-being, as well
as people's relationships with their spouses and neighbors. Hysteria was ascribed
to a jinn inhabiting the female body; infant mortality to the children's jinn step-
mothers who had murdered them out of jealousy; and diphtheria to a jinn sib-
ling of the sick child (also known as the *qarina*), who loved her so much that
he wanted to kill her and have her join him. Mothers, reports Ahmad Amin in
mid–twentieth century, came to despise their children whom they suspected of
having been replaced by their jinn sisters.[8] According to Amin, people saw the
jinn in stray cats and dared not interfere when these entered their home and
shared their dinner. They found old shoes in the streets and believed them to be
jinn corpses, and thus hung them around the necks of their horses, donkeys, and
even infants, to deter others.[9]

'Ali Mubarak similarly describes some healing practices, mainly popular
in the countryside, in his multivolume *al-Khitat al-Tawfiqiyya*. In the village of

Qusiya in Upper Egypt, for example, women believed that if a sick child were to be laid down on a certain spot at the village cemetery and fall asleep, he would be cured; if he were to fail to fall asleep, chances of recovery were slim.[10] Cairene women ascribed healing powers to a spring located near a monastery at the Greek neighborhood and dipped their sick children in it.[11] A spring at a local monastery at Athr al-Nabi was similarly believed able to cure female barrenness.[12] In the 1890s and 1900s, Egypt's literary journals, such as *al-Hilal* and *al-Muqtataf,* sometimes published letters questioning talismans, the *qarina,* the *zar,* and the *'ifrit,* which the editors dismissed as "superstitions" or scientifically labeled as mental illness.[13] One Ahmad Effendi al-Laqani, for example, asked *al-Muqtataf* editors about the *qarina,* which "some people believe to cause the death of infants in the first year of their lives," questioning "what is the *qarina* and what are its causes?" The editors replied that children die of malnutrition and neglect, and the *qarina* is nothing but superstition.[14]

Similarly, healing powers were attributed to women who were "married" to a jinn who revealed to them the world of the invisible and enabled them to diagnose and to cure. As healers, they donned men's clothing, as would their jinn partner who had taken over their bodies. Most famous is the *zar* ceremony, in which contact is made with the jinn inhabiting the troubled body through the induction of a trancelike state.[15]

This set of beliefs constituted some combination (or creolization) of orthodox Islam, Sufi Islam, and African beliefs brought by slaves. Some of these were not "ancient" or "traditional" at all, but rather recent: a product of intensified slave trade and African immigration to Egypt from the 1820s onward. As a public ritual, the *zar* served social functions alongside its healing potential. It brought women together in an exclusive female environment, which offered power that was denied them in other social arenas and sometimes momentarily destabilized race- and class-based power relations. It is no coincidence that most of these rites were performed by women and were related to the female body. Disempowered in most social domains, women used them to gain some control over those aspects of their individual lives in which they were supposed to be invested—marital life and motherhood. Sometimes associated with African slaves and servants, these practices further empowered those who had very little influence in other domains.[16]

In this exclusively female sphere, midwives were of utmost importance in mediating subjectivity and the female body. Pregnancy and childbirth were mediated through the presence of a community-based midwife and through the ever-present threat of maternal or fetal death. Midwife-assisted labor meant that women gave birth in a familiar environment, and the midwife was often a well-known figure in her community. Little is known about midwives or their work, and the little we know about the everyday of midwifery is mediated though elite or foreign observers. According to Edward Lane, large households employed a midwife in their harems, and lower-class families summoned midwives when birth was approaching.[17] Lane described a birth chair, which the midwife brought to the home of the expecting woman. The chair was covered with a shawl or an embroidered napkin and decorated with flowers of the henna tree. Rich women, claimed Lane, remained in bed from three to six days, whereas poor women resumed their ordinary chores after two days.[18]

A similar description is found some seventy years later in an essay by Gorgy Sobhy, a professor of medicine at the Egyptian University. Sobhy described childbirth as a process in which the laboring woman was encouraged to walk freely around the room, surrounded by her family members, and was seated on the chair only when childbirth was near. The midwife's help was both physical and moral as it included prayer and the invocation of saints. She visited the mother and child in the days following the birth, made the mother food, and supervised the customary celebrations. A child brought to dance between the legs of a woman in labor to hasten birth is one example of those practices that made midwives seem so superstitions in elite eyes.[19]

Lane, Sobhy, and others described "exotic" practices that captured their imagination. Some of these, however, constituted an important part of what many Egyptian women knew about their bodies. One's understanding of her body is mediated through discourse and practice, and these social agents helped construct women's knowledge of their bodies: how to interpret pain, what to expect from a nearing birth or from the nuptial night. For them, a baby dancing between their legs could hasten birth, and the sight of ugliness could disfigure their fetus. Modern medical practice and the hakimas supplemented—but far from replaced—what women knew about their bodies.

Midwives were often seen as guardians of women's conduct, as well as guardians of women's secrets. In familial and communal settings, midwives helped supervise women's conduct, but they could also help women conceal pregnancy, birth, and premarital defloration. In Western Europe, midwives were long associated with sorcery, illegitimacy, and death—abortion and infanticide. A midwife's role at childbirth also made her a potentially disruptive force that may help women get rid of unwanted offspring or help them keep illegitimate offspring secret.[20]

Alongside their obstetric and social roles, midwives also enjoyed a privileged status as expert witnesses on matters concerning their profession at the shari'a courts. The shari'a courts privileged oral testimony by eyewitnesses. In Islamic legal theory, a man's testimony was equivalent to that of two women, and most schools of legal jurisprudence did not accept exclusive testimony by women. Midwives were exceptions to this rule, and courts accepted their testimony because men were not allowed to view women's private parts.[21]

The role of the midwife in the shari'a court is significant for my discussion here because the legal sphere—the police and councils—was the main sphere in which they were to be replaced by hakimas in the period under review. Shari'a courts handled a variety of cases related to women's bodies. Some of these served as extensions of midwives' roles outside of court. Midwives testified in a variety of cases. For example, a virginity examination could support a woman's claim for divorce on the grounds of impotency. In cases of inheritance disputes, a midwife could testify that a child was born alive and was therefore a legitimate heir. A slave who had been illegally sold in spite of her pregnancy (making the sale null and void) could support her claim with a midwife's examination. Midwives' testimony, however, was not a routine part of legal procedure. Cases involving the female body did not necessarily require physical examination. The witness, moreover, was not always a professional midwife but rather a female member of the community, and many issues were left to the parties' testimonies or to the *qadi*'s good judgment.[22] The introduction of hakimas to the legal procedure, beginning from midcentury, introduced new notions of knowability, new conceptualization of the capability of medicine to know the body's history.

The French Doctor, the Egyptian Midwife, and the Black Hakima

"Their aptitude is amazing, especially with regard to current calumny by some pessimists who wish to deny any intelligence of the Negro race," wrote Clot Bey in his memoirs about the new students of the hakima school. "It is unquestionable that the Negro students of the school are no less apt than those of the other races, who seem to want to exclude them from the great family of intelligent beings."[23]

In an attempt to replace midwives, Clot Bey founded a school of hakimas, female medical practitioners, which provided its students with state-of-the-art medical training. Because he failed to find parents willing to send their daughters to a boarding school that had men and foreigners among its teachers, Clot Bey resorted to black slaves purchased at the slave market and to street girls, whose parents' permission was irrelevant.

Clot Bey's comment is quite remarkable in the context of dominant nineteenth-century medical theory and practice, particularly as it refers to a cadre of black slaves and street girls who received state-of-the-art medical training and became professional women's health specialists and forensic experts. This female expert became known as hakima—not merely a midwife, but a doctoress, the female equivalent of a doctor (hakim). Contemporary Western medical discourse referred to the white male body as the norm, and the female body, particularly that of black women, as its other. Physical difference was used to support existing gendered and racial power relations, including women's exclusion from the medical profession. Replacing female midwives with male obstetricians was considered a sign of progress. Women's incapability to practice medicine, as well as the perceived inferiority of non-European "races," were considered scientific facts. The creation of a professional cadre of female medical practitioners thus clashed with the medical common sense of the time.[24]

Mehmed Ali's main concern in hiring Clot Bey and initiating a medical reform in the 1820s was with the health of his army and with Egypt's growing involvement in the global economy. Diseases and epidemics weakened his army, whereas quarantine imposed on Egyptian imported goods in Europe damaged the economy. Clot Bey's medical reforms started with training medical personnel who would treat Mehmed Ali's soldiers, and he founded a medical school (first located in Abu Za'bal, later in Qasr al-'Aini), shortly after his arrival.[25]

The first doctors, health inspectors and teachers were foreigners. Clot Bey, however, strove to Arabize the medical system and create a cadre of physicians who would be able to communicate with the Egyptian population in its own language, and therefore be accepted and trusted. He strongly believed, moreover, that the system should be self-sufficient rather than rely on hired foreign doctors. Foreigners would be bound to return to their home countries following the termination of their contracts and thus could not be relied upon in the long run. Clot Bey was not a stereotypical colonial-minded reformer. He saw himself first and foremost as an employee of the Egyptian government, and his duty—to provide the pasha, whom he personally adored, the advantages of modern medicine. This mindset also explains his choice to train female doctors, who would be able to treat Egyptian women.[26]

The first doctors and health inspectors were European physicians hired for limited periods. These were replaced, beginning in the late 1830s, with Egyptians trained in Europe and graduates of the Qasr al-'Aini School. In 1832, the first mission of medical students left for France. Upon their return, they were appointed as instructors at the school of medicine, supplementing and later replacing the French staff. They also translated medical treatises into Arabic, as Arabic gradually replaced French as the language of instruction. One of them, Ahmad al-Rashidi, came to play a crucial role in the history of the hakima school as author and translator of treatises in gynecology and obstetrics, and was one of the school's first teachers.[27]

The creation of midwifery school was related mainly to two concerns—high child mortality rates and the spread of venereal diseases, particularly among soldiers. Clot Bey believed that the ignorance and low hygienic standards of midwives were to blame, and he hoped the hakimas would eventually replace midwives. As Foucault points out, following the French revolution and the formation of a mass conscription army, national strength came to be measured in numbers, initially numbers of potential soldiers. Such concerns brought, in turn, a growing concern with the individual body and made it into a site of intervention.[28] Female medical practitioners with modern medical training would be likely to lower infant mortality rates. Such a cadre—salaried and controlled by central authorities—would also register childbirths and report abortions and illegitimate births. As venereal disease was plaguing Mehmed Ali's army, Clot Bey believed that one could not effectively eliminate their spread in the army without treating women as well, both prostitutes and legitimate wives.

Clot Bey was particularly concerned with midwives' involvement in abortions, but this aspect does not seem to be perceived similarly by contemporary Egyptians.[29] Clot Bey was indeed appalled by what he saw as the selfish act of destroying a human fetus. "When a woman does not wish to become a mother," he argued, "these midwives see the destruction of the infant she carries as something natural for which they are not to be held accountable—neither in the eyes of society nor in the eyes of God."[30] In nineteenth-century Egypt, they were indeed not held accountable by law; and judging from the total absence of voluntary abortions from our legal records and if we are to believe Clot Bey, abortions were not considered socially condemnable either.[31]

Clot Bey soon realized that Egyptian gender segregation norms would enable him to achieve such goals only by using female medical practitioners, thus operating against the common sense of contemporary European medicine. Both Clot Bey and al-Rashidi's writings express particular concern with the reluctance of Egyptian men to allow a male doctor to examine the private parts of their wives and daughters. Because midwives did not have the expertise required to treat venereal diseases, they argued, men's refusal sentenced their wives to death.[32] Moreover, according to al-Rashidi, refusal to be examined by men was also against Islam, which "permits that which is forbidden" at times of necessity, especially when human life is at stake.[33]

The choice to recruit female doctors was foreign to Egyptian gender norms but, at the same time, operated within indigenous cultural codes: if men are not allowed to examine female bodies, let there be female doctors. Al-Rashidi's textbook, which was taught in the school, maintained that the "tender nature of women would not enable them to perform some of the very difficult tasks" involved in overcoming the obstacles of a difficult labor. At the same time, he argued that "if women study this profession in schools, master it and dare to perform major operations, it would be only just to incorporate them into the rank of doctors."[34]

Objections to girls' education stem in part from prevailing assumptions regarding female sexuality. Once aroused but not satisfied in marriage, maintains al-Rashidi's Bahjat al-Ru'asa', women's sexual desire is detrimental to their health. The taste for romantic novels, parties, dancing, and similar pleasures may cause both nymphomania and hysteria. He thus prescribes marriage as a cure, preferably shortly after puberty.[35] For similar reasons al-Rashidi disapproves of women's education, particularly outside the home. Because women's mental functions are inferior to those of men, their education or any excessive brain activity might be harmful to the functioning of their other organs.[36] Adolescent female sexuality, the text further maintains, could be contained only at home. Reading and social contacts of adolescent girls constitute unregulated spaces in the dangerous age of adolescence. When girls study with their peers, it states, they learn from each other the secrets of life, start associating with "those who are not their kind," and from there are easily led to immorality. The text does recommend limited education, within the confines of home, in topics such as geography, drawing, and history.[37]

Clot Bey recounts his frustration with parents' refusal to have their daughters trained as hakimas, in spite of the fact that girls did work in menial jobs outside of the home, especially as mason's assistants.[38] The educational dilemma was therefore resolved by resorting to kinless women, whose parents could not object to their education and who owed loyalty to the state alone—women whose education and intermingling with men would not tarnish any family's honor and reputation, namely, slaves and street girls. The school's students were therefore, at least initially, mainly female orphans, homeless girls, slaves, and a few male eunuchs from Mehmet Ali's palace. According to Egyptian gynecologist Naguib Mahfuz, in later decades some of the prejudice against the school subsided and more of its students were native born Egyptians, rather than slaves. More could then be recruited, and preference was given to orphans of soldiers.[39] One of the school's acute problems throughout its years of operation, however, continued to be its lack of new students. The student body never numbered more than a few dozen, many of whom were still orphans or girls literally picked off the streets.[40]

Because they were expected to inspect women's bodies on a daily basis, it became essential for the school's administration that their students remain respectable, as women were only likely to turn to hakimas who would not compromise their reputation. The school's administration insisted that the girls be virgins upon admission and marry medical doctors or sanitary inspectors upon graduation to ensure that they remain in service. Hakimas engaged to other men were encouraged to find alternative partners. Once married, they were granted the title of second lieutenant, a salary increase, and government-sponsored housing.[41] In her research on Egyptian medicine, historian Hibba Abugideiri argues this insistence on virginity and prompt marriage was a way to secure the school's legitimacy and attract more students.[42] The school, however, never truly appealed to the larger population, and Clot Bey and his colleagues had no reservations about relying on slaves and street girls. The supervision over the hakimas' conduct was significant, I believe, to legitimize their role as medical practitioners and to allow intimate interactions with Egyptian women—interactions of a kind restricted until then to community-based midwives.

The school curriculum was based on state-of-the-art nineteenth-century medical knowledge and technology and modeled after French midwifery training. The students first received Arabic literacy classes. They later learned the theory and practice of midwifery, pre- and postnatal care, treatment of simple diseases, dressing wounds, treating inflammatory tumors, elementary surgery, and vaccination and preparation of some of the most common medicines. The hakimas' license certified them to administer vaccinations, perform deliveries, and treat women and children.[43] School graduates learned how to use forceps, techniques for turning the fetus inside the womb during labor, caesarian surgery, and mechanical extraction of a dead fetus from the womb.[44] The school's main textbooks were *Kitab al-Wiladah* (Midwifery book); al-Rashidi's translation of Alfred Velpeau's 1829 *Traité élémentaire de l'art des accouchements;* and his *Bahjat al-Ru'asa' fi Amrad al-Nisa',* a gynecology textbook focused on women's diseases.[45] As I demonstrate in the following, more than techniques and basic anatomy, these women learned to see the human body as knowable through science.

Due to the small number of students, the hakimas never fully replaced midwives in childbirth. They were overworked and, in practice, intervened only in the most complicated deliveries, when families or midwives reached the police station or hospital and asked for their assistance. According to Mahfuz, some of them supplemented their income as midwives of well-to-do families. Most women, however, preferred midwives to doctors well into the twentieth century. Hospital delivery substantially replaced home delivery only in the 1920s.[46]

The reasons for women's reluctance to give birth in hospitals and to continue to rely on midwives are not difficult to imagine. First, the hospital environment deprived them of the family and community support described earlier. Second, it cut a woman off from a family that needed her care and support. In one archival record, a mother refused to send her five-year-old daughter to the hospital. The girl was too young to be left there on her own, she claimed, while she had younger children to take care of at home. The hakima, however, believed that an infection was risking the girl's life and sent her to the hospital, where she was treated and recovered.[47] More important, perhaps, hospital records from the period indicate that people patronized hospitals only when afflicted with serious diseases or injuries. Records of everyday activity at the hospital portray it as filthy and poorly maintained and contain many allegations of malpractice and spread of diseases.[48]

The functions that the hakimas came to play in Egyptians' lives cannot be reduced to Clot Bey's intentions. In search of the kinds of roles they came to play in people's lives, I found it necessary to turn to the police stations. This is, after all, where the everyday of childbirth, forensic examinations, vaccination campaigns, and other roles of hakimas and midwives were played out—where women had to decide whom to trust and whose examination to dismiss. "Professional" hakimas and "ignorant" midwives sometimes played very similar roles: hakimas came to play social and legal roles similar to the ones midwives had played in the past. Conversely, as the hakimas were few in number, midwives came to play roles that hakimas were supposed to assume, namely, the imposition of the power of a modern state.

The relationship between the hakimas and midwives was thus complementary rather than competitive. Midwives delivered most babies and called in hakimas only in cases of complicated birth. The central administration recruited midwives to vaccinate the population; they were supposed to report childbirths and could be punished for failing to do so. Those "superstitious midwives" were therefore never left "outside" the centralization process, but were part of it.

Instances in which hakimas did participate in childbirth helped consolidate their privileged status as medical experts, as well as their position as government agents. Consider the following examples. In one such case a woman named Zaynab bint Mustafa died after three days of labor. When the quarter's hakima arrived on the third day, she found the fetus to be already dead in Zaynab's womb, with a hand sticking out. In an attempt to save Zaynab's life, the hakima managed to extract the fetus mechanically from the womb. It was too late, however, and Zaynab died three hours later, probably of infection.[49] In another case, 'Abd al-Rahman called the hakima of Old Cairo's police station to assist his wife, Zahra, in her labor. She could not help her and called her superior, the hakima of Cairo's central police station, but both failed to save Zahra. Police investigation concluded that because Zahra had died in the presence of two hakimas, everything was done to save her life, and therefore no one was guilty of negligence.[50]

Clot Bey's efforts to undermine midwives' subversive potential were only partly successful. The incorporation of midwives into state mechanisms deterred women from using their services when secrecy was required. Midwives lost as least some of their role as neighborhood confidantes. Women who gave birth out of wedlock and wanted to avoid potential investigation did not call in a midwife, or they had to trust their midwife not to record the birth. Fahmy cites a case in which a soldier asked a midwife not to report the birth of an illicit child who died shortly thereafter.[51] In other cases, midwives were not called in at all. In February 1863, a divorced woman named Kashta gave birth to an infant in her stepfather's home. In an attempt to conceal the birth, she chose not to call in a midwife and trusted her newborn to her neighbor, who informally adopted him. The neighbor managed to keep the child for three months before Kashta's stepfather found out about what he believed to be his neighbor's illegitimate child and informed authorities.[52]

In a much more tragic case, a woman called Khadija bint Khalifa also did not call in a midwife. Her husband had left years previously, and she gave birth to an illegitimate child. A passerby heard her cries and rushed into her woodshed to find her in the midst of a difficult labor. She hastened to call a barber, but it was too late; when he arrived, both Khadija and the baby were already dead.[53] Here we see how the integration of midwives into the legal system directly affected women's lives.

The Body of Evidence

Despite being unable to replace midwives in childbirth, hakimas did replace them in the legal context. The main role they came to play in the lives of Egyptian women was related to their routine forensic examinations of women's bodies. Hakimas were stationed at Cairo's police stations and examined women in cases of unnatural death, miscarriage, and premarital defloration.

In late 1864, a midwife examined a woman who claimed she had miscarried as the result of having been beaten. The midwife confirmed the woman's allegation and further added that the fetus had human features and was therefore about four months old. The suspected assailants denied the accusations. The police had the woman reexamined, eighteen days later, by a male doctor. He found no indications of miscarriage and claimed the alleged fetus "had no human form whatsoever" and was actually "nothing more than a dry, hard substance, easily disintegrating, weighing about half a gram." He further stated that "the barber and the midwife have no expertise in conducting such examinations, and this midwife's testimony is merely proof of her ignorance." Following this case, the

Khedival Office issued a decree ordering that "from this moment on, midwives' testimony should not be relied upon."[54]

In this case, a midwife's testimony was totally discredited in favor of one by a male doctor. A 1856 decree stated eight years earlier that "barbers' wives are not qualified to examine dead women's bodies" and ordered the assignment of student hakimas in district police stations that did not yet have hakimas.[55] Nevertheless, midwives continued to examine forensic evidence, at least in the countryside, at least two decades later.[56] Hakimas supplemented rather than replaced midwives, and the police station supplemented the shari'a court as a legal forum for debating issues related to the female body. Hakimas' role in the police station supplemented midwives' role in the community and in court. As these examples demonstrate, these women were believed to have a superior knowledge about the body, a knowledge that enjoyed the backing of an investigating police: it had very concrete practical consequences and a police force to follow up an outcome of an investigation. As outsiders to the neighborhood community, they had no vested interest in supporting either of the parties involved.

The police station became a site in which hakimas' examination gained precedence over testimonies by midwives and over women's narration of their own bodies. Women brought forensic evidence to the police and specifically asked that a hakima examine their bodies for traces of the crimes committed against them. It was these everyday interactions between hakimas, their superiors at the police station, and individual women and families that came to consolidate the truth value and legitimacy of forensic examination.

The development of forensic medicine transformed the way in which legal systems in other parts of the world treated cases related to women's bodies. In nineteenth-century England, for example, courts relied on doctors' testimonies to determine whether women resisted sexual assault and to detect signs of induced abortion. Similar legal practices were imposed on colonized societies, notably India.[57] In precolonial Egypt, by contrast, a new forensic legal discourse relied on categories that made sense in Egypt's communal and familial life. Some of them were shari'a categories, namely, premarital defloration and coerced miscarriage, which somewhat paralleled the categories of abortion and rape. They touched on several points in a woman's life cycle and on patriarchal control of women's bodies and sexuality.

The differences between premarital defloration and rape, and between abortion and coerced miscarriage, are related to the legal and social significance of virginity and pregnancy. In nineteenth-century Egypt, lost virginity could have serious consequences for a woman's marital prospects: the question of coercion was important, but secondary to a damaged hymen. Similarly, as elaborated in the following, the Egyptian legal system was not interested in a couple's choice to terminate a pregnancy. It was legally permissible and might have not been socially condemnable either. In polygamous, slaveholding families, coerced miscarriage served the interest of co-wives and their children; illegitimate pregnancy, moreover, was also a cause for induced miscarriage, not always by the women themselves. The significance of the forensic categories was therefore specific to the time and place.

The status of the hakima's report was different from the role of a midwife in a shari'a court in several respects. As ad hoc witnesses, midwives did not develop any forensic expertise, nor were they expected to do so. The hakima, by contrast, provided specific expertise in forensic medicine, which required not only medical training but also familiarity with legal terminology and practice. She framed her report around details relevant to the investigation, such as the assumed cause and timing of death or injury. The hakima looked for evidence, documented it, and submitted a written report that incorporated legal language and reasoning. This need to document and create a coherent narrative that could be reviewed and appealed was new.

The nature of the knowledge that hakimas produced was also new. They were supposed to confirm facts, such as a ruptured hymen or an aborted pregnancy, and also to produce a narrative that specified cause and effect, the timing of a crime and its plausibility—in short, to weave the evidence inscribed on the body into a coherent story. Their reports therefore often outweighed the testimony of women they examined. The police and councils relied on their reports to reveal a truth that a woman might have been trying to conceal. People who filed their complaints in the police station similarly saw the hakimas' report as capable of proving a fact that they could not otherwise prove, or to reveal a truth that others tried to obscure. As outsiders to neighborhood life they might have been perceived to be less biased; their examination also gained the power and authority of an ensuing police investigation.

One concern that medical practice raised with central authorities was child marriage and its related health hazards. Age of marriage was often related to familial and communal considerations. In patriarchal societies, early marriage assures male control of women, as a girl is handed directly from her father to her husband and therefore turns from "daughter" to "wife" without any intermediate period of adult independence.[58] In discussing child marriage, Islamic legal discourse had to balance the welfare of a child against that of her future husband. According to Islamic law, girls could be married at any age, but the marriage could be consummated only after puberty. Husbands would appeal to a shari'a court when a young wife fled for her father's house, for example, and demanded that she return to the marital domicile. If the woman was too young to tolerate sexual intercourse, the *qadi* could rule that she may stay at her father's home until puberty. A *qadi* could summon a midwife to testify about a girl's competence for sexual intercourse or rely on his own judgment.[59]

In late nineteenth-century Egypt, child marriage and girls' capability to tolerate sexual intercourse became a medical concern. Al-Rashidi's *Bahjat al-Ru'asa'*, for example, cautions that sexual intercourse and pregnancy could be dangerous for young girls or for women suffering from physical deformities.[60] The central authorities became interested in child marriage after receiving hospital reports of young girls who had died as a result of sexual intercourse with their husbands, and the men themselves were convicted for homicide. Hospital reports then strongly recommended that girls not be wed before reaching puberty and becoming capable of tolerating sexual intercourse.[61] In one such case, a man appealed his conviction and claimed that he had not meant to cause the death of his twelve-year-old wife, arguing that "many are married at the age of ten or eleven, and nothing happens to them."[62] This argument not only contested his conviction but also challenged the superiority of medical knowledge and the state's attempt to limit his patriarchal privilege to access the body of a prepubescent girl.[63]

Premarital Defloration at the Hakima's Office

Virginity is a social category popularly assumed to be identical with the physical mark of an intact hymen. A damaged hymen, moreover, is perceived as a mark of penile penetration. The forensic procedure at the police station, somewhat ironically, reinforced and consolidated this assumption, which both contemporary medical literature and *fiqh* and fatwa literature had challenged.

Police reports and medical records referred to a damaged hymen as unequivocal proof of penile penetration, which could also provide indication of its timing ("recently," "a while ago," "two days ago").

Virginity examinations were not new to Middle Eastern societies. Historically, they were carried out as part of community surveillance of women's premarital conduct. This supervision could be subverted, but the possibility of subversion and manipulation does not eliminate the power of such supervision to control women's lives far beyond the physical mark of a damaged hymen.[64] Both Islamic legal theory and nineteenth-century medical discourse, however, questioned the validity of virginity examinations. Judith Tucker cites an eighteenth-century Syrian mufti who resented the practice of sending nonvirgins brides back to their parents on their wedding nights. He claimed that virginity cannot be determined with certainty and a damaged hymen is not necessarily evidence of sexual experience, but might result from an accident.[65] This legal opinion can be found in older Hanafi *fiqh* manuals as well. Twelfth-century Hanafi jurist 'Ali ibn Abi Bakr al-Marghinani, for example, claimed that a woman who had lost her virginity "either by leaping or by any other exertion, or by a wound, or by frequent repetition of the menses" should be legally considered a virgin.[66]

Nineteenth-century medical knowledge, and more specifically, the hakima school textbook, *Kitab al-Wilada,* completely rejected the validity of a physiological examination in determining a woman's sexual experience. According to Velpeau:

> Regarded as the seal of virginity by the vulgar ['amma in Rashidi's translation], and for a long time so considered by medico-jurists [al-atibba' al-shar'iyyin][67] and magistrates, the hymen has on more than one occasion been the cause of an iniquitous decision by the tribunals, either in condemning an innocent woman, or, on the contrary, in absolving one who was scandalously guilty. But at present it is universally admitted that a thousand causes foreign to the act of coition may destroy it, and that copulation itself does not always occasion its rupture. If this membrane be thin, delicate and broad, a sudden or extensive movement of the limbs, excoriations, the appearance of the menses, &c., may cause it to disappear.[68]

Parents and siblings, however, continued to bring young women to the police station to have their virginity examined, and young women sometimes demanded such an examination to prove they had been assaulted. The scientific (and clerical) assertion that a damaged hymen was no indication of premarital intercourse mattered very little to police practice and to those men and women. The hakima's knowledge and expertise carried the added weight of a formal police investigation. Premarital defloration could be a form of bodily injury for which women could demand monetary compensation in the shari'a court. As a violation of a person's honor, it was punishable by six months' imprisonment. It also compromised a girl's reputation and marital prospects. Medical examination, in this context, articulated some explanatory narrative as to the circumstances of the case. Coupled as it was with the social implication of premarital defloration, the opinion of scientists and 'ulama mattered very little.

The introduction of forensic medicine to rape trials in countries such as the United States or British-colonized India was used to dispute women's accusation of assault. Signs of struggle and violence were crucial in proving that a woman had not consented. In Egypt, the medical examination was used to confirm injury to the hymen and its timing because virginity itself was legally and socially significant. In one case, for example, the hakima noted that the man had used his finger. The damage to the hymen was presumably only partial and, more important, did not carry the possibility of illegitimate offspring. This piece of information was relevant in determining the shari'a-stipulated compensation, and presumably the girl's marital prospects. Historically, parents brought girls to court to have accidental loss of virginity registered for future reference, in case a future husband would question her virginity.[69]

A hakima's conclusion regarding the timing of defloration played an important role in supporting or refuting a woman's account. The police discarded women's testimony if a medical examination concluded they had been deflowered prior to the date of their alleged assault. Such conclusion supposedly indicated that they had not been virgins at the time of assault, thus absolving their assailants from responsibility for defloration. Police officers and council members, moreover, were more likely to believe a woman if a medical examination concluded her defloration had been recent.[70]

It is not my intention to assess the truth value of these assertions. My point here is that hakimas' conclusions about the injury and its timing gained a truth value that was meaningful to the police and to litigants. Hakimas gained their importance not only because of the police power they had behind them but also because they made sense to men and women who resorted to the police stations. In one case, a man accused of defloration confessed that he had indeed copulated with the woman but claimed that she had not bled and had therefore not been a virgin. However, when confronted with the results of the medical examination that showed she had been deflowered recently, he took responsibility for her defloration and agreed to marry her.[71]

The presence of a hakima at the police station also encouraged Egyptian men and women to rely on her examinations instead of, or at least in addition to, informal examinations conducted in the community. In several cases, girls had been examined by an unspecified "woman"[72] or the neighborhood's *shaykh's* wife[73] before their relatives brought them to the police station. Cairo's police headquarters even recorded one case in which a father invited a hakima to his own home under the false pretense of a medical emergency. When she arrived, he asked her to examine the virginity of two girls. She found that one of them was a virgin and the other was not.[74] This case implies that hakimas were also called in to inspect girls' hymens outside of a police setting and came to supplement midwives and *shaykhs'* wives as neighborhood guardians of female conduct.

Police officers and councils members often overlooked women's own accounts of events, especially when refuting evidence was supposedly inscribed unequivocally on their bodies. In the introduction, I cited a case of a girl named Siddiqa, who tried to contest a hakima's conclusion that she was not a virgin. Her statements at the police station give a sense of what she believed the hakima would be able to know about her body or of what she believed the policemen who interrogated her would like to hear. Although the common sense of the legal process assumed she had been a virgin before she left home and lost her virginity following sexual intercourse, she claimed the cause to be battering. Most important, Siddiqa's narrative at the police station also challenged the hakima's claim to superior knowledge of her own body. Siddiqa attempted to claim that the hakima may not have superior insight into her past.[75]

During the first years of the British occupation, one can find several cases in which a girl's consent to sexual intercourse constitutes one element in the hakima's report. As demonstrated in chapter 5, a girl's consent to premarital sex was a very important element in her investigation, but it was only rarely debated in terms of physical evidence. In one such case, the hakima commented that a woman was strongly built and sexual assault would have left marks of coercion and struggle on her body. Because the hakima found no such traces, she concluded the woman had probably consented to sexual intercourse. A lower-instance council then convicted her of premarital defloration. The woman chose to appeal the verdict and claimed that the results of the medical examination were not an accurate indication of events, that she was never reexamined, and that the hakima's conclusion was simply not true. The Supreme Council accepted the appeal, but on different grounds.[76] I did not find a sufficient number of such cases to determine whether it was the influence of the British legal system that changed the focus of the medical report. Again, the hakima's report produced a narrative, a cause and effect relationship, that could presumably be read on the body. The girl's appeal, moreover, challenged the hakima's capacity to read her body but at the same time validated the capacity of an examination, by a different person or by different means, to reveal the truth. The forensic examination at the police station created new kinds of thinking of the body and of the knowledge it could manifest.

Both cases discussed here demonstrate points at which women adjusted their narration of their bodies and of sexual assault to fit into new modes of comprehending causality and the body. Siddiqa first claimed that her body was misunderstood but then "confessed" that she had really been involved in premarital sex; in the second example, the girl trusted a medical examination (though a different one) to be able to tell the truth regarding a recent assault. The legal procedure itself had here a "pedagogical" role in "educating" women how to make their experiences of their bodies comprehensible to the legal system. These examples also illustrate agency and resistance articulated within the categories and terms already set by the legal system itself.

Miscarriages

On 23 July 1879, twenty-five-year-old Fatima accused two men and a woman of beating her to the point of miscarriage. The defendants denied the charges. The hakima of al-Jamaliyya quarter examined Fatima's "outside" *(zahir)* and "inside" *(batin);* noted the bruises on her thighs, back, and stomach; described the condition of her genitalia; and concluded that she had indeed recently miscarried, that her fetus was about a month and a half old, and that her physical examination indicated her pregnancy had been a few weeks old. Her examination, however, could not establish a causal relationship between beating and miscarriage because "causes of miscarriage are numerous. They include strong psychological turbulence, carrying a heavy item, falling on a solid object or any other reason that might be clarified in the course of the investigation." When the police confronted her with the defendants' denial, Fatima argued that she did not have further proof against them but that "the facts that were confirmed in the hakima's examinations are sufficient." This was not the case, however, and the council acquitted the defendants.[77]

Fatima arrived at the police station with a specific purpose in mind—pressing charges against those who allegedly caused her miscarriage. She was surprised to learn that the medical examination did not lead to conviction. The fact of miscarriage was established but not a narrative, a cause and effect relationship of a kind that hakimas produced in defloration cases. Punishment may have been one outcome she had in mind, monetary compensation another. A woman's status within her family could be elevated once she became a mother, especially if she gave birth to a son. Many in a woman's environment had a vested interest in causing her to lose her pregnancy. If she was a co-wife or a slave, other co-wives or their offspring could be threatened by her new status or by a potential heir. An enslaver, as I further elaborate in the next chapter, also had an interest in ending a slave's pregnancy because a slave who had his child could not be sold and the child was his heir. Much more than abortions, then, the police dealt with women's accusations that they were beaten to the point of miscarriage, or that they were forced to abort.[78]

Fatima's case is a typical one. It is interesting because it demonstrates the extent of women's trust of the police and the forensic procedure in addressing an assault on their bodies. Typically, again, this trust was misplaced because the hakima did not find any evidence of causal relation between assault and miscarriage. Fatima voiced what others might have thought—that the medical examination would confirm their experience.

At the shari'a court, a victim of coerced miscarriage was entitled to monetary compensation, depending on gestational age.[79] The notion that many factors might cause miscarriage, as the hakima's report in Fatima's case stated, was not new. Ibn Sina's eleventh-century *al-Qanun fi a'-Tibb* (Canon of medicine) ascribed miscarriage to emotional as well as physical traumas including a jump backwards, a serious blow, anger, fear or grief, as well as excessive physical exercise or sexual activity.[80] The wording of the hakima's formulaic account of miscarriage can be traced to *Bahjat al-Ru'asa'*, which mentioned further possible factors: "greasy or bad-quality nutrition, alcoholic or hot beverages, purgatives, vomitives and excessive bloodletting; sleeplessness, hard work, fierce movements with the purpose of carrying something heavy; dancing, jogging and jumping, especially backwards . . . strong psychological turbulences and excessive sexual intercourse."[81] Present-day medicine has not yet fully understood the causes of miscarriage nor devised ways of preventing it. For nineteenth-century Egyptian women, resorting to the police station might have been way of explaining the inexplicable or finding someone to blame.

As in defloration cases, hakima reports differed from midwives' testimonies at the shari'a court in their insistence on accuracy and their attempt to construct a coherent narrative. In addition to determining the fact of miscarriage and the fetus's age, the hakima had to trace evidence of causal relations between beating and miscarriage. The requirement for such evidence was new, as the shari'a procedure required only evidence of beating and that miscarriage actually took place. In the council, on the other hand, even if eyewitnesses supported assault allegations, its relationship to the miscarriage was very hard to prove.

As in the defloration cases discussed previously, the hakima had to read on a woman's body physical evidence of the circumstances of the crime. In miscarriage cases, however, such a causal relationship was very hard to determine, and convictions were therefore very rare. Although signs of beating and miscarriage were clearly read on the woman's body, the causal relation necessary for conviction often was not. It is interesting that whereas the fact of defloration and its timing were always assumed to be known through the hakima's examination, in cases of miscarriage, in which such conclusive findings would have been to the advantage of women, the results were in most cases ambiguous. Reading the body otherwise might have been too threatening to prevailing social norms.

To what extent were women aware of the forensic procedure and of the implication of the hakima's medical examination? It seems that women like Fatima, who came to the police station after a miscarriage and brought the fetus as evidence, knew about the examination and believed the circumstances of the crime could be read on their body. Fatima assumed the police hakima would see what her assailants denied—signs of the assault and consequent miscarriage. Her knowledge of her body and her intimate experience of proximity between beating and miscarriage made her assume that a medical examination would reveal the truth, which eyewitnesses and defendants could not or would not provide. It seems, however, that at least in miscarriage cases, the victims placed too much trust in the hakimas. Women's intimate knowledge of their bodies, here, was not autonomous from social meanings of pregnancy and motherhood, as well as from decades of police presence and of forensic examinations.

Some of the medical examinations concluded that women who pressed charges against alleged assailants for causing miscarriages did not actually miscarry or were not pregnant at all. In one such case, a woman filed a complaint against her husband and claimed that after he had beaten her she miscarried a five-month-old fetus. Her husband denied her accusation. The hakima examined her and concluded that the woman's words were "not correct" because her blood was menstrual and there were not signs of miscarriage or of beating on her body.[82]

Why did these women resort to the police station? One possible explanation is that these women misinterpreted their bodies. Most of the cases (though not all) dealt with early pregnancies. In the absence of reliable pregnancy tests, women might have misinterpreted a belated menstruation as pregnancy and bleeding as miscarriage. Others might have been afraid that a certain incident had caused them to miscarry and were relieved when the medical examination proved them wrong. Another interpretation is that these women were lying, did not realize their lies would be detected in the forensic examination, and therefore underestimated the hakima's knowledge. Most of them were bleeding when they arrived at the police station and may have assumed their menstrual bleeding would be mistaken for miscarriage.

Another set of possible reasons is related to the status of pregnancy in Egyptian society and to women's status once pregnant or as mothers. Some women may have pretended to be pregnant to gain some of the social benefits associated with this status and then used a fight as "proof" that they had miscarried. Others may have assumed the police would take miscarriage complaints, which are related to the loss of fetal life, more seriously than other forms of domestic violence.

This question is related to a larger one: why did women file complaints of miscarriage that were rejected in the overwhelming majority of cases? Why did women go to the trouble of going to the police station, sometimes with their aborted fetuses, after having suffered a physical and emotional trauma, if the likelihood of conviction was so small?

Violence against pregnant women was not rare. Women who lost their pregnancy as a result of a violent assault might have assumed that a medical examination would be able to show what they could not prove by other means. Perhaps they trusted the medical authority of the hakima and believed the results of her examination would be as conclusive as their own experience of their bodies. Another possibility is that they believed that the hakima's examination would do no more than a midwife's examination in the shari'a court—determine the fact of miscarriage and the age of the fetus. Finally, they might have been interested in more than a conviction. The complaint at the police station and the medical examination that followed it may have served a social function as well. The assailant, a husband or a rival, could be publicly summoned to the police and questioned about behavior the assailant thought would go unpunished.

My argument here is that the power of the police station to infiltrate family and community life was consolidated in exactly such moments. The police and the hakimas became a part a familial dispute as women took advantage of these newly formed institutions to seek refuge against violence—no matter how partial and unsuccessful this challenge might have been. The police and the medical examination became a part of women's commonsense understanding of assault and the means to address it.

In both miscarriage and defloration cases, then, the hakima's examinations created social dynamics that neither Clot Bey nor Ahmad al-Rashidi had predicted. Both women and men adopted the forensic medical procedure to resolve disputes involving the female body. The hakimas supplemented existing mechanisms for monitoring the sexuality of unmarried adolescent girls and were believed to be able to read the circumstances of a crime on a victim's body. In both defloration and miscarriage cases, the hakima's examination of women's bodies disregarded women's accounts of events. In the case of virginity examinations, a woman's recent rape experience was overlooked when a hakima concluded that she had been deflowered at some earlier date; women's claims that their hymens were injured as a result of anything other than sexual intercourse were totally ignored, and in some cases, their claims that they did not consent were questioned as well. In cases of miscarriage, women's own testimonies—their perception of a causal relationship between violence and miscarriage—were ignored, privileging their bodies' silent testimonies and the written report of the hakima who had read it.

"Informal Medicine" in Court

As discussed earlier, many women saw the invisible world of the jinn as a factor that could explain their physical and mental well-being. During the second half of the nineteenth century, modern medical discourse permeated both police reports and women's own accounts of their bodies' histories. In this last section, I focus on legal cases that confronted "superstition" with state-sponsored medical-legal institutions. It was here that litigants were told their healing practices could be considered health hazards, that *zar* healers could be held accountable and punished as charlatans. These meeting points, moreover, created and reenacted boundaries between "folk medicine" and Western medicine that only the modern training of the hakima would be able to reveal. This boundary was real enough to make women in labor and parents of sick children turn to the police and to the hakima when their healing procedures had failed.

In official discourse, those who mediated between the world of the living and the invisible world of the jinn were charlatans. According to the 1880 Police Act, they "pretended to have knowledge in matters of the spirit," extracted money from unsuspecting women, and sometimes even "seduced dimwitted women to commit all sorts of despicable deeds."[83] Only officially sanctioned scientific medicine was deemed capable of rational healing of the body, whereas informal medicine was labeled as nothing but false. Police handling of these healers no doubt reflected a real concern with public health. Some of these practices could be life threatening, and they sometimes replaced scientific medicine that in some cases, even in the nineteenth century, could indeed have provided superior care. At the same time, this anxiety also reflects a need to draw a line, which was never that clear, between reliable and unreliable medicine, between the hakima and the superstitious healer or midwife.

Some traces of popular medicine are evident in council and police records. In one case, a man named Yusuf 'Abd al-Rahman al-Sharbatly brought his seven-month-old daughter to a woman named Umm Hana, who introduced herself as a hakima. His daughter's health only deteriorated as a result, and he brought her to the police station. The baby died in hospital five days later. The doctor's report indicated that she suffered from two newly inflicted burns on her face, which caused her death. Umm Hana was convicted of practicing medicine without a hakima license. The council was convinced of her good intentions, however, and sentenced her to only two months in prison.[84] *Tibb al-Rukka* mentions facial burns as means of convincing the child's jinn sister to let go of him and relieve him of diphtheria, although it is difficult to determine whether this was the case.[85]

This case is interesting, first, because it mentions a form of popular practice that rarely reached official records. It is also interesting because of Umm Hana's choice to present herself as a hakima—a choice that, in a way, reaffirmed the distinction between the superstitious and reliable. She took on a category (namely, a "hakima") that was legitimized in official practice but one that was not what she would call herself in traditional society. The police investigated this case as a form of impersonation. Finally, this case indicates an official interest in safeguarding boundaries. Court cases dealing with medical negligence were not new, but this was not the situation here. It dealt with titles, with definitions, and with legitimacy. It also dealt with the abstract new notion of public health.

In another case, a woman named Khadija pressed fraud charges against her healer. She had been possessed by the jinn a year before, she explained at the police station, and chose to consult a *zar* healer named Hasna. Hasna approached her at a *zar* ritual she was attending at a neighbor's place, presented herself as an expert *zar* healer, and offered to help. Hasna promised to cure her but only took her money and failed to deliver on her promise. Although Khadija could not prove her claim because their interactions were private, the police took the investigation very seriously. Hasna's neighbors confirmed that she was known to be possessed by spirits and had a reputation as a healer who used written notes, medications, and oils. Others testified to having seen her walking around the neighborhood in men's attire. Hasna denied these allegations and denounced them as vicious rumors. She was finally convicted, not for stealing Khadija's money, but rather for her practice, which was "detrimental to public order."[86] The money Khadija gave Hasna could have been a "gift" to the jinn, and her use of men's attire, an instance in which the jinn supposedly controlled her body.[87]

Again, beyond an ethnographic anecdote, this case represents yet another encounter, another reenactment of the division between "real medicine" and "the charlatan." Khadija resorted to the police, we are told, to complain about the financial fraud: she paid for a treatment, but ended up being robbed of her money but not of her cure. In her story, she did not doubt the capacity of the *zar* to cure her; in her own understanding of her mental and/or physical problems, it was the jinn who caused her misery. The police, by contrast, were concerned with "public health," a vague concept that a centralizing modern state apparatus had conceived and then reenacted in instances such as this one

Conclusion

The interaction between hakimas located at the police station and individual women constructed the superiority of hakimas' medical expertise and the relevance of police intervention in the intimacy of the female body. At the same time, these interactions also created new narratives, new understandings of the body and of causality. These interactions enabled and then consolidated the professionalization of forensic medicine and the medicalization of legal discourse. They made "the state," through the hakima's speculum, a relevant presence in young women's experience of lost virginity; they created a knowability of bodily processes.

At the same time, these processes led to unintended outcomes and tensions. Women were trying to use the system to their own advantage; some were resisting a hakima's interpretation of their bodies, and others continued to consult other medical practitioners and healers, who were now dubbed "backward" and "superstitious," instead of or in addition to the hakimas. Midwives became an unofficial extension of state power, which meant women were sometimes reluctant to contact them when they did not want a birth to be known to the authorities. At the same time, modern medical knowledge became part of the non-elite understanding of the body and medicine. As this chapter also illustrates, state power and the power of modern medicine created new ways of comprehending the body, and with them, a language that translated into the capacity to act: sometimes challenging, sometimes reclaiming their bodies. As several examples in this chapter illustrate, women asked for their bodies to be comprehended otherwise and their assailants to be punished.

3

Female Slaves, Manumission, and Abolition

On a summer day in 1877, Saluma, a Sudanese freed slave, knocked on a stranger's door in the Palestinian village of Tira in the Ottoman Nablus Province. Saluma had been kidnapped from Cairo about five months earlier. She was smuggled through al-'Arish to Tira, along with five other women, to be sold there as slaves. Her kidnappers had sent her to get some bread from a local bakery, and she was now waiting outside a stranger's house, hoping for a friendly face. The woman who opened the door listened to her story and hastened to inform the local authorities in Nablus. The authorities then sent the six women and their kidnappers to the Cairo police station, and from there they returned to their homes. Two of the other women were named Fatima, and the others were Zayn al-Mal, Bakhita, and Sa'ida.[1]

In this chapter, I examine the case of Saluma and her friends with two objectives in mind. The first is to see how, beginning in the 1850s, international efforts to abolish the slave trade transformed the official treatment of slaves, especially in Cairo. I focus on the Cairo police station and detect subtle but significant transformations in the official conceptualization of slavery and of police role vis-à-vis the slave trade and slaves themselves. Until 1854, the police, the shari'a courts, and the councils upheld the shari'a in protecting the ownership rights of masters and protecting slaves from excessive abuse. Here again I am looking at the role of the police station and the legal system at large in maintaining the institution of slavery—and the role of slaves themselves in legitimizing the distinguished function of the police and with it, of state power in neighborhood life. As I show here, from the mid-1850s onward, the legal system started perceiving its role as protecting slaves and former slaves, such as Saluma and her friends, as free persons.

My second concern here is with the effect of the prolonged process of abolition on slaves and former slaves. Following historian Ehud Toledano, I understand enslavement as a form of legalized violence and, at the same time, as a form of attachment. Enslavement stripped the individual of her earlier life—family, community, even name and religion—while at the same time integrating her into new social networks, most notably the family. It also entailed forced migration into a new cultural context, which required creative coping mechanisms, acculturation, and integration. Thus, although manumission meant freedom, it ruptured the newly acquired bonds.[2] I question here how social bonds were created with enslavement and how they were affected by the slow process of abolition.

The case of Saluma and her friends provides a detailed example of women's fate following manumission. They were kidnapped because they were black, kinless, and hungry in a society where most black women were still slaves. Most of them were kidnapped as they were looking for employment. Most experienced months and years of employment uncertainty after their manumission. Their situation unfolded in the same year Egypt signed a convention committing itself (anew) to abolishing the slave trade.

In her oft-quoted essay "Can the Subaltern Speak?" Gayatri Chakravorty Spivak criticizes historians' attempts to reconstruct subaltern's "pure, retrievable form of consciousness" without deconstructing colonial and postcolonial discourses and privileges. In reading sati narratives, foreign accounts of widow burning in colonial India, she demonstrates how widows' own voices remain muted; even their names, she argues, were translated and/or misspelled to unintelligibility. Between the colonial versions of "they wanted to die" and "white men saving brown women from brown men," women's subjectivity remains in the shadow.[3] Lata Mani's reading of Spivak suggests we keep reading elite and colonial discourses against the grain but takes Spivak's assertion as a warning that we cannot counter discourses of domination simply by letting the subaltern speak. What we can read, instead, are shifting subjectivities, which are sometimes hidden in colonial reports, written for other purposes altogether.[4]

Eve Troutt Powell demonstrates how useful (and depressing) this reading can be for historians of slavery but expresses the hope that histories of slavery will be written in which slaves themselves will be seen and heard and not relegated to the background of political and cultural affairs. She therefore urges historians to seek "original, independent voices" and "real, autobiographical narratives" in our archival records.[5] In this chapter, I use both archival records and travel accounts to reconstruct not slaves' voices but, rather, multiple forces that shaped women's choices within changing social and political realities of slavery.

Enslavement

Historians have little evidence regarding the experience of enslavement and life in bondage. Ottoman slaves did not write their memoirs; their experience of enslavement did not interest the authorities and therefore left little mark in writing. Legal sources present moments of conflict and document extreme abuse but say little about everyday life. Even the very detailed case of the six women is laconic with regard to their lives as slaves and virtually silent on their life before slavery.[6] Sa'ida's enslaver, for example, was a Jew who manumitted her after eighteen years of service. Fatima was bought by a pasha-ranked official "after she had arrived from her country" and was manumitted fifteen years later. Bakhita was simply "manumitted eight years ago."[7] These laconic phrases conceal the violence of the slave trade, the dangerous journey to Egypt, and enslavement itself.

For most slaves in precolonial Egypt, life in bondage started in forced rupture, transfer, and then readjustment to a new social environment. After explaining the legal status of slaves in precolonial Egypt, I proceed to describe the violence of enslavement in precolonial Egypt, as reported by nineteenth-century travelers. In spite of their bias, they provide the only written evidence of the early stages of enslavement.

Slavery in the Ottoman Empire, including Egypt, operated within the boundaries prescribed by Islamic law. The shari'a views slaves as both property and persons. Although it establishes slave owners' property rights, it also offers slaves some protection against abuse. As property, slaves could be owned, sold, given away as a gift, and bequeathed. As persons, their legal rights and obligations were limited. Slaves could convert to Islam, and once they had, they were obliged to perform most religious duties. Slaves could also get married, but only with their owner's permission, and a male slave could marry only two wives (as opposed to four for free men). Slaves also enjoyed legal protection against neglect and abuse. A slave could demand to be resold on the grounds that her enslaver did not provide for her basic needs; and in some schools of jurisprudence, severe neglect made manumission compulsory. The slave was not protected against her owner in criminal law, however, because murder and bodily injury were considered private matters for which only the owner could press charges.[8]

Islamic law also provided the slave with a semi-kinship relationship with his or her owner in the form of legal tutelage *(wilaya)*, which a slave retained, at least formally, after manumission as well. This status offered a substitute for family protection that freeborn men and women enjoyed under law. Thus, a former enslaver was to pay blood money when his or her manumitted slave could not—an obligation of the extended family in the case of freeborn Muslims. A slave owner inherited the property of his or her manumitted slaves, but not the other way round. Enslavers served as their slaves' guardians at marriage—a duty that was normally assigned to a free person's male relative. Manumitted slaves were also identified throughout their lives by the name of their former owners, in a way similar to a free person's identification by his or her father's name. Their first names had already been replaced upon enslavement and the names they were given upon birth often long forgotten.[9]

The status of female slaves was distinctly different than that of males. Men were allowed to cohabit with female slaves they owned as long as the latter were not married, and they therefore served as concubines. Female slaves, moreover, were particularly valued as domestic servants. They were not subjected to the same gender segregation norms as free women, and they were able to perform outdoor chores that allowed their mistresses to stay at home. For these reasons, female slaves outnumbered males three to one. A slave who gave birth to her owner's child gained the privileged status of *umm walad* (a child's mother). This status meant that she was free upon her master's death and was not to be sold to another for as long as he lived. Children of these unions were free and considered their fathers' legitimate heirs. A child of a female slave born to a man other than her owner, on the other hand, became the enslaver's property but could not be sold separately from his or her mother.[10]

In Islamic legal theory, manumission is considered a meritorious act. Most manumitted slaves were freed through verbal declaration by their masters; many female slaves became free upon their owners' deaths as *umm walad*. Slaves had the option of buying their freedom, but only few could afford it. Historian 'Imad Hilal argues that because manumission was considered meritorious, a slave owner who insisted on having a slave pay for his or her freedom was looked down upon.[11]

Although Islamic law does not recognize any distinctions among slaves, in practice slaves were differentiated by race.[12] Most esteemed (and most expensive) were white slaves imported from the Caucasus or Georgia. Those were often conscripted to the ranks of the elite—the men as soldiers and bureaucrats and the women as concubines. This practice gradually faded away in the first half of the nineteenth century. According to historian Gabriel Baer, the number of white slaves in Egypt was about two thousand in 1839 but declined considerably thereafter, to about 2 percent of the slaves freed between 1877 and 1882.[13] Following them in the racial hierarchy were Ethiopian slaves. Ethiopian women were more expensive than their Sudanese counterparts and considered more suitable as concubines. At the bottom of this hierarchy were black Africans, imported from Central Africa (mainly present-day Chad) and the Sudan. Baer estimates the number of black slaves in the 1850s between twenty thousand and thirty thousand, about half of them in Cairo. Egypt's population at the time was about 5 million, with 276,000 living in the capital.[14]

Slave ownership was not merely the prerogative of the Muslim elite. Members of all classes could own Sudanese and Ethiopian slaves, and many slave owners were Jews and Christians. Slave ownership was a status symbol for people of all classes. Baer and Hilal found slave owners among Bedouins, peasants, merchants, clerks, state officials and army officers of all ranks, religious functionaries, and others. Lower-class households could not afford more than one slave.[15] The freed slaves found in Tira reflect this diversity. Fatima's former owner was a pasha-ranked official, and Saluma's was an effendi. Bakhita's former owner was a lumber merchant and the owner of the second Fatima was a translator. Zayn al-Mal was owned by a Copt, and Sa'ida was owned by a Jew.[16]

The manumission option and low fertility rates among slaves created continuous demand for imported slaves. A child of a slave and her enslaver was a free person and could not be counted as slave. Furthermore, the lower ratio of males among slaves and the relative isolation of slaves led to low marriage and procreation rates. Non-elite families owned no more than a slave or two, so slaves were relatively secluded and slave marriages rare. Enslavers' unlimited sexual access to the bodies of unmarried female slaves further discouraged them from permitting marriage between slaves.[17]

The slave trade was therefore crucial for maintaining the institution of slavery. The enslavement of freeborn Muslims being illegal, slaves had to be imported from non-Muslim lands. They were acquired mainly through raids, kidnapping, or capture as prisoners of war. In nineteenth-century Egypt slaves were imported mainly from sub-Saharan Africa, particularly from Sudan and Ethiopia. The largest slave caravans reached Egypt from Darfur, through a desert route known as *darb al-arba'in* (the forty-day road), which led to Asyut in Upper Egypt. Many others reached Egypt from the Kurdufan region, and still others arrived via the Nile or the Red Sea. Many perished on the way.[18]

Archival sources are rather laconic about life before enslavement and say virtually nothing about rupture from family and kin, the road to Egypt that not everyone survived, the adjustment to life in bondage, and the erasure of one's former self. These aspects of slaves' lives were of no interest to free Egyptians. Here foreign accounts are particularly useful, in spite of (and partially because of) their bias: their stated aim was to prove the cruelty of slavery. As Eve Troutt Powell cautions us, slavery itself is the subject in abolitionist writings, whereas slaves remain objects relegated to the background. Slave voices are restructured to serve the abolitionists' narrative.[19] Lata Mani's reading of sati description demonstrates how these can be read against the grain to reconstruct women as subjects. Foreign observers' narratives, she demonstrates, convey stories of coercion and of women's escape from the pyre that subvert the texts' own assertion that resistance to sati was merely an act of the European observer and that women voluntarily sacrificed themselves. While the texts' authors conclude that sati was a religious act, their conversations with women present the complexity of economic and familial pressures.[20]

For my purposes, travel accounts complement parts of the picture that Egyptian sources tend to ignore. It is an important aspect in understanding slaves' lives because many, if not most, African slaves in nineteenth-century Egypt were the first generation in bondage and still remembered their native home, enslavement itself, and the substitution of a new and unfamiliar identity for their old one.

Consider the following example. Sixteen-year-old Barilla was born to a Muslim family in Gallabat village in Eastern Sudan and was kidnapped at the age of six. American traveler Alvan S. Southworth purchased her in Khartoum in March 1872 in order to liberate her immediately afterwards. He recounts her story in the first person:

> One bright summer day, nearly ten years ago, when those dreadful men came, my father had gone to market to get the day's provision; all of my eight brothers

had gone to the mosque to read the Koran, and my mother was in the plantation gathering coffee . . . I was playing with the sheep near the door of the house; my back was toward the entrance. Suddenly I was grabbed by two big hands. A piece of iron was thrust into my mouth like a horse's bit. I felt very sick and frightened. I was carried out of the house covered up with clothing, so that no one could see me. Then I was put in a hut and tied up and kept until nighttime. I sobbed bitterly. I was crushed with grief. My father! My father! My brothers! My mother! My home! My sheep! My dresses! My happiness! I knew nothing! I became bewildered and prayed to heaven. The men came in the nighttime and took me away and put me on the back of a camel. They did not meet anyone. When they saw a caravan coming they moved out of the way, because they knew my father would come in search of me. I was all alone and the only girl they stole at that time. When I got out in the desert the iron was removed from my mouth. I was given to eat.[21]

This story represents a first stage in a slave's life: a violent rupture from home and family. Similar narratives appear in other abolitionists' writings and represent a dehumanizing aspect freeborn Egyptians preferred to ignore. According to Southworth, Barilla was a Muslim, and her enslavement was therefore illegal—but not unheard of.

The next stage was readjustment to life in bondage. English traveler Sophia Poole describes a slave girl shortly after her arrival to Cairo, in her first household in Cairo, an upper-class Ottoman-Egyptian household. "We begged to know the cause of her distress, and gently tried to remove her hands, but to no purpose. She only pressed them close to her face, and gave no reply." Mrs. Poole then learned that the girl was a new slave "and either grief for the loss of friends, or her fears for the future, overwhelmed her."[22]

British traveler Lady Lucie Duff-Gordon received an eight-year-old female slave named Zaynab in March 1863 and handed her over less than a year later to a "Turkish household." Duff-Gordon narrates the next stage in a slave's life—a young girl's transition into life in bondage. In this process, Zaynab had to learn to tell friend from foe, to learn new languages and new religion and to forget old ones. Throughout the text, Zaynab's former self as a free Sudanese child is gradually erased, and a new one emerges. She is now a slave but also an opinionated Muslim and anti-Christian girl in whom Duff-Gordon was no longer interested.

Unknown photographer, *An Arab Woman,* ca. 1900. Courtesy Silver Print Collection, Ein Hod.

Zaynab was sent from Khartoum as a present to Mr Thayer, the American consul general in Cairo, who had no other female servants in his household. He invited Duff-Gordon to see the girl, and when she noticed how coarsely his cook and groom treated her, she decided to take her in. Initially, Zaynab's most notice-able behavior was fear. When she noticed Duff-Gordon's earrings, she pierced her own ear with a pin because she believed it would please her new mistress. The incident shocked Duff-Gordon, who wondered, "what extremities of terror had reduced that little mind to such a state?" "When she first came, she tells me, she thought I should eat her; now her one dread is that I should leave her behind," Duff-Gordon wrote her family on 13 April 1863. She was so "slavish" and so obe-dient, Duff-Gordon further observed, that she had no will of her own. Alongside this fear, we find vague traces of Zaynab's past. In her first letter about Zaynab, Duff-Gordon described the girl singing "quaint Kordofan songs all day." Such appearances of her native identity do not appear later in the text.[23]

The few descriptions that follow in this and later letters convey less of Zaynab's past and more of her process of acculturation into Muslim Egyptian society and her enslavers. In two weeks' time, Zaynab learned to use a needle and to sew "very neatly and quickly."[24] Duff-Gordon left her for a while with her daughter Janet in Alexandria, and Zaynab quickly picked up the multiple languages spoken in the international community there.[25]

Zaynab was apparently spared some form of social erasure; she was allowed to retain her name and was not forced to convert to Christianity. In a letter from 21 May, Duff-Gordon mentions that one of Zaynab's former enslavers called her Salaam al-Sidi, "but she said that in her own village she used to be Zaynab, and so we call her." The tragedy of forced identity erasure is further illustrated through a minor character, a former slave named Mahbrooka, who took interest in Zaynab because "her fate had been the same." She was bought by an Italian man, was his slave until his death, and then got married and embraced Islam. She bore the pain of forced conversion to Christianity, forgot her original name, and was relieved when Duff-Gordon reassured her there was no intention of baptizing Zaynab by force.[26] The tensions and struggles to which Zaynab and Mahbrooka were exposed were related to their enslavement by foreigners: Zaynab's social environment included both Duff-Gordon's household and her peers—slaves of neighboring households.

The religious tension led to frequent conflicts between Zaynab and Janet's Christian servants and, later, with Duff-Gordon herself. "Zaynab is much grown and very active and intelligent, but a little louder and bolder than she was owing to the maids here wanting to Christianize her, and taking her out unveiled, and letting her be among the men," she wrote on 1 October.[27] Later, Duff-Gordon wrote her family that she decided to hand over Zaynab to a Muslim household. Zaynab, she explained in a letter dated 1 December 1863, "is very clever and I am sorry, but to keep a sullen face about me is more than I can endure, as I have shown her every possible kindness."[28]

Lucie Duff-Gordon's description conveys some empathy with the young girl. Apparently, she wanted to be an enlightened enslaver. She allowed Zaynab to keep her name, extracted her from a male-only work environment in which she was clearly miserable, and did not force her to convert. Slavery, however, always entailed violent erasure of the slave's former self, no matter how well intentioned an enslaver may have been. If at first Zaynab believed that piercing her ear with a pin would please her new mistress, she soon enough learned that using needle and pin for sewing would be more appropriate for this purpose.

Zaynab's own voice is not heard at all. She is frightened, efficient, lazy, or grumpy, but the only words she is recorded as having said are "How piccolo *bint?*" each word taken from another language she picked up in Alexandria. She is mostly mute (or produces odd sentences), but her textual presence reveals some aspects of slavery of which the author herself is only partially aware: the process of enslavement, the process of erasure of the slave's former self, and glimpses of a slave's past. The actual story is of two children (Zaynab and the now-adult Mahbrooka) sold to slavery, forced to forget their former culture and embrace a new social role and a new culture, and at times even a new name and a new religion. Unlike Zaynab, Mahbrooka is allowed to speak of her pain through the text and to protect Zaynab against a similar fate.

Taken together, these three narratives, though not typical, give a sense of the process slaves underwent as they were taken from their homes in the Sudan to an Egyptian or an Ottoman-Egyptian household (more often than not, more than one). This process was not uniform: some slaves were born into slavery and knew no other existence, but tens of thousands were first generation in slavery. This processes, in one form or another, helped shape one's sense of self. It created new identities and new subjectivities and erased old ones. It was a distractive process but also a formative one. The violence embodied in the early stages of enslavement is significant if we wish to reconstruct what slavery meant to slaves themselves.

Evidence of life in bondage is scattered and fragmented. Archival sources mainly describe moments of conflict and pain because these were the instances that reached the police or court. Records of runaway slaves rarely mention motivation for escape. When they do, archival records employ no more than a word or two: unhappiness (*'adam rahatihim*) or hardship (*ta'b*). Such tropes conceal more complicated life stories, but in legal language they simply mean that a slave had the legal right to ask to be resold. In rare cases, slaves mentioned physical punishment or beating but did not offer any further detail.[29]

There is some tacit evidence of pain in cases of real or alleged suicide. Although such cases are very few, they convey the sense that such a drastic step was believed common among slaves. When police officers asked leather merchant Jibril Fadlallah about the death of his slave whom he was later convicted of murdering, he had a ready answer. She committed suicide, he said: "It is known that people of her kind/race *(jins),* when they hate their masters, sometimes eat something that makes them die. That's probably what happened to her as well."[30] Jibril's comment, which he hoped would sound credible, implies that suicide was believed to be much more common than the handful of documented cases. He was not the only one to generalize this way. When Bakhita, a black slave of a man named Bakhit Ruman, hanged herself, he was not surprised: "Maybe she hanged herself because that's what happens with female slaves sometimes."[31]

Other suicide cases offer more details but not an actual narrative. One slave threw herself out of a window "due to her illness." Her owner's mother testified that "she asked for water, and when we were about to bring her some, she suddenly threw herself out the window."[32] When a slave owned by a man named Sa'id al-Danqalawi killed herself with a knife, he told policemen that he had "never been insolent or offensive towards her, in a way that would have made her do such a thing."[33] In a similar case, a slave named Bakhita hanged herself from the banisters of a staircase. The slave who found her testified that there had been no enmity between her and any other member of the household and that she had not been mistreated; the neighbors further testified that they heard no suspicious noises the night before. When asked whether a woman six feet tall could hang herself from a banister four-and-a-half feet tall, the police doctor argued that "it cannot be denied that in cases of emotional distress, people may do things that would put their lives in danger."[34]

Archival and travel sources relate some stories of extreme violence. Sophia Poole mentioned brutality toward female slaves. A neighbor, she claimed, beat a female slave so severely that she lingered in pain for a week and then died. Another man beat one of his slaves until she threw herself out the window and was killed on the spot. Both men, she then mentioned with great indignation, were Christian.[35] One council record mentions a slave named Maryam who drowned and was hastily buried without contacting the authorities and therefore without a proper autopsy. One of her owner's neighbors claimed that the owner's wife had had a fight with the slave, had beaten her with a stick, tied her hands behind her back, and had her legs bound with iron chains normally used to restrain horses. The neighbor could not support his claim, however, and the autopsy that the police hakima conducted on the exhumed body could not prove it either.[36]

When a slave named Khayra died, the doctor concluded that severe beating was the cause of her death. Her owner, however, claimed that she was indeed beaten but only very mildly, as punishment for her frequent escapes. The bruises found on her body, he further claimed, were a result of her escape route, which included climbing from her window to a nearby palm tree. Because there was no further proof of beating, the owner was acquitted.[37]

There is also some evidence of sexual abuse, as socially and legally defined in a society that did not see slavery itself and the sexual access of enslavers to their female slaves as a form of abuse. Sexual abuse cases that reached police and courts involved a man who had sexual intercourse with a slave he did not own. Most often this was a slave who belonged to another member of his household, such as a wife or parent. Even then, he could claim in court that he believed himself to be a legal co-owner. In this case, qadis and muftis applied the principle of doubt and absolved him from responsibility. The question that arises is whether this legal doubt also affected social handling of such illegal intercourse. Police and council records describe some horrid cases, in which such illicit intercourse ended in forced abortion or even infanticide—which might imply that such instances could carry social sanctions that men did not want to face. In one such case, a man sexually assaulted his uncle's slave, impregnated her, and subsequently threw the newborn child into a well.[38] Although he might have been legally able to get away with impregnating his uncle's slave, perhaps he also hoped to avoid some social sanctions related to this illegitimate pregnancy, not to mention the financial burden of another heir.

Alongside pain and abuse, archival sources relate stories of escape or attempted escape. Slaves who attempted to escape were often aware of their legal rights and opted for absconding because they believed that even if caught, resale or even manumission were bound to improve their lot. In his discussion of Ottoman slavery, Toledano views absconding as a calculated act by people at least partly aware of the consequences and risks involved. They escaped in order to improve their lot inside the slavery system, sometimes with another enslaver, and sometimes to improve their living conditions within their own households once captured and returned.[39]

In one such case, a slave jumped out the kitchen window on the second floor of her owner's household, about twenty feet above street level, and fractured her thigh. She escaped after her owner went to work and left her with his wife, who would not let her sleep in her quarters.[40] A white slave named Fatima managed to escape through a cellar. Other slaves noticed this and informed the police, who caught her in the street in the company of two men.[41]

Some cases also involved theft. Stolen property could guarantee the slaves' economic survival in the days and weeks following their escape.[42] Not all theft allegations were true, however. Foreign observers noted that slave owners filed false accusations against runaway and manumitted slaves to force them to repay or return to servitude. Accordingly, the 1877 Anglo-Egyptian Convention obliged Egyptian police to investigate theft charges seriously only after guaranteeing the slave would be legally manumitted. In this way, a slave's freedom was not contingent on whatever charges had been made against him or her.[43]

Slavery and the Khedival State

During the first half of the nineteenth century, Mehmet Ali Pasha's state-building efforts heavily relied on slave labor and the slave trade. Mehmet Ali occupied the Sudan in 1821, as part of an attempt to create an empire within, and later autonomous from, the Ottoman Empire. A few decades prior, the Ottoman Empire prohibited the export of white slaves to Egypt in order to weaken the rebellious Mamluk elite, which depended on steady supply of slaves. The occupation of the Sudan was therefore designed to replace the declining slave trade from Georgia and the Caucasus. Mehmet Ali also hoped to monopolize the slave trade income and to conscript slaves to his newly founded army and employ them in his agricultural and industrial projects. Many of the slaves his army captured in the Sudan did not survive the journey to Cairo, however. The failure to create a slave-based army led him to create a mass-conscription army modeled after the French example, although several slave regiments persisted to the 1830s.[44]

During the middle of the century, the African slave traffic to Egypt and the Ottoman Empire increased. Egypt's occupation of the Sudan in 1821 and the Ottoman reoccupation of Tripoli facilitated the importation of slaves to both Cairo and Istanbul. The Ottoman ban on slave exports to Egypt and the subsequent Russian occupation of Georgia and the Caucasus reduced the trade of white slaves and led to increased demand from other sources. The cotton boom further increased the demand for slave labor in the Ottoman provinces, particularly Egypt.[45]

As previously noted, the police station came to play new roles in Egypt's urban life as it became a site to which people could turn to address injustice or to resolve disputes. Slavery was no exception: slave owners and traders brought sales disputes to the police; runaway slaves were caught in the streets of Cairo and brought to the police station; and slaves themselves resorted to the police station to address abuse. This communal recognition and the capability of the police to provide assistance endowed it with power and made Khedival state-building efforts into a meaningful presence in family and community life.

As police and court records indicate, at least until 1854, the Egyptian police handled slavery-related disputes in close cooperation with the slave traders' guilds. Midcentury police records contain correspondence with mainly two individuals: 'Ali Effendi, the head of the white slave traders' guild, and Sulayman Agha Abu Dawud, who headed the black slave merchants' guild until his death in 1877.[46] The slave merchants' guild temporarily lodged runaway or manumitted slaves awaiting legal procedures. Because most of those slaves had not committed a crime, the police could not hold them in custody, but they had no home to which they could return.[47]

The police acted, for example, as arbiters in cases of sale disputes, which were then forwarded to the shari'a courts. If the buyer managed to convince the police that the slave he had purchased was "damaged," the police could demand that the buyer receive his money back and return the slave to the merchant.[48] The parties could use the services of the medical personnel at the police station to detect physical defects on a slave's body and especially to determine whether a female slave was pregnant. If impregnated by her owner, she could gain the status of *umm walad,* making the sale null and void.[49]

At least before the mid-1850s, runaway slaves took up a lot of police time and work. To many of them, police offered the shari'a-sanctioned option of resale. Those who brought runaway slaves to the police station were often law enforcement personnel, such as neighborhood *shaykh*s, guards, soldiers, and policemen, who patrolled the city at night and were bound to notice unusual movements. A few came of their own accord to file a complaint or to demand their legal rights. During one summer week of 1854 (10–17 June), for example, twenty-three runaway female slaves reached the Cairo police headquarters following a failed escape attempt. Five of them were Ethiopian and the rest Sudanese. Two of them came on their own initiative, and the rest were captured on the streets of Cairo and brought to the police station.[50] The police then acted as mediators. They collected the standard award of twenty-five piasters from the slave owner and handed it to the capturer.[51] If a slave chose to return to her owner, the police handed her over. If she chose to be resold, she was sent to the head of the slave merchants' guild in the al-Sultan market. The merchant then gave the sales money to the former owner, having deducted some fee. The police also took measures to ascertain the slave's identity to ensure that the money would be transferred to the right hands. When slaves ran away from a slave merchant, the police confirmed their identities but also confirmed that the merchant was a certified guild member.[52]

The police forwarded to the shari'a court cases of runaway slaves who claimed their enslaver had denied them their legal rights as *umm walad* and sold them.[53] In other cases, women claimed their enslavers' heirs illegally kept them in bondage after the enslaver's death. Some cases involved paternity disputes, as when the owner or his heirs refused to recognize the child.[54] In other cases, women claimed that they had been legally manumitted but that their masters withheld their documents. In such cases, the police often demanded owners to supply the relevant documents; when they refused, if the freed slaves could provide evidence of a verbal manumission, the police issued such documents in their stead.[55] Among those accused of mistreating their slaves, one can find a member of Lower Egypt's Council of Adjudication[56] and the patriarch of the Greek Orthodox Church.[57]

Baer argues that one of the reasons for the relative failure of early abolition attempts during the second half of the nineteenth century was the strong interest group of slave merchants and the involvement of state officials in slave ownership and trade. The officials who had to take measures against the slave trade owned, purchased, and even traded slaves themselves. The patriarch and the council member are two examples. One can imagine that officials at the customs service, or ones stationed in the Sudan, owned slaves and had a hard time figuring out why they should venture to stop the trade.[58]

The abolition of the slave trade and the institution of slavery were related, in part, to a transformation in elite discourse in the Ottoman Empire, including Egypt.[59] Abolition entailed reconceptualization of personhood in terms of universal freedom, not only among the elite, but in many other social strata as well. Slaveholders as well as slaves had to reformulate their understanding of family life for such a transformation to occur. The initiative originated outside the Ottoman Empire and was imposed on Egypt in a series of international conventions. By the 1880s, the Egyptian Khedival family and, later, the *effendiyya* class hailed the monogamous family as a sign of modernity. An 1880 decree, for example, already termed the slave trade an "offense against humanity," a terminology that can be found in the Ottoman center of the period as well.[60] The process of abolition, however, was one whose effects were felt beyond elite circles in the everyday of police work and in life choices of slaves and enslavers alike.

The Road to Abolition

The case of the six slaves belongs to a period of increased international efforts to suppress the slave trade. In August 1877, Egypt signed the Anglo-Egyptian Slave Trade Convention and agreed to take assertive measures against slave trade. This was an important moment but not the first effective step toward abolition. This convention followed over two decades of British pressure and local efforts, from the 1854 banning of slave trade to its abolition in the early 1890s.

Efforts to abolish slavery in British colonies started in Britain itself in the mid–eighteenth century. Abolitionists first faced opposition by West Indian planters, who saw slavery as ordained by God and as a Christianizing-civilizing mission. Indeed, the British government was at first reluctant to infringe upon slave owners' property rights. By the early decades of the nineteenth century, rejection of slavery became a part of British middle-class value system and was then incorporated into English national identity, closely associated with Enlightenment ideas, and into the colonial civilizing mission. Slavery was abolished in Britain and its colonies in 1833, and British efforts were then directed to the American South. Following the American Civil War, these efforts came to focus on the Ottoman Empire, including Egypt, and helped to establish British hegemony in the region, as part of its imperial project.[61]

Most scholars tended to focus on the 1877 convention as a turning point in state policy toward slave ownership and the slave trade, and they argue that earlier measures were of questionable efficacy. In the Sudan, at least, Ottoman-Egyptian officials were not very effective in enforcing the ban, and the Khedive Isma'il hired British officials in their stead.[62] In Cairo, however, everyday police work was changing, as well as policies on slavery. Although many state officials had vested interests in slave ownership, police and council records do indicate a policy shift. The police station was a crucial site in this transformation. The success of abolition and transformations in the lives of individual women (and men) depended, in part, on the ability of runaway slaves to trust the police and rely on police willingness to help them.

In December 1854, following international pressure, Egypt's governor Sa'id Pasha issued a decree banning the importation of slaves from the Sudan. The decree further ordered that slave caravans be stopped at customs and all slaves emancipated and returned to the Sudan. The effectiveness of this ban was limited. Following the decree, many merchants asked for a grace period to sell the slaves they had already purchased, then used this grace period to buy and import even more slaves. Subsequent orders indicate that the ban was somewhat effective in discouraging the slave trade, but far from watertight.[63]

The Egyptian administration in the Sudan was forced to readjust to its new role. Until the 1840s, Egyptian troops in the Sudan conducted raids and captured slaves for Mehmet Ali's army and for his new industrial and agricultural projects. Sa'id's decree now ordered the same functionaries to suppress the trade and to fight against the traders. The customs service similarly shifted from collecting customs for slaves and vaccinating slaves against smallpox to preventing slave caravans from reaching Egypt. The new orders from Cairo ran counter to their commonsense understanding of their role and of power hierarchies. Dismissal of some of these officials was among the first measures to curtail the slave trade.[64]

Khedive Isma'il, Sa'id's successor, took more assertive measures against the slave trade and ordered the governor of the Sudan to arrest slave merchants, free their slaves, and imprison the traders. He also sent military expeditions to sub-Saharan Africa, with the proclaimed purpose of combating the slave trade at its origins. The failure of Egyptian administrative and military measures to stop the trade during the 1860s led Isma'il to appoint European officials as governors and leaders of military expeditions against traders. He hired British officers, such as Sir Samuel Baker and Charles G. Gordon, to suppress the slave trade in the Sudan. As Troutt Powell argues, he also had imperial goals in mind, seeing it as his mission to civilize the peoples of East Africa. Isma'il hoped that abolition would make Egypt a recognized part of Europe, as a colonizing, civilizing nation.[65]

These measures were only partially successful due to continuous demand and persistent trafficking. Four-year-long Anglo-Egyptian negotiations led in August 1877 to the signing of the convention with the purpose of stopping the slave trade from reaching or passing through Egypt. Egypt agreed to suppress the trade, punish merchants, and free slaves caught in these caravans. It also allowed British ships to search all ships sailing through the Red Sea. Slaves caught leaving Egypt were issued manumission documents and a passport certifying their status as free persons. The convention also provided for a twelve-year grace period for internal slave trade and the sale of slaves between families.

In addition, the convention and the decrees that followed it provided for the foundation of manumission bureaus that would supplement the police in handling slaves and manumission. These bureaus were authorized to issue manumission documents to all slaves wishing to be freed, even against their owners' wishes. The bureaus' officials were also to help freed slaves find salaried jobs. Women were to be employed in "government centers" or as domestic servants in "respectable homes"—jobs that were extensions of the role they used to play in Egyptian society and the role that freeborn Egyptians were used to see them playing. Men were to be given agricultural, industrial, or domestic jobs, and children were to be sent to government schools.[66]

In 1891 Lord Cromer declared the slave trade had been abolished and slave ownership was in its last days. In November 1895 British and Egyptians signed the Anti-Slavery Convention. It prohibited all slave trade, even between families. The convention classified any infringement on the freedom of an individual as a crime, and the slave trade became infrequent and clandestine. By that year, slave ownership had significantly declined. The emerging Egyptian nationalist intelligentsia started condemning slavery as un-Islamic. Illegal trade and illegal enslavement persisted, albeit at unknown scale.[67]

The effectiveness of abolition efforts and their impact on families and on slaves themselves cannot be assessed merely through official policies; it was low-ranking officials and, again, women who chose to resort to the police station to demand their rights, who made abolition relevant. As early as 1854, police reliance on the slave merchants' guild and the slave market significantly weakened. At least theoretically, the police could no longer send slaves to the slave market to be resold, and indeed fewer cases of runaway slaves reaching the police station are recorded after the fall of 1854.

Police correspondence from that fall indicates some confusion as to the role the police were to play, from that point on, in slave ownership disputes. In a letter to the Khedival office from October 1854, the Cairo police commissioner asked for instructions. Until that day, the letter read, he handed runaway slaves whose owners lived outside of Cairo to the head of the slave merchants' guild. The latter would then detain them in the market until their owners reclaimed them. The last female slave sent to the market, a runaway slave called Nur al-Sabah, was sent back with the information that the slave trade was banned and the slave merchants' guild could therefore no longer hold slaves for the police station. The confused police commissioner then claimed he was not aware of the ban and its implications and asked for new instructions for handling runaway slaves.[68]

The cooperation between the police and the slave merchants' guild lasted beyond the 1854 ban, but the extent of this cooperation is not clear. In a case recorded in March 1858, the police sent a slave called Bakhita, who was unhappy with her enslaver, to the slave merchants' guild "to have her employed as she sees fit." It is unclear whether she was to be manumitted and employed as a free woman or resold as a slave.[69] According to Baer, in the 1860s the government relied on the *shaykh* of the slave traders' guild to lodge and feed liberated slaves until they found the means to fend for themselves.[70]

Court verdicts from the 1850s and 1860s similarly indicated a shift of emphasis. In the winter of 1864, for example, two female slaves, Sa'ida and 'A'isha, ran away from their masters. A Sudanese man named Musa al-Barnawi persuaded them to accompany him to Cairo, where he promised he would marry Sa'ida. When they got to Cairo, however, he tried to sell both but was caught. A Council of First Instance convicted al-Barnawi of theft, according to article 11 of chapter 3 of the Sultanic Code, which concerned theft of "items whose worth is about a few hundred piasters."[71] The Supreme Council of Adjudication accepted the lower-instance ruling but concluded that the man should be convicted of abduction instead, according to article 6 of chapter 2. This particular article referred to persons, rather than chattel, and to anyone who "abduct[s] a Muslim or non-Muslim girl to another region or another country claiming to have married her without her relatives knowing it."[72] In this transitional moment, then, the same women were considered property in one legal instance and persons in another. This case, moreover, illustrates a pedagogical process: the Supreme Council instructs a lower court instance to view them as persons rather than property.[73]

With the decline of the legal slave trade, continuous demand for slaves initially led to brisk illegal trade. The import of slaves from the Sudan and the kidnapping of slaves and freed slaves appear in police and court records from the 1850s onward, although it is difficult to determine whether and how much the ban on slave trade was enforced. In one case, a slave named Halima was kidnapped from her owner in Samannud in Lower Egypt, brought to Cairo, and sold to a slave merchant. She was subsequently resold several more times, until she managed to inform one of her buyers that she was actually a stolen slave. She was then returned to her kidnapper, but she managed to escape and inform the authorities, who arrested her kidnapper and returned her to her original owner.[74] In another case, a slave named Bakhita reached the police station and claimed she was unhappy with her owner and would like to be employed elsewhere. A short investigation revealed that she had been smuggled from the Sudan and purchased illegally. The slave dealers who sold her were convicted for violating the "widely known" Khedival decree against slave trade.[75]

A May 1873 decree stated that the wide land of the Sudan, and the multiple ways leading to Egypt, made it very difficult to stop the trade. It then ordered the immediate release of all slaves coming in to Egypt, such that the men be conscripted to the army, the boys sent to schools, and the women wed to "those who wish to be married."[76]

In August 1878, only a year after the Anglo-Egyptian Convention, Scottish missionary John Hogg caught two Sudanese men smuggling three slaves and brought them to the American consulate in Asyut. The men claimed that one of the women was his wife, but Egyptian authorities suspected that they intended to sell her and sentenced them to two months' imprisonment, in accordance with the convention. The involvement of foreigners, both missionaries and foreign consuls, in enforcing the ban was also noted in other parts of the Ottoman Empire in this period.[77]

The 1880 Police Act describes the border-crossing stage: "Some charlatans, especially of West African origins, deceitfully collect Sudanese women and children and sell them to Bedouins, who then smuggle them to Gaza and other places to sell them there."[78] The six slaves described in the beginning of this chapter followed exactly this route.

In their interrogation at the police station, all six women narrated similar stories. They were unemployed, even hungry, and met a woman who offered them jobs in al-'Abbasiyya, a new neighborhood on the outskirts of Cairo. When they reached the desert, Bedouins attacked them, stole their jewelry, and took them to a cave in al-Huwaytan Mountain in the Sinai. During their weeks-long stay there, more women were brought in, about two or three a week. When their number totaled about forty, their kidnappers distributed them among several traders. Their particular group traveled to Tira. Almost all six mentioned two free children, ages six and eight, who were kidnapped in Manshiya and then sold in al-'Arish and Gaza. Hawwa, another freed slave kidnapped under similar circumstances, told the police that two women of her group were too old to endure the journey and were murdered by their captors before leaving al-'Arish so they would not hold up the entire group.[79]

Some of the illegal traders mentioned in police and court records were Sudanese and West African immigrants, and others were freed slaves themselves. Illegal trade provided some former slaves with an easy source of income, when most legitimate trades were not available to nonguild members or those outside of kinship networks. They took advantage of weaker compatriots with whose vulnerability they were all too familiar. Women who tended to trust others who shared their skin color and fate were therefore easily deceived.[80]

Manumitted Slaves

As difficult as life in bondage may have been, freedom presented its own challenges, particularly economic. The persistence of abolition efforts turned manumitted slaves into a large-scale social problem—rather than merely an individual predicament. In a satirical column by nationalist thinker 'Abdallah Nadim in 1892, cited by Troutt Powell, a manumitted slave called Bakhita claimed free life to be harder than slavery. For her, the uncertainty of independent living was almost intolerable. Although domestic labor did not differ much from her experience as a slave, it was confusing and difficult to work in a different household every month.[81] Half a century earlier, French physician Clot Bey (see chapter 2) similarly captured some of the hardship facing manumitted slaves in the Egyptian society. European tourists, he wrote, bought slaves to emancipate them, believing they were performing charity. Clot Bey argued that they were actually condemning the freed women to further misery: "In a country in which a woman cannot live without male tutelage liberty forces the manumitted slave to choose between two lamentable alternatives—poverty or prostitution."[82]

Both comments, though written by free men, reflect what manumitted slaves described in police and council records—economic insecurity and the absence of family, community, and guild networks, which made life very difficult. Some historians have assumed that the reintegration of slaves in the free society was not problematic because free status and common religion erased all stigmas. The centrality of skin color to the system of slavery and the importance of social networks to individual identity and to economic and social survival render such a generalization meaningless.[83] According to Baer, the difficulties of integration into the free society were related to the absence of a labor market capable of absorbing free labor. As I further demonstrate in the following, finding employment outside the guild and outside social networks was a daunting task indeed.[84]

The 1877 Anglo-Egyptian Convention ordered the Egyptian police to ask manumitted slaves, upon their release, whether they have any means of livelihood and to verify their claims. If they were found to be unable to support themselves, the convention then stipulated they should be employed in agriculture or in domestic labor.[85] This specific stipulation attests to the extent of the problem and to official understanding of the consequences of mass manumissions. It also implies that freed slaves continued to play the kinds of roles they had played in Egyptian society as slaves—as domestic and agricultural workers.

This chapter's opening story may be read as reflective of economic insecurity, as all six freed slaves were captured while seeking employment. Sa'ida had been manumitted a year before and worked for a butcher for three and a half months; when he left for the Hejaz she remained unemployed. Fatma's Nubian husband had divorced her a year before and left for his home country; she worked for the Egyptian Bank scribe for six months, then left and was unemployed for a month. Bakhita had been manumitted eight years before and had worked as a servant ever since.[86]

Manumission meant detachment from all-important social support networks. Outside these networks, freed slaves had to persevere mostly on their own. As outsiders to the guild system, for example, they had a hard time finding employment.[87] According to Baer, moreover, the market for free labor was virtually nonexistent before the late nineteenth century. It was only when the labor market was capable of assimilating them that freed slaves integrated into Egyptian society.[88]

Skin color also impeded social integration because it affected the ways in which freeborn Egyptians saw Sudanese men and women.[89] Troutt Powell argues that in late nineteenth-century Egypt, Sudanese were viewed as a part of the domestic scene, as the servants and doormen of Egyptian society, and therefore had a hard time integrating as equal members. Egypt's colonial relations with the Sudan further led many Egyptians to see Sudanese as barbarians civilized by Egyptian occupation.[90] This stigma is also reflected in official terminology. Police and court records often use the term *jariya* (female slave) to describe free black women, sometimes in tandem with the term *ma'tuqa* (freed slave), connoting both race and past slavery status.

Blackness of skin also put manumitted slaves in actual danger. First because they were readily identified as they wandered about looking for employment. Two of the women found in Tira were clearly traced by their kidnappers because they were black. Zayn al-Mal was approached by "a man who recognized her, but [whom] she did not recognize"—a man who recognized her vulnerability or even learned of it from a third person. Sa'ida met the woman who had kidnapped her on the street as she was looking for employment, and both women started talking because she was a Sudanese "of the same race," which might imply not only a slave status but also a specific ethic group.[91] Here, more clearly, it was race, combined with hunger and despair, that made Sa'ida conspicuous and vulnerable to her kidnappers.

Black manumitted slaves could easily be resold as slaves. A black woman was assumed, by default, to be a slave, unless she could prove otherwise. Runaway slaves were found as government-paid guards and policemen kept a watchful eye on blacks who could not satisfactorily explain their whereabouts or display manumission documents.[92]

Identification as a slave was not based on skin color alone, however. As Troutt Powell demonstrates, slaves' clothing also made them immediately recognizable. She cites a court case in which a doorman recognized a woman to be a slave because she "came in a black robe and a white veil, like the clothing of a slave."[93] It may have also been a woman's habitus, her body language, the way she moved in public space that made it easy to distinguish her from free Muslims.

Therein lay the importance of manumission documents for the very survival of freed slaves. In a society of growing physical mobility, in which communities were shattered or displaced, documents came to replace the authority of the local community in authenticating a person's identity. Ottoman shari'a court records document numerous manumission deeds *(i'taknames)* and manumitted slaves probably also held copies of such deeds.[94] For black women wandering the streets of late nineteenth-century Cairo, these documents meant freedom. Oral testimony to the verbal act of manumission was not always easy to come by in a city of more than three hundred thousand inhabitants. These documents were crucial for finding a job for women who had no other means of support. Accordingly, the 1877 Anglo-Egyptian Convention defined denial of manumission documents as equivalent to denial of freedom. Anyone who took away or withheld a freed slave's documents was punishable as slave trader.[95]

Freed slaves who came to the police station and complained that their documents had been withheld stated that they literally could not survive without them. In one such case, three freed slaves claimed that because they had not received their manumission documents, they could not find employment as free women and were on the verge of starvation. The police station conducted a brief investigation that verified their claims and granted them such documents.[96] In another case, a man illegally resold his manumitted slave and withheld her manumission documents. A government official was about to purchase her on the slave market when she informed him of her actual status. After an initial denial, her former owner agreed to provide the documents, which would "enable her to work for her living" and would also protect her from illegal trade.[97]

Without means of support or community networks, many freed slaves had to fend for themselves. Some chose to remain with former owners as servants, fearing the economic insecurity of freedom. Domestic service was the kind of work they were expected to find outside their former enslavers' home anyway. Manumission bureaus, founded in 1877 following the convention, as noted previously, actively referred freed slaves to domestic labor.[98] Some women settled into marital life, and others resorted to prostitution. Many of them formed their own alternative networks that sometimes failed, as the friendly face of a fellow freed slave sometimes turned out to be that of a trader, as our opening case demonstrates.

Some runaway slaves and manumitted slaves saw the Sudan as a viable alternative to life in Egypt. It is hard to determine, however, how widespread this choice was, how many survived the journey back home, and what they found when they got there, as the slave trade probably dramatically affected their native communities. Some of their family members and friends might not have been there when they returned. In one case, the police reproached a slave owner who waited a week before asking their help in finding his runaway slave for not reporting her escape earlier, "although he knew that when slaves, both male and female, run away from their masters, they normally go to the Sudan."[99] A black woman called Badi Sabah was found on a Nile boat; she immediately confessed that she had indeed escaped from her mistress with the purpose of "going to her country" and had stolen some of her mistress's clothes and jewelry, probably to finance her long journey.[100] A manumitted slave named Bahr al-Zayn asked the Cairo police to send her back to the Sudan and to help her find a husband in the Sudan regiment. The police station granted her request and sent her to the Sudan.[101]

The extent of this phenomenon is not known, yet is it safe to assume that it was a reasonably accessible option. Manumitted male slaves were often conscripted to the Egyptian army and made the journey back home as soldiers. Some of them might have traveled to Egypt, married free women, and settled there, and their stories might have inspired some of their peers. It was a long, expensive, and dangerous journey, however, and those who chose to take it were probably few in number. In some cases the authorities might have been more than willing to help those who wanted to return to the Sudan, sparing Cairo's streets from yet more vagrants.

For some manumitted slaves, marriage was an option, but sometimes only a temporary one. Of the six women found in Tira, Fatima married a Nubian man after her manumission, but he divorced her a few years later when he returned to his country. The other Fatima was married to a man named Muhammad al-Bayumi and was kidnapped when he was away traveling; upon his return he informed police of her absence, and it was his complaint that initiated the investigation from the Egyptian side. Zayn al-Mal married a Sudanese servant who died shortly after his conscription; after his death, her former owner chose to throw her out of his residence, and she had to find a place on her own. A freed slave called Hawwa was found in Jaffa in the course of the investigation. She was married to a Sudanese soldier who had left for the Sudan. One of the traders told her that several men, including her husband, had deserted, and promised her that he was waiting for her in al-'Abbasiyya, where she had been kidnapped.[102]

Some manumitted slaves had children, some of whom were born of their former masters. Some tried to keep their children after manumission, although custody belonged to the father or his household. In other cases, women had to support children unacknowledged and unsupported by their father's family. In one case, a freed slave named Fatima lost custody when she married a former officer of the Cairo police station. She came to court claiming that they had divorced and demanded custody. A neighbor then testified that Fatima and her ex-husband were still living in the same household, which might have implied that they had pretended to divorce for the sole purpose of regaining custody.[103] Of the six women found in Tira only one, Saluma, was a mother. She had borne her

Adullah Brothers, *A Group of Women,* ca. 1880. Courtesy Dan Kyram's collection.

enslaver a daughter, now twelve years old, and had to leave his residence because of frequent conflicts with his wife. He got her an apartment in Azbakiyya, and both Saluma and her daughter worked as tailors to support themselves.[104]

To find work, freed slaves had to rely on new networks and institutions. Nineteenth-century travelers in Istanbul described self-help organizations of freed slaves that provided help against enslavers and also against sickness and life's misfortunes, in the form of popular religious practices.[105] In Cairo, foreign observers noted the existence of a guild of domestic servants, which became stronger in the late nineteenth century following the abolition of the slave trade.[106] According to British traveler Edward William Lane, who wrote in the 1830s, servants in large towns were under the authority of a *shaykh,* who helped potential employers find servants and then became responsible for the conduct of the servant he had recommended and held accountable in case of theft.[107]

I could not find evidence of a servants' guild, but I did find some references to an employment agent *(mukhaddima)* prior to the foundation of the manumission bureaus in 1877. These agents helped manumitted slaves find employment, mainly as domestic servants. In one case recorded in the council's archives, a freed slave called Fatima found a job through an employment agent after presenting her manumission documents. Fatima did not hold the job for long, however; she stole a precious ring from her employer and escaped.[108] In another case, an employment agent called 'A'isha illegally sold a slave to a woman who had asked for her help in finding a servant and settled for a slave.[109] Hawwa, the freed slave kidnapped to Jaffa, managed to contact the British consulate and was returned to Cairo. Once there, she asked the police to refer her to a *mukhaddima,* who helped her find a job.[110]

There is some evidence that some former slaves resorted to prostitution and that others worked as servants in brothels.[111] One murder case, for example, refers to an Ethiopian freed slave named Za'faran as a prostitute,[112] and another mentions a Sudanese slave called Halima as the brothel's servant.[113] Most tragic, perhaps, is the story of a Sudanese woman named Bakhita, who was murdered by a Sudanese soldier because she had not kept her promise to leave the brothel and marry him. She was a slave in an Alexandrian household, and her enslaver manumitted her and several other slaves before his death. She had been unhappy in his household and left soon after his death to work in a brothel in the al-Turtushi slum in Alexandria; from there she moved to Ma'ruf slum in Bulaq.[114] Bakhita, prostitution, brothels, and the slums they inhabited will be the focus of the next chapter.

Finally, popular medicine, fortune telling, and the *zar* were other survival mechanisms for slaves and manumitted slaves. Official decrees and medical textbooks refer to such practices and rituals performed by black slaves, former slaves, and Sudanese immigrants, alongside Islam, which many of them came to embrace.[115] The 1880 Police Act cautioned against African fortunetellers as "charlatans who read people's fortunes in the sand and in the books and claim to be knowledgeable in matters of the spirit."[116]

'Abd al-Rahman Isma'il's 1892 book on popular medicine (see chapter 2) also attributed fortune telling specifically to Sudanese. He described Sudanese men "sitting on the open road, by the walls of a house, in front of them a bit of yellow sand. All sort of riffraff, idling fools, come to see them and ask them to foresee their black future and painful fortune." Street performances of black men in African attire also feature in travelers' accounts and in Orientalist paintings from the period.[117] Sudanese women, mostly elderly, read people's fortune in seashells and minerals, which they spread in front of them on the ground. "Like their fellow countrymen," wrote Isma'il, "they sit on the open road. in front of them seashells and small pieces of colorful minerals, in green, red and black, each having its own name and its own meaning."[118]

As noted in chapter 2, scholars have suggested that many of the popular beliefs that foreign and local sources ascribed to Sudanese and Ethiopian slaves and manumitted slaves were actually a blend of religious practices and belief systems that slaves had brought with them and Egyptian popular religious practices. Because there is no evidence of the *zar* in Egypt before the nineteenth century, Richard Natvig speculates this was a belated development that followed the Egyptian occupation of the Sudan and the increased influx of slaves.[119] Pamela Constantinides similarly hypothesizes that the cult of spirit possession known as *zar* was an indigenous belief system developed in Egypt and then disseminated to other parts of the Ottoman Empire, as well as back to the Sudan, partially through slaves' pilgrimages to Mecca. According to Toledano, this was one way of domesticating the unfamiliar, creating new meanings that made foreign land seem like home.[120]

Conclusion

The abolition of the slave trade and large-scale manumission changed the face of Egyptian families and communities. It created a large group of kinless women (and to a lesser extent, men) who were not affiliated with any social networks. The newly founded manumission bureaus chose housework for women and military service for men to help "clear" the streets from potential beggars and prey for illegal trade. This process also meant that many free Egyptians had to get used to the idea that black women and men were no longer slaves.

The abolition of slave trade in precolonial Egypt was a prolonged process of readjustment. First, it was a process in which the Egyptian administration, and more specifically the legal system, had to readjust their mechanisms and conceptualization of slavery. From a legal system that sanctioned slavery and the inherent inequality between free person and slave, it turned to abolishing the slave trade as an unjust and inhumane practice. State authorities, moreover, came to see slaves more as persons and less as property. As part of this process, Egyptian society as a whole had to readjust to the illegality of slavery and also to viewing black men and women as free persons.

At the same time, slaves themselves were undergoing a process of readjustment to their new lives as free persons as individuals and as a social group. Some chose to stay on with their former enslavers and preferred the security of their masters' households to the insecurities of the job market. Others chose to return to the Sudan. Still others remained in Egypt and had to cope with racial prejudice and inaccessibility of social networks. To do so, they formed networks of their own, with varying success.

Police and council records shed a new light on slavery. As we have seen, they shift our focus from shari'a-defined justice and women's roles inside the family to questions of labor, as well as social networks and women's capability to survive without them. They also provide insights into women's agency and coping mechanisms. Although archival records fail to offer unmediated voices of slaves, they portray a system that was attuned to their plight and helped them to address their hardships. The story that opened this chapter is about slavery and manumission, free labor and readjustment to free life; it is also a story about race. Most important, it is a story about female agency—that of a woman named Saluma who mustered the courage to knock on a stranger's door one summer day in 1877.

4

Prostitutes and Other Women of Ill Repute

Zanuba, a *qadi*'s wife by second marriage, left her husband and started working as a prostitute for her cousin Nafisa, who owned a brothel in Bulaq, one of Cairo's poor neighborhoods. Her husband and father informed the police and asked that she be punished. Along with Nafisa and Zanuba, the police recommended convicting Zanuba's first husband for encouraging her to move into her cousin's establishment, "in spite of the fact that he knew that she was a respectable woman *(hurra)* and Nafisa was a prostitute."[1] In another case, a couple turned over their daughter, Sayyida, to the police and claimed that she had turned to prostitution after her divorce. She was convicted because she "used to be a respectable woman, and passed from the path of moral rectitude to immoral deeds and the disgraceful path of drinking, illicit sex and disobedience to her parents." The brothel owner, Zaynab, was also imprisoned for six months, having disregarded "former warnings to her and women like her not to allow non-dubious women into their houses and to immediately contact authorities in order to prevent respectable women from illicit sex, through seduction and the like."[2]

Both cases deal with boundaries of respectability, with social handling of those who dared cross them, and with the role of police in enforcing such segregation. I look here at prostitutes and brothels as sites of social control, in which individual family members, neighbors, neighborhood communities, and state officials raised competing and sometimes complementary claims. In a way, all were concerned with separating respectability from vice: banning prostitutes from "respectable" neighborhoods and "respectable women," such as Zanuba, from brothels. Safeguarding these boundaries corresponded with growing tension between the influx of rural immigrants and manumitted slaves and the

79

growth of the urban slums, on the one hand, and a demand for a rational (and hygienic) urban space, on the other. Reconfiguration of power in the nineteenth-century shifted surveillance responsibilities from the neighborhood community to a hierarchy of a modern state; it also manifested itself in police and neighborhood handling of prostitution, making the brothel a site of state formation—one in which the presence of the state in communal life was configured.

Prostitutes and Other Nonrespectable Women

As in other times and places, "prostitute" in late nineteenth-century Egypt referred to both a person and a metaphor. In both popular and official discourse, the prostitute was the ultimate outsider to the normative patriarchal family, diametrically opposed to the *hurra*, the respectable wife, mother, and daughter.[3] When official records use the word "respectable" in the plural they imply the dominant classes, or "those whose lifestyle and/or welfare were judged to be more seriously threatened by prostitutes," as argued by Khaled Fahmy in his article on prostitution in nineteenth-century Egypt.[4] Respectability, however, was also a gendered term, and when used in the feminine tense, the *hurra* was the chaste daughter, mother, or wife who accepted her role in the patriarchal bargain.[5]

Respectability and prostitution were supposedly opposed, but the prostitute was threatening because women's sexuality was believed to be treacherous and easily led to temptation, especially when contrasted with its male equivalent. Several proverbs listed in Johann Burckhardt's 1817 lexicon mark the *hurra* and the *qabha* (the public woman) as opposites but as two sides of the same coin, as evidenced in popular sayings such as "a decent public woman rather than an indecent honest woman."[6] Other proverbs claimed that "an honorable man is honorable, even though mishap should befall him,"[7] as opposed to "if thou shouldst prove a virtuous woman, hang a jar on my ear."[8]

Archival records of late nineteenth-century Egypt provide some examples for the ambiguous boundaries of respectability. Women and places of ill repute could easily be mistaken for respectable, and vice versa. The 1880 Police Act, for example, warned policemen and *shaykh*s that prostitutes might pretend to be respectable women and rent an apartment in a good neighborhood under such false pretense.[9] Similarly, maidens whom the police had found in a brothel sometimes claimed they mistook it for a respectable place. In one case, for example, a prostitute who heard her daughter was seen in one of the neighborhood's houses had to ask a man she saw nearby whether it was a respectable place because she could not determine what it was by its appearance.[10]

The terms used to describe nonrespectable women are similarly ambiguous, which implies that prostitutes were not always clearly distinguished from other lower-class women. Only few court cases use explicit terms such as "prostitute" *(hurma min al-fawahish, bagha', mumis),* "madam" *('a'iqa),* or "brothel" *(karkhana).* Most cases use more ambiguous terms such as "dubious" *(mashbuh)* women or such who "have strayed off the straight path" *(ghayr mustaqimat al-ahwal).* Both terms implied a gendered notion of respectability. When referring to men, these terms usually described habitual criminals, whereas in the case of women, they often connoted sexual misconduct but not necessarily prostitution.[11]

The picture is further complicated by the tendency, also prevalent in other times and places, to equate nonmarital sex, or even casual interaction with men, with prostitution. A woman who "strayed off the straight path" could be, for example, one of the public performers who captured the imagination of contemporary travelers. Some of these were musicians who performed to a female-only audience in private parties or inside the harem. Others were street performers but were not involved in commercial sex, and some worked as prostitutes as well. Foreign travelers often tended to view all these women as prostitutes, and some of them might have been considered nonrespectable in their communities as well.[12]

Although "dubious" and "prostitute" were interchangeable, in many cases there is no indication that a specific woman was actually involved in commercial sex. In one case, a woman described as one who had "strayed off the straight path" professed to be an orange vendor.[13] Another woman thus labeled claimed to be a street sweeper.[14] It is unclear, however, how these women acquired their reputations and whether they were actually involved in commercial sex. Lower-class women often worked outside the home as servants, peddlers, or unskilled laborers. Upper-class women, on the contrary, could afford to observe stricter gender segregation norms, and their presence outdoors could compromise their respectability. This ambiguous definition of prostitution affected the regulation of women's conduct in the urban space, which was rapidly transforming during the second half of the nineteenth century.

Sex and the City: Prostitution and Urban Transformation

Council and police records from the late nineteenth century portray prostitution as a predominantly urban phenomenon. Although partly reflective of
the urban bias of these sources, this portrayal also reflects social realities and
historical developments associated with modernity. Scholarship on prostitution
in other historical societies points to the effects of industrialization and rural
migration on urban prostitution. Social and economic upheavals following the
Industrial Revolution created a growing supply of migrant women, many of
whom viewed prostitution as a viable economic alternative to poverty. Industrialization and the migration of rural laborers and peasants also created a large
population of unattached and sexually deprived males who sometimes chose to
visit prostitutes.[15]

Similar processes were affecting Egypt's urban landscape. Mass recruitment
to the corvée and army drove many peasants to the city. Some escaped recruitment, and others chose not to return to their home villages after years in service.
The 1877 abolition of slave trade and subsequent manumissions swelled Egyptian
towns with freed slaves—men, women, and children. European businessmen
and travelers inhabited the newly built neighborhoods, and European prostitutes
quickly followed. Improved sanitation contributed to increased natural growth.
The railway further facilitated mobility and brought new immigrants to the city,
improving central authorities' access to the countryside.[16]

On the night of 1 April 1874, Iranian merchant Qasim Nasrallah stabbed a
Turkish-Ottoman officer to death in a brothel in Suez. For several months, Qasim
had been regularly visiting Fatima, one of the brothel's employees, and was allegedly in love with her. Four days prior to the murder, he had threatened to kill
any man he saw with her, and Fatima had angrily asked him to stop visiting her.
In their trial, Qasim was sentenced to ten years' imprisonment, and Fatima and
her madam to two months—for having failed to prevent him from visiting the
brothel and what seems to have been a predestined death.[17]

More than just another crime of passion, the Turkish officer's murder reflects
vast social transformations in the Ottoman-Egyptian city. All men and women
present in the Suez brothel that night of 1874 were touched by the developments
Egypt was undergoing in the second half of the nineteenth century: the opening of the Suez Canal in 1869, Egypt's integration into world economy and its

growing dependency on European powers, the abolition of the slave trade, and the growing number of foreigners. Indeed, none of them was native to the city. Hajj Qasim Nasrallah, the killer, was an Iranian who had owned a store in Cairo's Khan al-Khalili bazaar for three months before moving to Suez two years earlier. Two of the prostitutes whom the police interviewed that night, Anisa and Fatima, were Cairene. Fatima had moved to Suez six years earlier and had been working at Anisa's brothel for only six months. Za'faran, a third prostitute, was a freed slave who had been living in Suez for the past three years and had moved into the brothel only three weeks before. Most of the brothel's patrons were Ottoman soldiers on their way back from Yemen, part of which the Ottoman army had occupied only two years before. The Ottoman officer and the Iranian merchant quarreled in Ottoman Turkish, which the prostitutes admitted they did not understand.[18] This heterogeneity reflects the transient nature of port cities, but is also reflective of a specific historical moment.

The city of Suez, on the northern tip of the Red Sea, experienced nineteenth-century transformations in a particularly dramatic fashion. It had served as Egypt's port to the Red Sea and thereafter to the Indian Ocean for centuries. Goods imported from Arabia, India, and Sudan, as well as pilgrims and soldiers on their way to the Hejaz, passed through here. Yet three developments changed the city's destiny in the 1860s: the railroad connection to Cairo established in 1854 meant vastly increased traffic of people and goods; the 1864 opening of the Isma'iliyya Canal brought fresh water from the Nile, boosting the city's development and the growth of crops in nearby fields; and the opening of the Suez Canal in 1869 enormously increased maritime traffic. The city was vastly reconstructed, with new residential buildings, hostels, and shops, as well as coffeehouses, taverns, and European-style hotels. Both native and foreign merchants moved their businesses to Suez to take advantage of the opportunities it now offered. Governorate offices, a police station, a shari'a court, and a hospital were opened to serve the needs of its growing population. Foreign consulates and churches served the growing foreign communities of Europeans, Ottomans, and Iranian nationals. According to 'Ali Mubarak, Suez transformed from a village of 1,500 residents in 1833 to a town of 12,000 in 1867, shortly before the opening of the canal. According to Baer, in the 1870s its population somewhat declined: after work on the canal had ended, many foreign nationals left the city. Suppression of slave trade further reduced one of the city's sources of income.[19]

Suez is but one example of the drastic transformations that also affected Egypt's largest cities, Alexandria and Cairo. Both cities experienced two growth trends: on the one hand, the expansion of upper-class, European-modeled neighborhoods, and on the other, growing shantytowns inhabited by rural immigrants. Over the course of the nineteenth century, Alexandria experienced unprecedented expansion, from about 25,000 inhabitants in 1825 to 232,000 in 1882, due to the Egyptian governors' industrial and maritime enterprises. Both internal and international immigrants began to inhabit newly established neighborhoods outside the old city walls. Most of them immigrated from delta villages and inhabited Alexandria's new slums, and a small minority of Europeans inhabited its renovated quarters.[20]

At the same time, Cairo's population increased from about 260,000 during the short-lived French occupation of Egypt (1798–1801) to 374,838 in the census of 1882.[21] Most contemporary observers tended to associate prostitution with Cairo's luxurious quarter of Azbakiyya, due to the proximity of hotels and venues such as coffeehouses, taverns, and the Azbakiyya Park that opened in 1872.[22] Council and police records also point to Bulaq's new slums, probably due to the concentration of lower-class immigrants and the proximity of the Qasr al-Nil barracks. By 1884, Azbakiyya and Bulaq became the most populated quarters in Cairo. Azbakiyya, however, housed a much wealthier population—government income from Azbakiyya was three and a half times that collected from Bulaq. Both quarters also offered the largest numbers of coffeehouses and taverns.[23]

The Azbakiyya quarter was dramatically reconstructed in the course of the nineteenth century. Once the residential quarter of Ottoman aristocracy, Azbakiyya Lake was drained in the 1830s and turned into a European-style garden. Later in the century, Azbakiyya became a hub from which new roads radiated, and the garden was turned into a park modeled after the Parisian Parc Monceau. Hotels, coffeehouses, and taverns opened around it. Brothels shortly followed, mainly on Clot Bey Street, Muhammad 'Ali Street, and in the nearby Was'a Square, located northeast of Azbakiyya Park.[24] Mid-nineteenth-century travelers complained that Azbakiyya was not hospitable for Europeans, as prostitutes, peddlers, acrobats, and beggars wandered among its coffeehouses and harassed tourists. In later decades, however, travelers began to lament that Azbakiyya had become a totally European quarter, no longer reminiscent of the "real Orient" of their imagination.[25]

Bulaq experienced a different kind of development. Once a small village on the Nile and the city's main river port, it became industrialized, with textile factories, an iron foundry, and Egypt's first printing press. Until the 1840s Bulaq also retained its earlier status as a center of commerce, manufacture, and transport. By the 1850s, however, it was integrated into Cairo and quickly became one of Cairo's slums. The inauguration of the railroad during the middle decades of the century brought about a decline in river traffic. By midcentury, travelers described Bulaq as a "dilapidated" suburb. As Cairo expanded, Bulaq was incorporated into the city and became a poor immigrant neighborhood composed of temporary housing, or 'ishash.[26]

Many prostitutes, in both Alexandria and Cairo, worked in shacks called 'ishsha or takhshiba, usually made of mud bricks or wood and rudely furnished, in new shantytowns around both cities. In Cairo, prostitutes' hovels were located mainly in Bulaq. In 1884 'Ali Mubarak counted 3,878 woodsheds in Cairo, about 7.5 percent of listed buildings.[27] In Alexandria, continuous immigration brought about the establishment of clusters of shanties around city walls: near the city's harbors, around the Mahmudiyya Canal, in the east, and in the vacant lands of the walled city. Prostitutes lived mainly in the Kum Bakir, Kum Nadura and al-Turtushi neighborhoods.

Police and council records imply that neighborhood dynamics, combined with police enforcement, created some informal zoning that pushed many prostitutes to parts of the city in which their presence was deemed less disturbing, that is, poorer neighborhoods and/or in the proximity of women "like themselves." Prostitutes tended to open new brothels near existing ones and were therefore concentrated in certain city streets or blocks. In one assault case, for example, a prostitute called for help and managed to summon several prostitutes and coffeehouse patrons from nearby establishments, who rushed to assist her.[28] When a "dishonorable" woman of Akhmim village in Jirja was murdered, the police interrogated her neighbors—three men and nine women "like herself."[29]

Within this urban setting, three institutions came to be most associated with prostitution—the brothel, the coffeehouse, and the tavern. The brothel itself could be a small hovel or a two-story house. Some police and court cases mention several rooms with doors that could be locked from the inside.[30] Other cases refer to a two-story building, the second floor of which had a large room where the prostitutes and their clients could enjoy dinner and drinks.[31] The roof was sometimes used for sleeping, especially on hot summer nights.[32] Some cases mention male or female servants,[33] and other establishments owned slaves, perhaps an indication of relative affluence.[34]

The word used for "brothel" was the Ottoman *karkhana,* or "a prostitute's place" *(mahall al-fawahish);* in many cases, the prostitute's residence was not mentioned at all. Very few cases explicitly mention a madam *(karkhanjiya* or *'a'iqa).* Other cases refer to a "landlady" who rented out rooms to prostitutes. The distinction between the two may have been blurred: landladies were not always pimps, and tenants were sometimes self-employed. In one murder case, for example, prostitutes claimed that the victim, a Syrian prostitute named Susana, had been their landlady. They did not share the same apartment but rather lived in small, adjacent apartments.[35]

In addition to the brothel, prostitutes were associated with two distinctly male spaces—the tavern and the coffeehouse. Historians of other Ottoman cities have noted that due to the Islamic prohibition on alcohol, the Ottoman coffeehouses often served social functions similar to those of taverns and tried to imitate the atmosphere of the tavern in all but the drinks served. Men frequented such places for gambling, drug consumption, and obscene puppet-shows, and coffeehouses sometimes offered a safe haven for political discussions and dissidence. During the nineteenth century, new European-style coffeehouses were opened, especially in Alexandria, that also offered billiard tables and foreign journals. Women's presence in coffeehouses and taverns was generally associated with immorality. Police and court records describe how young women were lured into such establishments and then deflowered—either there or in a nearby brothel.[36] The Police Act similarly notes prostitutes' habit of spending the night in coffeehouses and taverns, a habit that according to the act should be eliminated.

Council and police records describe coffeehouses, taverns, and brothels as a part of men's nightly routine. In one theft case, for example, two men testified that they had coffee in a coffeehouse in Muhammad 'Ali Street near Azbakiyya Park, then drank some alcohol in a tavern in the nearby Was'a Square, and finally went together to a brothel where they drank more alcohol and had sex with prostitutes.[37] In another case in Alexandria, three men reported having had coffee together in a coffeehouse, then getting drunk in a *buza* (a tavern serving a beerlike beverage) in a Kum Bakir neighborhood, and finally going to the nearby prostitutes' hovel.[38] Brothels, taverns, and coffeehouses were often adjacent. In one case, the tavern was located on the first floor and the brothel on the upper floor.[39] In other cases, prostitutes or their servants were sent out to buy food and alcohol from nearby establishments.[40] In two cases, patrons of a coffeehouse rushed to the rescue of a prostitute when she was assaulted by her client and cried for help.[41]

Such a detailed description of prostitutes, their dwellings, and their clientele is not available for earlier periods. It is therefore difficult to assess the impact of nineteenth-century transformations on the geography of prostitution. It is noteworthy that such details become important enough to be registered in this period and that petty quarrels at brothels reach the authorities. Indeed, in precolonial Egypt supervision of prostitutes and control of their conduct becomes more a part of modern state apparatus.

The Neighborhood Community and the Gaze of the State

> God grant us no neighbor with two eyes.[42]
>
> —Nineteenth-century Egyptian proverb

In January 1871, Cairo police headquarters received a petition from a quite unusual coalition, composed of the Shafi'i mufti, the deputy patriarch of the Roman Catholic Church, and residents of Darb Mustafa neighborhood in Azbakiyya. They complained that the neighborhood *shaykh* had violated state regulations by allowing brothels and taverns to be opened near a mosque, near the church, and in the proximity of respectable homes. Patrons of the brothels and taverns, they added, knocked on neighbors' doors and harassed women on their way to the church. A representative of the petitioners even took police officials on a guided tour through the neighborhood and identified eleven brothels and three taverns. The petitioners asked the police to "clean up" the neighborhood, relocate all dishonorable women, and discharge the *shaykh*. The council found their complaint justified. The *shaykh* was dismissed, and the illegally opened brothels were closed down.[43]

The case of the Darb Mustafa neighborhood illustrates a complex and multilayered system of control that struggled to segregate urban space and minimize interactions between respectable and nonrespectable members of society. First, the neighborhood community exercised its privilege to expel unwanted elements. Second, the officially appointed neighborhood *shaykh* could either allow or forbid a prostitute to reside in his neighborhood. Finally, when the latter had failed, the police and councils were authorized to review the *shaykh*'s conduct.

In nineteenth-century Britain, the Venereal Disease Act signaled a new level of state intervention in social problems, an extension of government responsibility, and the creation of new institutions to regulate women's bodies. In Egypt, regulation and medical examinations were enforced only following the British occupation. Even before, however, police involvement in the case of Darb Mustafa neighborhood and in similar cases articulates new notions of state power, in which regulation of women's nonmarital sexuality played an important role. The self-regulatory mechanisms of the urban neighborhood became part of a hierarchy of supervision and control. In Egypt, such a dynamic created a new kind of relationship within neighborhood communities, which were reconfigured as part of a new kind of state power. In this new dynamic, the neighbors' choice to turn to the state reaffirmed its role in neighborhood life.

In Ottoman cities, neighborhood surveillance played a significant role in maintaining order. Social networks, such as the neighborhood community or guild, disciplined their members, and central authorities relied on this internal discipline to enforce law and order. Community surveillance was subsumed in legal procedures, and people could be held legally responsible for crimes committed in their neighborhood or by relatives. The Ottoman Code viewed crimes such as murder, robbery, theft, or assault as subject to collective responsibility. Inhabitants of a house, a village, or a neighborhood were compelled to help find suspects of murders that had taken place in their midst. People residing near a crime scene were required to locate the offender. Finally, an escaping criminal's relatives were also held responsible for bringing him to justice. Neighborhood communities thus had a vested interest in maintaining public order.[44]

Ottoman legal practice, moreover, allowed neighborhood communities to expel unwanted elements, such as criminals and prostitutes, to preempt such trouble. Historians of Ottoman shari'a courts have reported cases in which neighborhood communities demanded the expulsion of individuals such as prostitutes, alcohol distillers, and "dishonorable" men and women. The local *qadi* was to decide whether to order such expulsion and then to enforce it.[45] Direct state intervention, particularly in Egypt, was limited to taxation. During the seventeenth and eighteenth centuries, female singers and dancers were under the fiscal control of tax farms, and prostitutes were organized in a taxed guild.[46]

During the 1830s and 1840s a growing concern with public health became prominent, and in this context, prostitutes came to be seen as health hazards. They endangered the health of army troops and the students of the newly founded state schools, and they were viewed as the main agents of venereal diseases. The establishment of the hakima school described in chapter 2 clearly reflects this concern. In 1834, Mehmed Ali banned prostitutes and female public entertainers from Cairo and other cities in Lower Egypt, in which his troops and new schools were concentrated. His officials closed down brothels and put prostitutes under the supervision of their neighborhood *shaykh*s. Those who continued their practice were punished, as were *shaykh*s who failed to enforce the ban. An 1836 decree ordered prostitutes to be expelled to the town of Isna in Upper Egypt.[47] The ban was still enforced, at least partially, in the 1850s, and police records offer several cases in which men and women involved in illicit sex were imprisoned, expelled, or chastised. In most cases, it is not entirely clear whether money had actually changed hands, that is, whether the parties had been involved in commercial sex as opposed to nonmarital sex.[48]

Beginning in the late 1850s, police became less concerned with commercial sex as such and more concerned with instances in which prostitutes threatened the peace of the city's respectable classes. Alongside their efforts to contain crime, police activity was directed at preventing complaints such as that filed by Darb Mustafa's residents. By enforcing this informal zoning, the police strove to minimize interactions between respectable women and those who had "strayed off the straight path."[49]

Darb Mustafa's residents' request to have their neighborhood "cleaned up" corresponds with new ways of perceiving public space. Official decrees and regulations echo contemporary travelers' accounts and describe the Egyptian urban space as chaotic, overcrowded, and smelly, in other words, a space that should be cleaned, ordered, and disciplined. Mehmed Ali and his heirs built new modern neighborhoods that featured broad boulevards, spacious squares, statues of public figures, and French-style public gardens. They introduced gas and electricity services, linked Egypt's major cities to new railroads, and installed a water supply system.[50] Concerned with public health and the spread of epidemics, the Egyptian administration also cleaned Cairo's streets and issued regulations with regards to proper discharge of domestic refuse. Waste disposal was no longer considered a private matter but rather a public health issue.[51]

These efforts extended to public order as well. The police patrolled city streets at night to detect any suspicious movement in the otherwise dark and empty streets. Pedestrians were required to carry lanterns after dark, and those who did not were immediately deemed suspect and could be arrested.[52] Most vulnerable to police control and surveillance were vagrants, beggars, and street performers who had no permanent place of residence, no work, and no connections. They were disturbing the peace in the streets that the state was trying to clean up and discipline.[53]

The 1880 Police Act described Cairo's urban space as a chaos that should be disciplined. Public fights were endangering public order; fortune tellers were taking advantage of superstitious women; and wedding processions were also problematic as participants would stop at taverns and bars, get drunk, dance, steal, and start fights. The police were also concerned with unwanted elements "wandering about public spaces without work, home, or source of income." These were poor immigrants from Upper Egypt, Sudanese immigrants, and freed slaves wandering about Cairo's alleys, begging, performing, and supposedly also stealing, attacking innocent passers-by, illegally trading in slaves, and committing innumerable other atrocities. The act further warned that public performances of dancers, singers, monkey trainers, or bear trainers caused overcrowding, which lead to traffic jams and accidents and risked young children. People's habit of leaving their children outdoors unattended only aggravated the problem.[54]

On a discursive level, this was an elite concerned with disorder, with rationalizing Egypt's social chaos. The city was becoming full of rural immigrants and manumitted slaves who had no permanent place of residence. This description also reflects the ways in which the urban elite came to perceive social order and defined how the city should look. The act reflects an elite gaze that adopted, in part, foreigners' perceptions of Egypt, at a time of its growing political and economic dependency.

Low-ranking policemen and *shaykh*s were supposed to enforce the new regulations. However, like the abolition of the slave trade, which had conflicted with many Egyptian's commonsense understanding of family life, many low-ranking officials continued to patronize brothels and saw prostitutes as a normal part of neighborhood life. Still, many Cairenes wanted the streets cleared and vagrants arrested. They saw the nightly watch and the police stations, and they also could see their complaints were taken seriously. By complaining against a *shaykh*'s

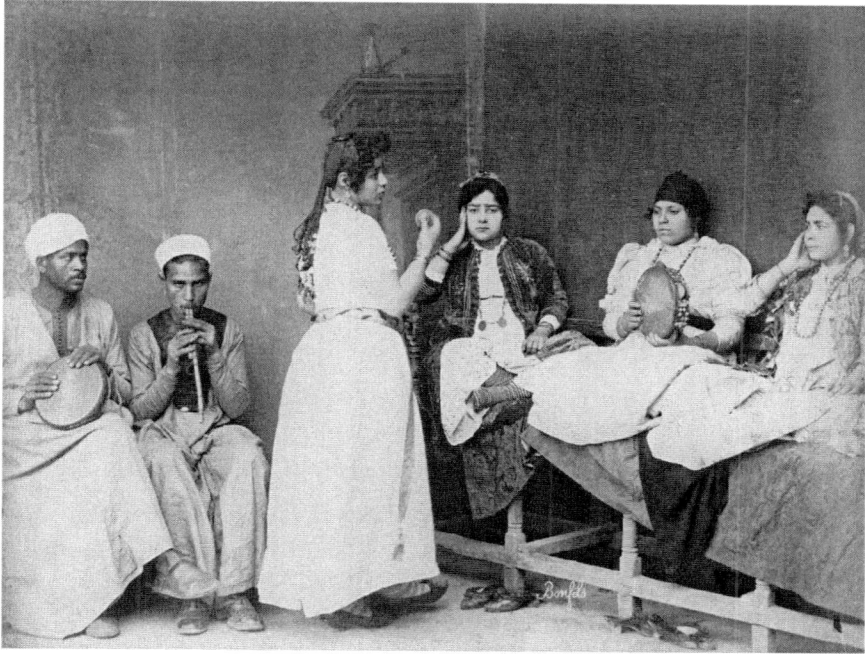

Felix Bonfils, *Musicians, Singers, and a Dancer*, ca. 1880. Courtesy Dan Kyram's collection.

conduct, they were reaffirming the power of the police and its legitimacy, as distinct from that of the neighborhood.

The Police Act similarly sanctioned (or rather formalized) the role of the *shaykh* and the police in monitoring prostitutes' places of residence and public conduct. The act addressed prostitutes' visibility and mobility in public space and allowed them to practice their trade only when hidden from the public eye. According to article 19, many prostitutes walked the streets of Cairo in what was considered an unsatisfactory and uncivilized state, repulsive to the public eye and disruptive of public order. These women, the act stipulated, should henceforth appear in public only in an orderly manner and properly covered, or they might be taken to the police station. Article 61 forbade prostitutes to walk outdoors unveiled and uncovered, and it further stated that they should not appear in such a state outside their houses or at their windows.[55]

The Police Act also mandated police involvement in segregating brothels, taverns, and coffeehouses from respectable neighborhoods. Article 8 instructed *shaykh*s and police commissioners not to allow prostitutes to dwell among respectable residents and warned that some of them might try to rent a place under the guise of respectability. Article 13 singled out major thoroughfares, such as Clot Bey and Muhammad 'Ali streets, located around Azbakiyya Gardens, where Christian and Jewish women had recently opened many brothels. It then instructed the police to close them down for the sake of public security. Coffeehouses and taverns, which shady characters allegedly tended to frequent and which were frequently the site of malicious acts, could not be opened near mosques and holy shrines, and those already operating in such locations were to be closed down. Finally, male and female singers were banned from spending their nights in coffeehouses and taverns and from committing immoral deeds therein.[56]

Beginning in the 1850s, as the ban on prostitution was no longer in effect, prostitutes were allowed to live in the city, but their choice of residence was, at times, contingent upon the approval of the neighborhood *shaykh*.[57] The neighborhood *shaykh* was responsible for mediating between landlords and potential tenants, and he received an annual fee of one month's rent from the tenants. The Darb Mustafa neighborhood example indicates that the *shaykh* had to obtain neighbors' consent to open a brothel in a "respectable" neighborhood. In a similar petition submitted to Cairo police headquarters, community members accused their *shaykh* of hiring outsiders to impersonate as neighbors, which implies the existence of an actual legal procedure for allowing new residents into the neighborhood.[58] *Shaykh*s' role in monitoring prostitution augmented their power within their communities, backed by the law enforcement authorities, and gave them leverage over local prostitutes.

At Darb Mustafa, the *shaykh* benefited from rental fees from incoming prostitutes and had little regard for the decency of the neighborhood that official decrees and regulations had entrusted to him.[59] In a similar situation in Cairo's al-Darb al-Ahmar quarter, residents claimed that in order to avoid police intervention, their *shaykh* had turned his own home into a sort of tribunal, arbitrating conflicts between prostitutes without resorting to the police.[60] Both examples supposedly attest to the corruption of the traditional *shaykh*s and their resistance to state intervention. These *shaykh*s, however, were operating within new power structures rather than outside of them. Their power within their communities cannot be separated from the role they were entrusted with in monitoring vice.

These social relations mirror, rather than contradict, the role they came to play in neighborhood life.

The centrality of prostitution in defining the role of *shcykh*s in the Police Act serves as one indication of the place of prostitution in molding the state's role in communal life. *Shaykh*s were supposed to control prostitutes' dwellings, their conduct, and their appearance in public space. The "traditional" figure of the *shaykh,* supposedly a residue of informal or traditional power, acquired unprecedented authority over individual women, backed as it now was by state power. This new form of power was molded through neighborhood conflicts and in individual quarrels, which situated different parties on different sides of a state/ society dyad.

Similar processes affected police personnel as well. In one case, a policeman from Tanta in the Nile Delta was dismissed for supplementing his income with fees received from prostitutes for services whose nature was disputed in the course of the investigation.[61] In another case, a policeman from Shibin, also in the delta, accused his superiors, the police commissioner and the sergeant, of arbitrary arrest, torture, and intimidation of prostitutes innocently walking the town streets, on such pretexts as failing to sweep the floor in front of their residence or failing to hang a lantern by their door. In this particular instance, the police commissioner was accused of many other abuses and violations. It seems that harassment of prostitutes served as a way of intimidating the town's population and asserting authority over those who refused to obey.[62] This detailed case, which includes no less than thirty-two separate offenses, illustrates more clearly how much the power to intimidate and harass prostitutes played a role in asserting one's authority in communal life. Public women were harassed in public in order to deter others.

It is not a surprise that just as prostitutes tended to be removed from respectable neighborhoods, respectable members of the community tended to leave the neighborhood when prostitutes started to move in. At Darb Mustafa, for example, the petitioners claimed that some of their neighbors had left their homes and rented apartments elsewhere. Even when regulations were enforced and prostitutes had to leave the neighborhood, landowners had a hard time finding new residents; there were still many brothels in the neighborhood, and respectable families refused to move back in. Landowners, who did not want their properties to remain empty, subsequently agreed to rent them to prostitutes.[63] Although no official zoning policy was in effect, such dynamics created informal zoning of prostitutes in precolonial Cairo.

Finally, supervision of prostitutes' mobility and visibility affected "respectable" women as well, especially when they chose to cross over. Police and council records refer to "respectable" women found in brothels who had been seduced or kidnapped or had moved there of their own free will. The police intervened after a woman's relatives called them in. Such cases seem to have most vividly confirmed public fears that the proximity of respectability and vice would lead to a breakdown of patriarchal authority over the respectable wife and daughter. These anxieties were probably coupled with genuine concern for the well-being of the girls and women involved.

In one such case, a midwife and her husband accused their neighbor Amna of manipulating their daughter into copulating with a certain effendi. Neighbors testified to seeing her talking to the girl on the roof through a party wall, and the girl confirmed that Amna invited her to visit each time her parents were away until she finally agreed. Amna and the effendi were sentenced to one year in prison and the girl to four months.[64] In another case, a woman named 'Adila who used to take a girl called Hanim to perform in private parties took her one day to a brothel without her mother's knowledge, and sent a servant to tell the mother that Hanim was staying with her aunt. In the brothel, 'Adila drugged Hanim and threatened to accuse her of theft if she refused to come again.[65] In both cases, the prostitutes were not convicted of merely luring girls away from the straight and narrow but of mediating their defloration. In one case where the parties involved testified that defloration had taken place before the couple had reached the brothel, the madam was acquitted, and so was a servant who claimed that because the girl looked mature, she had assumed the girl was not a virgin.[66]

In the next chapter I demonstrate how communal supervision of women included not only those who "strayed off the straight path" but also extended to other women's conduct outside of the home. Neighbors kept an eye on women's conduct and were happy to report an illegitimate child or a conspicuous-looking female servant. Such behaviors were possible in a city in which prostitutes' dress became an official concern, not only a moral one. The new dynamic between prostitutes, their neighbors, *shaykh*s, and policemen redefined the rules of the game: who had power over whom, in what circumstances, and how such power could be abused or subverted. Prostitution was therefore one arena in which the neighborhood community's role in modern state formation was defined.

Prostitutes and Social Networks

The socioeconomic upheavals of the nineteenth century affected the lives of individual Egyptian women. "Nonrespectable" women were often those who resorted to prostitution because personal misfortunes or nationwide transformations had deprived them of any other means of survival. Narratives of prostitutes, however, are rare. Because the police did not criminalize prostitution as such, biographic details of individual prostitutes were rarely registered as they were usually irrelevant to the investigation. When such details are mentioned, four groups of women figure most prominently: widows, divorcees, manumitted slaves, and immigrants.[67]

Consider the following example. On the night of 8 October 1877, a soldier and former slave named Ahmad Isma'il shot Bakhita, a prostitute and former slave, in a brothel in 'Ishash Ma'ruf in Bulaq. He did so after realizing that she was never going to leave the brothel and marry him as she had promised. Jundiya, the brothel owner, heard the gunshots and summoned the police. Ahmad Isma'il confessed and was convicted in the shari'a court.[68]

This murder case relates the story of two women, Bakhita and Jundiya, who had been relegated to the margins of normative, patriarchal family structure through manumission and divorce, respectively. As internal immigrants, moreover, both were also outsiders to the urban neighborhood community support networks. Bakhita's enslaver manumitted her shortly before his death. She stayed with his family for a short period but was not happy there. In chapter 3, I argued that such manumitted slaves sometimes chose to stay on for lack of better alternatives. Staying at the same household, however, came with a price: old habits die hard, and manumitted slaves were probably treated as they had always been. Power struggles within the household made life more difficult, especially since the power balance had changed and since leaving had become an option. Bakhita, specifically, was manumitted upon her enslaver's death, which might have deprived her of whatever support she had from him when he was still alive. She then left for a brothel in Turtushi, a lower-class neighborhood in Alexandria, and from there moved to Cairo and stayed in Jundiya's brothel for three years until her murder.

Jundiya came from a small village near al-Bahnasa in the al-Minya Governorate in Upper Egypt. She had moved with her family to Cairo seventeen years before the tragic event. Five years later, her husband died during his army service, which forced her to resort to prostitution to support her two sons, one of whom was later conscripted in lieu of his father; the other was blind.[69]

In chapter 3 I quoted Clot Bey's comment on the connection between manumission and prostitution. According to Clot Bey, both manumission and divorce deprived women of male protection and of subsistence. He claimed that manumitted slaves sometimes turned to prostitution as an alternative to poverty. Many prostitutes, he further observed, were divorced women who could not remarry. In short, exclusion from social networks left women unprotected.[70]

Not only individual misfortunes, but also mass mobilization and conscription resulted in the breakdown of support networks. This particularly affected women and girls. Rural immigration and conscription deprived families of their chief breadwinners and sometimes forced women into prostitution.[71] Unattached women—divorcees and manumitted slaves—who immigrated to the city on their own had few employment alternatives. A woman like Jundiya, who had immigrated to the city with her husband, was left upon his death without the protection of community-based networks.[72]

The prevalence of immigrants among prostitutes is apparent in many other records. Earlier in this chapter I described a murder in a Suez brothel where one of the prostitutes involved was a manumitted slave and two others were immigrants from Cairo.[73] In other brothels, we find immigrants from the countryside alongside immigrants from other parts of the Ottoman Empire, North Africa, and Europe. In one murder case in Alexandria, for instance, the brothel owner was an Ottoman subject from Syria, and her tenants included an immigrant from the village of Damietta on the Nile Delta, another from Cairo, and a manumitted slave. One of their neighbors was of Moroccan descent.[74]

European prostitutes, unlike their Ottoman and North African counterparts, enjoyed the protection of their respective consulates in accordance with the capitulation agreements. In some cases, this meant the police had to resort to the mediation of foreign consulates in order to interview a foreign suspect or witness. There are no details about the background of foreign prostitutes, probably because part of their interrogation took place in their respective consulates or because such details were deemed irrelevant. Police records mention mostly

Italian and Greek prostitutes, two national groups that constituted the majority of lower-class immigrants in Egypt at the time.[75] Notably, in precolonial Egypt, foreign prostitutes shared residential areas and even brothels with native prostitutes. With the 1882 British occupation of Egypt, the British imposed regulation on Egyptian prostitutes but not on their foreign counterparts.[76]

'Imad Hilal sees prostitutes as women who did not wish to fulfill their natural role as wives and mothers. To Hilal, prostitutes' children were undesirable outcomes of illicit relations. He cites cases of infanticide in support of this claim, and he argues that prostitutes who had living children were exceptions—women "overcome by their maternal instinct."[77] Because many prostitutes were widowed, divorced, or manumitted, I would argue instead that it is safe to assume that at least some of them had their children as wives and slaves and that they resorted to prostitution, at least in part, to support children whose father could not or would not support them. Police and council records indicate that some prostitutes had children; some had them before being divorced or manumitted. These children sometimes lived with them in a brothel. Bakhita's madam, Jundiya, for example, was the mother of two adult sons.[78] Another case mentions a child living in a brothel with his mother, a prostitute called Zaynab, who had three older brothers.[79] A third case mentions a prostitute who lived with her minor daughter and next door to her sister.[80]

Some prostitutes viewed motherhood as a central part of their identity. However, their practice could deny them custody of their minor children. Muhammad al-'Abbasi al-Mahdi, the supreme mufti of Egypt throughout most of the latter half of the nineteenth century, agreed with a husband that his wife's involvement in prostitution was a valid cause to deny her custody rights.[81] Prostitutes did, however, fight their ex-husbands in court in an attempt to regain custody. In one shari'a court case, a man demanded custody of his minor son. He claimed that his ex-wife, Hasna, was a prostitute *(min ahl al-fisq wa-l-fujur)*, but he could not support his claim, which was therefore rejected.[82] We can also find prostitutes concerned with their daughters' reputations, even if they could not guarantee respectable status for themselves. In one such case, a girl living in one of Alexandria's shantytowns with her mother, a prostitute called Zubayda, was found in a neighboring brothel, and her mother asked that the men whom she believed to have deflowered her be punished.[83]

Individual life stories are difficult to trace, let alone patterns or statistics. Historians of Ottoman societies noted, for example, that women who "repented" could have their repentance registered in a shari'a court and get married—which implies that prostitution could sometimes be recognized as a temporary occupation. My tentative and partial sampling of cases involving prostitutes in nineteenth-century Egypt indicates that they were affected by the major transformations that Egypt was undergoing at the time. As described here, these changes transformed individual lives as well as the faces of nineteenth-century cities, neighborhood communities, and what came to be known as the modern state.

Conclusion

This chapter traced three sites of ambiguity on which state officials, local communities, and individual families have attempted, with varying success, to impose clear demarcation lines. The first is the line separating respectable women from prostitutes. As demonstrated, "prostitute" was not a clearly defined category because "women who strayed from the straight path" were not necessarily involved in commercial sex. Moreover, respectable women did cross the boundaries of respectability, interact with prostitutes, and work as prostitutes, at least on a temporary basis. Some of them even started or supported families of their own.

The second demarcation line separated the respectable neighborhood from the brothel, tavern, or coffeehouse. As shown here, these urban institutions constituted a part of neighborhood life that was not necessarily segregated from family homes and houses of worship. Prostitutes and other nonrespectable women were concentrated in certain neighborhoods, streets, or alleys and tended to live close to one another, but this did not create hermetically enclosed quarters or actual spatial segregation before prostitution became officially regulated.

Finally, this chapter exposes the ambiguity of the seemingly neat distinction between state and society. The state relied on the neighborhood community to enforce public order. The *shaykh,* who acted both as state employee and neighborhood representative, sometimes allowed prostitutes to dwell in respectable neighborhoods, blurring distinctions the central administration was trying to impose. Ongoing efforts to regulate prostitution, if not suppress it, have been shown to be the result of both top-down regulations and bottom-up demand by communities transformed by nineteenth-century modernity.

5

Virginity, Honor, and Premarital Defloration

On the night of 24 June 1863, Alexandrian merchant Muhammad Harun claimed that his newly wedded wife, Asma, was not a virgin on their wedding night. He also concealed the "evidence" of her virginity—her blood-stained garments. Her mother and maternal uncle hastened to contact authorities. A hakima who examined her at the police station confirmed that Asma had been deflowered only twelve hours previously, that is, on her wedding night. Muhammad Harun admitted he had lied to take revenge on her mother for a loan she had denied him. This admission came too late, however, as the rumor of Asma's alleged promiscuity had already spread. Consequently, she and her relatives demanded that Muhammad Harun be punished and Asma's reputation *(sharaf)* restored. According to article 2, chapter 2 of the Sultanic Code, Muhammad was sentenced to two months' imprisonment for violating a person's honor.[1]

The focus of this chapter will be premarital defloration, as presented in precolonial police, council, and shari'a courts. The legal procedure normally included a medical examination (see chapter 2), a police investigation, a shari'a procedure, and a council ruling. Defloration cases were about 0.5 percent of the cases handled by the Supreme Council of Adjudication. They were mostly filed by women's guardians or closest kin or, in cases involving domestic servants, by their employers; the rest were filed by the young women themselves. Some of them asked for the assailant to be punished, and others asked to have the woman punished for disobedience and unruly behavior. I use Asma's case, as well as cases of premarital defloration, to question how different notions of honor, virginity, and defloration were transforming through everyday interactions between the legal system and individual litigants. As in previous chapters, my argument here is that these sites are where modern state power was constituted.

What Is "Honor"?

Common in the literature of Middle East history and anthropology is a gen-dered distinction between *sharaf*, a man's honor gained through his actions, and *'ird*, a woman's honor as manifested through her (real or alleged) sexual conduct, which also bears on her family's reputation.[2] This distinction is useful for under-standing social regulation of women in precolonial Egypt. It is not sufficient, however, to understand what honor meant to policemen, council members, or individual litigants. It was certainly not a coherent concept but rather one that various individuals and institutions interpreted somewhat differently.

As a starting point, I prefer to see honor as an organizing concept, a form of cultural capital that helps define a person's status. Honor operates as a link between the individual and the community and a moral framework for behavior, and it provides a basis for acceptance in collective life. Because social standing depends on public recognition, an offense against one's honor threatens not only an individual's good name but the very foundational rules of social life. Restoring honor involves reclaiming public recognition that has been wrongfully denied.[3]

Ottoman legal practice treated sexual crime as disruptive of social har-mony, and it defended the individual against both slanderous talk and sexual acts. Islamic law recognizes damage to one's reputation mainly in the context of illicit sexual relations. *Qadhf* is a Qur'anic *hadd* offense that specifically refers to false accusation of illicit sexual relations *(zina)*. Because *zina* is one of the gravest offenses, punishable by death, *qadhf* is considered of similar gravity. In legal prac-tice, other elements of a person's reputation were relevant as well.[4] Leslie Peirce demonstrates how, in sixteenth-century 'Aintab, people used the shari'a court to clear their reputation, for example, by claiming they were not fully responsible for the actions that compromised their honor.[5]

As shown in chapter 1, Tanzimat Codes, beginning from the 1839 Gülhane Edict, included new concepts that were integrated into Ottoman legal tradi-tion and sometimes transformed in the process. Whether Ottoman concepts in Enlightenment wording or Enlightenment concepts couched in Islamic-Ottoman rhetoric, these codes were introducing new concepts to Ottoman legal life. The most notable innovation was the nominal equality of all Ottoman subjects that departed, in its spirit, from religion-based distinctions inherent to Islamic and Ottoman legal practice. The Gülhane Edict, and the later 1840 and 1851 Ottoman

Codes, guaranteed protection of a person's "life, honor and property." Whereas protection of life and property are rather straightforward, protection of honor is a more ambiguous concept.

Article 1, Chapter 2 of the 1855 Sultanic Code reads as follows:

> Whereas all the subjects of the Ottoman Empire have acquired the shari'a-stipulated rights consisting of the safety of their life and property and the protection of their honor ['ird] and good name, and whereas consequently they can claim their rights, regardless of their status, in accordance with freedom as circumscribed by the shari'a and not in accordance with absolute freedom, and whereas a person's honor and good name are as dear and respected to him as his own life, and whereas protection and safeguarding of this honor is required by virtue and humanity, and whereas slander [qadhf] violates a person's respect and prestige and hurting or abusing him without good reason is regarded as an injury to one's honor and an assault on his respect, it is therefore necessary that anyone against whom it has been proven, according to the shari'a, that he has the audacity to injure a person's honor in a manner that makes the application of the hadd punishment obligatory, shall be punished with the hadd punishment according to the shari'a.[6]

The wording of this article of the code is a direct translation from Ottoman Turkish, and like other Tanzimat texts it stresses that the universal principles evoked are also rooted in Islamic and Ottoman legal tradition. Honor here is conceived as an individual right deserving protection rather than something whose violation is a crime against God or the customary notions of women's honor. It is "as dear and respected" as one's life; it is translated as both 'ird and namus; and it is also equated with the Islamic concept of qadhf. In Enlightenment terms, a person's honor and dignity is a human right that should be protected from the arbitrary power of rulers. In this particular article of the code, I would argue, the Enlightenment concept of human honor and dignity was translated to Islamic legal terms. In the Egyptian context, this article of the code was used primarily to adjudicate cases related to women's honor ('ird). This was not the Enlightenment concept of personal honor, but rather a social concept that made sense to Egyptian men and women who brought their cases to the police and courts.

Simply noting that "honor" was interpreted almost exclusively as women's sexual honor does not begin to cover the complexity of the term. Litigants themselves were making all sorts of claims as to what this honor was. Councils' verdicts, in turn, sometimes similarly employed 'ird as women's honor, but these also referred to a generalized, public honor that connoted an abstract notion of a "state"; at the same time, it was also personal honor and dignity, which was as dear to one's person as life and property.

In a case from the early 1860s, the Mansura Council chose to convict a girl for her part in her own defloration "since she had enabled a distasteful deed, by giving herself to whoever it was that committed the act in her, without informing any of her family members or contacting the authorities until her pregnancy became visible." In its verdict, the council stated that it could not find any article of the law applicable to the case, but still believed that the girl deserved to be punished. If the offense would be termed "a violation of a person's honor," the girl would be made into both a victim and a perpetrator, which was at odds with the spirit of the law. The dilemma here was how to reconcile the abstract notion of "a person's honor" with the very concrete commonsense understanding of honor: a girl compromised her honor and should therefore be punished. In this case, the dilemma was solved by concluding that she did not really consent, and she was sentenced to two months' imprisonment. When the case was forwarded to the Supreme Council of Adjudication, the council members chose to believe the girl's claim that she had not consented and convicted the man of abduction. The verdict then stated that the relevant article for the case was article 6, which dealt with abduction.[7]

Councils readily convicted women of violating their own honor. A woman named 'A'isha, for example, was accused of violating her own honor because she had entered the store in which she was assaulted of her own free will.[8] Another woman was accused of violating her own honor because the act was committed "with her consent and without coercion."[9] I discuss below the kinds of narratives women were to produce in order to convince the legal system that they were unwilling partners. Here I am interested in demonstrating that although unintended in the code itself, council verdicts turned violation of honor into a legal principle that reaffirmed patriarchal control of women. A woman could violate her own honor only when she was seen as giving away something that was not hers to give. "Violating her own honor" often really meant her family's honor, and some council verdicts explicitly say so. In one case, in which a girl had left her home and moved to Cairo with a Christian man, council members stated the woman had violated her own honor alongside her family's.[10]

The notion of family honor also figures in council verdicts concerning honor killing, discussed in chapter 1. Council verdicts sometimes concluded that protection of honor was a motivation that justified a mitigated sentence. In one such case, the council concluded that because the murderers were "the closest ones to [the victim], some of them being her shari'a heirs, it would not have been easy for them to commit any act against her unless she had done some terrible deed that led them to do what they have done in order to protect their honor."[11] In another case, convicts' verdicts were reduced because the killers were "infuriated by her neglect of her honor and feared scandal and shame."[12]

What I trace in Supreme Council verdicts is a creative interpretation of the Sultanic Code, which was authored in Istanbul and drew its inspiration from Paris, and its readjustment to the concerns of Egyptian litigants. The Supreme Council recognized honor as justification for murder; its verdicts also recognized defloration as violation of honor—which was, strictly speaking, foreign to the spirit of the law. They therefore adjusted the code to what litigants kept bringing to the police station.

Several council verdicts, moreover, portrayed defloration as violating a generalized, unspecified honor. In one such case, a couple confessed they had been involved in consensual defloration and were sentenced to six months' imprisonment for their "despicable deeds," which had "violated human honor and dignity" (al-'ird wa-l-namus al-insani).[13] In another case, a man married a young woman, whom he immediately handed over to his Greek employer, who deflowered her on her wedding night instead of her legal husband. The Cairo Council concluded that both men had violated public order (nizam 'umumi), a person's honor, and all laws, both human and divine (kamil al-shara'i' wa-l-qawanin).[14] In both cases, council verdicts referred to a generalized human honor and public order, which were absent from most other verdicts. These verdicts brought in the "public" as a legal abstraction, independent from the persons of the litigants, and introduced the state as an abstract entity, as an interested party.

To complicate matters even further, honor was a concept litigants used to make claims that challenged councils' conclusions. In one case, a man appealed his daughter's conviction of defloration and claimed that only the man who deflowered her should be punished. He claimed that his daughter had been punished severely enough: nobody would marry her, not even if he tried to pay him off. Imprisonment, he added, would be an additional and unnecessary torment.

"She is now deprived of a home and a husband like all other women, who were not harmed as she was."[15] In a similar case, a man appealed his sister's conviction and claimed that a prison term combined with the girl's unfortunate defloration would be detrimental to her reputation, honor, and future *mahr*.[16] Here, whereas councils concluded that a girl should be convicted for violation of honor, the girl's guardians turned this argument on its head: it was the sentence, much more than premarital sex, that could be detrimental to their honor. Both appeals were accepted but on different grounds, and both are further discussed later.

Another indicative example is of a British father named Ferdinand Helvston(?), who sued his servant in the shari'a court for deflowering his eight-year-old daughter. In his appeal, he explained, "It is shameful *('ayb)* for us too, and a hindrance of future marriage." He therefore demanded monetary compensation "for our current and future expenses."[17] I find this case an interesting example of a creative use of the legal system by a person who clearly did not fully understand its meaning. His choice to turn to the shari'a court should not surprise us: it was only there that he could ask for monetary compensation. What I find interesting is his translation of honor and *mahr al-mithl* to concepts that make sense in his world. This cultural translation was part of how multiple ways of understanding honor and virginity had coexisted.

Premarital Defloration

Women's honor was closely related to virginity. In precolonial Egypt, loss of virginity, normally within marriage, constituted a social and legal boundary marker. The male act of penetration transformed a woman's status and identity from a *bikr* (virgin) into a *thayyib* (nonvirgin) and from a "girl" *(bint)* into a "woman" *(hurma)*.[18] A woman's first sexual intercourse with a man allegedly awakened her dormant sexuality and therefore changed her person and identity. Premarital loss of virginity was normally associated with reduced marital prospects and bore on both the girl's and her family's reputation.

From a legal point of view, defloration turned "girl" into "woman." In the Hanafi school of legal jurisprudence, for example, a virgin's silence could be considered consent to marriage. Nonvirgins, on the other hand, had to explicitly voice their consent. Twelfth-century Hanafi jurist 'Ali ibn Abu Bakr al-Marghinani reasoned that a virgin's "assent is rather to be supposed, as she is ashamed to testify her desire," whereas the *thayyib,* "having had connection with men, has not the same pretense to silence or shyness as a virgin," and her silence is therefore insufficient for consent.[19]

Because the concept of honor is closely associated with public recognition, a woman's virginity on her wedding night had to be publicly recognized and her premarital chastity acknowledged. Public display of a woman's inner garments at her wedding night and the public shame associated with alleged premarital defloration served to supervise and control the sexuality of all women.

As present-day feminist authors have noted, virginity norms regulate not only women's sexual relations but also their social lives, their associations with men and women outside their families, and their mobility in public space.[20] Even when subverted or manipulated, these norms nonetheless cast their shadow on women's everyday conduct. People's appeal to the police, shari'a courts, and councils to reclaim a woman's honor can be partially understood in this context.

Nineteenth-century travelers, as well as indigenous elite authors, commented on what they perceived to be archaic practices soon to be tamed and disappear. Nineteenth-century European travelers were stunned by the public nature of marital defloration. According to Swiss traveler Johann Burckhardt, who resided in Cairo during the second decade of the nineteenth century, lower-class Muslims carried the bride's bloodstained innermost garments in triumph to neighbors' houses. More respectable families exhibited the bride's garments only in the bridegroom's house, whereas upper-class Egyptians condemned this practice and no longer allowed it.[21] Writing in midcentury, French physician Clot Bey similarly observed that on the wedding night, the man deflowered his bride with his index finger covered with a white handkerchief, which was then proudly presented to the parents and guests and exhibited around the neighborhood. "Defloration is not at all surrounded with prudish mystery," he observed, comparing Egypt to his homeland. "On the contrary, the public is some sort of a witness, invited to certify the results."[22]

'Ali Mubarak's *al-Khitat al-Taqfiqiyya,* published in the late 1880s, documents similar ceremonies in the countryside. In the village of Dashna in Upper Egypt, for example, the groom deflowered his bride with his finger in the presence of a maid. The men stood outside the house while women stood outside the nuptial room, beating heavy drums to drown the bride's screams. The bride's mother and sister then carried the bloodstained garment around as testimony of the bride's honor *('ird* and *sharaf).*[23] In the village of Ja'fariyya, the bride's closest female kin showed her bloodstained garment while singing and ululating. Village women then colored their eyelids with the bride's blood as a cure for blurred eyesight.[24]

In Asma's case, which opened this chapter, the girl and her parents protested exactly because they were denied this public ritual, because the groom concealed her blood-stained garments. In another case, an oil merchant from Cairo married off his daughter Nafisa to a man from al-Mansura in the delta, who insisted the marriage be consummated in his hometown. On her first night there, the groom handed the bride over to his employer, a Greek merchant, who proceeded to deflower her himself. Nafisa's mother and sister returned to Cairo with Nafisa's "evidence of virginity"—probably a bloodstained garment—to display around the neighborhood "as is customary" before turning to the police. Nafisa's parents pressed charges against the men who had disgraced their daughter but at the same time could publicly reclaim her honor by providing indisputable evidence of her virginity.[25] Such cases made the police and councils, alongside the neighborhood or village community, an arena for negotiating and debating girls' virginity.

Historians of Ottoman courts describe the shariʿa court as a public forum that served, together with the neighborhood or village streets, to display or dispute women's respectability. In his study of eighteenth-century Aleppo, for example, historian Abraham Marcus cites a case in which a man brought his daughter to the shariʿa court following rumors of her sexual misconduct, had four midwives verify her virginity, and then had it registered in an official document. In another case, a woman came to court to register the fact that her four-year-old daughter had lost her virginity as a result of an accident and brought four eyewitnesses to confirm this.[26]

In a sense, police and councils served a role similar to the one shariʿa courts had played in previous centuries. Ruiz, Fahmy, and others demonstrate how parents used the police to control their daughters, whereas young women contested, undermined, or appropriated the state's legal control mechanisms. State involvement in cases of premarital defloration, they argued, enabled central authorities better control over individual and family life. This was yet another arena, the argument goes, in which the modern, centralized state asserted its control over family life.[27]

My argument about state formation was fleshed out in earlier chapters, and here I am more particularly interested in what police and council involvement in premarital cases entailed for young women themselves, or rather, in how they chose to narrate their experiences in the police and courts. I wish to begin with a young woman named Nasra, who appealed her conviction of premarital defloration to the Supreme Council of Adjudication. I am interested here in the underlying logic that guided her successful appeal, and I will place it within the context of other defloration cases from precolonial Egypt.

Girls and Their Hymens Facing the Law

In November 1884, Nasra, a girl of Turkish origin from al-Maniya village near Fayyum, appealed her conviction for premarital defloration to the Supreme Council of Adjudication. The lower-instance council had based its conviction mainly on the hakima's report, which noted the lack of any signs of struggle on her body; it was therefore assumed she probably consented. Nasra based her appeal on the following arguments. First, she questioned the medical examination's validity in determining consent, and she further argued that she had not been reexamined for a second opinion. Second, she claimed she was a chaste girl who rarely left her father's residence and was therefore unlikely to be willingly involved with men. Third, she claimed the defendant assaulted her after she had refused his marriage proposal, in an attempt to force her to marry him—thus establishing his motive. Finally, she claimed he confessed in the shari'a court that he had indeed deflowered her by force, agreed to pay her *mahr al-mithl* as compensation, and offered to marry her. It was this last argument that convinced the Supreme Council of Adjudication to reverse the lower council's verdict and to acquit her.[28]

Nasra was convicted for violation of honor in accordance with the Sultanic Code. She was not, however, convicted of *zina*. Theoretically, Islamic law treats premarital defloration as both a crime and a tort. As a crime, it is a form of *zina*—illicit sexual intercourse between a man and a woman who is neither his wife nor his slave—or, to use the shari'a formulation, a man's intercourse with sexual organs that he does not own. It is considered a crime against God (a *hadd* crime), punishable by death when one of the partners is married or by lashes if both are not.[29]

In practice, few jurists and judges treated extra- and premarital sexual intercourse as *zina*. According to Islamic rules of evidence, conviction in *zina* requires no less than four witnesses to the act itself or confession in four separate court sessions. At the same time, false accusation of *zina (qadhf)*, as noted above, is also considered a crime against God. In addition, courts did not apply the *hadd* punishment in cases when doubt was involved (e.g., if a man claimed that he wrongfully believed his partner was legitimate), when the witnesses could not provide the exact location and means of the crime, when their testimonies conflicted, or when the crime was committed under duress.

Cases in which no proof was available or the principle of doubt was applied were subject to an extra-shari'a punishment, handed over to the *qadi*'s discretion, and ruled on according to their particular circumstances.[30]

As a tort, premarital defloration entailed monetary compensation for bodily damage that equaled proper bride-money *(mahr al-mithl)*. Such compensation was obligatory if a woman had lost her virginity as a result of an accident, but not in cases of consensual sex.[31] In general, then, Islamic law relegated enforcement of illicit sex to private justice. *Zina* was hard to prove, and cases of premarital sex were most often resolved in the form of private compensation or marriage. If the plaintiff chose to drop charges, the shari'a court did not independently pursue the case.[32]

The main function of the shari'a court procedure was often to restore social order and help a girl and her family reestablish their status and reputation. Monetary compensation could help a victim with significantly reduced marital prospects survive economically. Public recognition of nonvoluntary defloration may have also helped girls restore their reputation.[33] For similar reasons, a common solution in such cases was marriage, which might have been devastating for some of the women involved but served to contain the damage inflicted on the family's reputation. As demonstrated in the following, some cases did involve consent, and marriage might have been the solution the women themselves had desired.[34]

In Khedivial Egypt, in cases in which a *hadd* crime could not be established, the defendant would be liable to extra-shari'a punishment, which could take the form of flogging, imprisonment, or expulsion (chapter 2, article 2 of the Sultanic Code).[35] Article 6 of the same chapter refers to "unpleasing deeds, such as abduction of a Muslim girl, or a girl of another religious community, to another region or another country, with the false claim of marriage, without the knowledge of her relatives." Such offenses were punishable by six months' imprisonment.[36] Council verdicts relied on both articles in adjudicating cases of premarital defloration.

Applying these legal procedures to Nasra's case, we may reach some preliminary conclusions. First, we may conclude that Nasra's assault was not conceptualized as rape. Because the offense was defined as nonmarital sex, it was the fact that the parties were not married, rather than her consent, that distinguished lawful from unlawful sex. Defined as such, Nasra had to prove that she was forced into an illegal act. In other words, both parties could be held accountable, unless the woman could convince police and court that she had been coerced. This is exactly what Nasra was doing—trying to convince the authorities she was forced into sexual intercourse.

In other defloration cases from the period, young women and girls had to narrate their loss of virginity in ways that would convince police and councils that they were not culpable, against hegemonic assumptions regarding women's sexuality. This bias of the legal system brings to mind Susan Estrich's notion of "real rape." In her study of rape in the American legal system, legal scholar Susan Estrich argues that implicit assumptions, often not written in the letter of the law, influence everyday interactions between rape victims, the surrounding society, and law enforcement authorities. These assumptions determine whether rape victims perceive themselves as such, as well as the ways in which they are treated in court and in police stations. They likewise affect the credibility of the narratives and "corroboratory evidence" victims are expected to produce so as to correspond to the "perfect model" of "real rape." A "real rape," she further argues, one that is seriously investigated and punished, is one that takes place outdoors, in which the assailant is unfamiliar to the victim, and that involves evident physical coercion. Moreover, to prove that she did not consent, claims Estrich, the victim must prove that she physically resisted her assailant, that her conduct had not been sexually "provocative" immediately prior to the assault as well as in everyday life, and that she complained immediately afterward. Distrust of women, claims Estrich, is incorporated into the judicial system's unwritten, unofficial definition of rape and rules of evidence.[37]

As Nasra's case indicates, assumptions similar to those Estrich outlined in her study of the American legal system were implicit in the interaction between the nineteenth-century Egyptian legal system and assault victims. Her failure to display signs of physical resistance, for example, undermined her claim that she had not consented.

Similarly, Nasra mentioned her chastity and tendency to stay at home to support her claim that she had indeed been assaulted, as home was conceived to be a safe space that could easily protect women from unwanted sexual acts. Council verdicts often did not believe women who claimed to have been assaulted at home. The watchful eyes of the community and the family were supposed to offer protection, or at least bear witness. Sexual assault did, however, take place inside the home. Women sometimes accused men of breaking into their homes and assaulting them in their sleep.[38] In two cases, women claimed that premarital defloration occurred within the protective fold of their families, as their cousins had deflowered them several years previously during a family visit while both children were "playing together."[39] In one case, a young woman accused the *shaykh* of the village guards of breaking into her home a few months previously and attacking her in her sleep. The council chose not to believe her, stating in its verdict that sexual intercourse inside the house could not have taken place without consent "since the house in which she claims to have been attacked at night is full of people; if she is telling the truth, she would have screamed, and they, as well as the neighbors, would have heard her."[40]

Physical or vocal resistance was another set of behaviors that assault victims were expected to display. Council members and police officers expected assault victims to scream, and those who did not went to great length to explain why they failed to do so. The possibility that the girl was too frightened to scream was never suggested. A girl who was assaulted in her neighbors' basement claimed that her assailant put his hand on her mouth to prevent her from screaming. Because the room to which he had dragged her was underground, she further emphasized, nobody would have heard her even if she had screamed.[41] Council members chose not to believe women who did not scream. In one such case, Asyut Council opined, "it is improbable that such an act would be imposed on her without her screaming and calling for attention, and without the neighbors hearing her."[42]

A delayed complaint could cast further doubt over the plaintiff's credibility, such as when a woman or her relative complained only after her pregnancy became visible[43] or after the man who impregnated her forced her to have an abortion.[44] Immediacy of complaint made it more reliable. Thus, for example, a hakima's report that stated the victim was still bleeding when she arrived to the police station supported her credibility.[45]

In most council and police cases I examined, girls described physical coercion or claimed they had been drugged or intoxicated, and were therefore incapable of resisting and learned of their defloration only the following morning.[46] A drug inserted into an innocent-looking pastry was a common trope in girls'

testimonies.[47] The similarities in the scripts that women were expected to produce is related to inherent distrust of women, common to many legal systems. It
is also related to a common underlying assumption of rape as a form of nonmarital sex that happens to be committed against a woman's consent.

Another question Nasra's appeal raises is related to class. Nasra was from
a Turkish-speaking family and claimed that she rarely, if ever, left home—both
indicative of relatively upper-class status. Nasra claimed that privilege, which
allowed her to leave home rarely, made her beyond reproach and unlikely to consent to illicit intercourse.

The question of gender segregation, class, and mobility in public space is
highly pertinent. Because female sexuality was believed to be treacherous, wom-
en's confinement to their homes was designed to minimize their interactions
with men who were not their closest kin and was believed to guarantee their
premarital chastity and marital fidelity. As historians of women and gender in
the Middle East have demonstrated, however, cultural norms regarding women's
seclusion were more strictly enforced on upper-class women, who participated in
public activity through servants and intermediaries. Lower-class women, on the
other hand, often worked outside the home as peddlers, bathhouse attendants, or
servants in upper-class households. Peasant women worked the fields and simply
could not afford to stay at home.[48]

Upper-class families, moreover, may have been able to resolve cases involving premarital defloration privately, which the poor could not afford. Consid-
ering the crowded lower-class neighborhoods, in which neighbors could more
easily see and hear unusual commotion in one's private residence, this explanation sounds plausible. Council and police records provide it some support. In
one case, for example, a woman privately told her mother of her defloration. In
response, the mother screamed in shock and grief, neighbors assembled, and the
police intervened.[49]

Council and police records imply that lower-class women and girls worked
outdoors, outside the house, and that their presence in public space was acceptable but also made them more vulnerable to assault. Girls and young women
worked in factories, onboard steamships, in public works projects, and in construction.[50] One man assaulted a girl collecting straw in the field;[51] another
assaulted his neighbor's daughter who knocked on his door asking for salt;[52]

and in another case, a baker assaulted a servant girl who fetched bread for her employer.[53] Men who could not afford to leave their fields for the corvée sometimes sent their daughters in their stead. They slept separately from the men but were still vulnerable to abuse.[54]

Lower-class women's presence outside the home did not imply lack of supervision or control. Both state authorities and local communities kept an eye on these young unmarried women. Neighbors contacted the police when they saw a girl acting in a manner unbecoming of a virgin: outdoors, unsupervised, associating with the wrong people, or in inappropriate places. When referring to young women, the phrase "wandering about as one pleases" connoted (perceived) sexual misconduct.[55] In one case, for example, the head of Bulaq Police Station arrested a young woman who had opened her cousin's store after dark. She had done so with her cousin's permission, but her unsupervised presence outdoors at night led the police to examine her virginity and investigate the circumstances of her defloration.[56]

Neighborhood communities and neighborhood *shaykhs*, alongside the family, played a central role in monitoring lower-class girls' conduct and mobility. In cases of eloping couples, for example, neighbors readily testified about earlier interactions between a girl and her alleged seducer. In one such case, neighbors testified that the girl had been visiting a neighbor, a single man living with his brother, although her mother had forbidden it.[57] In another case, neighbors noticed the girl speaking to her neighbor, a woman of questionable character, on the roof when her parents were away—suggesting this neighbor might have been responsible for the girl's subsequent disappearance.[58] The proverbial neighbor's eyes seem to have been relevant not only to supervision of prostitution but also to supervision of the conduct of lower-class young women who ventured to the public sphere.

Two groups of women that figure most prominently in such cases are orphans and servants. Some servants were former slaves, whereas others were freeborn women, sometimes of rural background, who often worked for better-off family members who had immigrated to the city. Their assailants were either members of their employer's household or service providers, as servants were also the ones who went out grocery shopping while their upper-class mistresses stayed at home. One female servant at *'umda*'s household, for example, accused one of his slaves of assaulting her in the fields.[59] Two other women accused men they had worked for as nannies.[60] Finally, one servant girl claimed the head butler of the house in which she used to work several years before had deflowered her.[61]

Domestic service was the most widespread form of labor for young girls in the Ottoman Middle East, including Egypt. It was the most available and socially acceptable trade for lower-class women and girls. Historians of Ottoman societies have found evidence of poor families who handed their daughters, sometimes at the tender age of six or seven, to well-to-do families for whom they worked for little pay or room and board alone. For the girls' parents, this meant one less mouth to feed. For the employer's family, it meant very cheap labor. For the girls involved, however, this could entail daily hardship and abuse. Domestic labor mimicked the intimacy of the domicile but deprived girls of family protection and care. Although some employers perceived this form of servitude as charity, girls who brought their cases to court presented them in terms of exploitation. Some servants were orphans or manumitted slaves and therefore enjoyed no family protection and were left at the mercy of their employer. Rural girls did not fare much better.[62] The intimacy of the domestic assignment, together with unequal power relations of age and gender, exposed girls to sexual abuse, court cases of which abound.[63]

Orphans figure in many cases of premarital defloration. Some of them worked as servants to support themselves, and others were informally adopted by relatives or neighbors and became victims of sexual abuse in their foster families. One girl was adopted by the neighborhood *shaykh*'s family after her parents' death and was assaulted by the *shaykh*'s son.[64] After her mother's death, eight-year-old Fatima was left with no one but her disabled stepfather, and she was forced to beg for a living. Eventually, a Moroccan man picked her off the street and employed her as a servant; she then accused him of deflowering her.[65] Again, the intimacy of home could prove treacherous to young women who lacked family protection.

⁓

I would like to conclude with two similar appeals, one by a brother and another by a father, against the conviction of young women for involvement in premarital defloration. I mentioned these cases earlier in the chapter because in both these men claimed that imprisonment would be more harmful to their female relative than their alleged involvement in premarital sex.

In one case, Hasan Ghurab accused another man called Sa'd Abu Tajjar of enticing his sister Hasna to leave home and steal her brother's money. Sa'd kept trying to draw the girl's attention from the street, looking up at her window and entertaining her until the late hours of the night, until he managed to convince her to leave the house. In her testimony, Hasna admitted she had befriended Saʻd, their next-door neighbor, over a couple of years. One day, as she visited his house to get some dough from his mother, she found him alone, and he took advantage of the opportunity, deflowered her, and promised to marry her.

The Appellate Council convicted Hasna because she was "seventeen years old, and not a minor, who is incapable of understanding what would dishonor her." In response, Hasna's brother appealed to the Supreme Council of Adjudication, claiming that Hasna was not seventeen years old but younger, still a minor lacking the mental capacities and reason of an adult woman. She was an innocent victim of a deceitful man who took her by force and lured her with his marriage promises. Following her brother's appeal, the Supreme Council ratified Hasna's conviction but reduced her prison sentence from the usual six months to three.[66]

In a similar case, a Jew called Ibrahim Haim accused a twenty-eight-year-old Iranian named Muhammad al-Baghdadi of abducting his fourteen-year-old daughter, Esther. Muhammad was a neighbor, and like Saʻd, neighbors frequently saw him by her window. Esther claimed she used to play with his female servant, along with her younger sister, and that he introduced himself as a Jew named Harun, talked to her, and even gently touched her hair. She became curious, and one day she "was not of her right mind," as she claimed, and went looking for him. He allowed her into his house and then deflowered her. When a policeman was brought to Muhammad's house, he found the girl there. As she noticed the policeman approaching, she signaled to Muhammad to remain quiet and tried to hide behind the door, but it was too late. A lower-instance council found both parties responsible and convicted them. Esther and her father chose to appeal. She was of tender age, they claimed, and that man had seduced her and caused her a permanent damage. When she was brought to the Appellate Council, this record concluded, it became clear that she was indeed very young and was indeed deceived as she had claimed, and she was acquitted.[67]

Both appeals revolved around the girls' ages and their capability to consent to sexual intercourse. Implicit to these appeals was the assumption that young girls, unlike older girls and women, are not sexual beings and are therefore unlikely to commit such an act of their own will. About one-fifth of the cases in my sample involve four- to ten-year-old girls. The law did not define an "age of consent," but in practice, policemen and council members treated cases involving younger boys and girls differently than those involving older girls and women. Police treatment of child molesters, moreover, was consistent, regardless of the child's gender. Unlike adult women, children did not have to prove that they had not consented, and councils often reasoned that children were incapable of false complaint in sexual matters.

In one assault case of a five-year-old girl, for example, the council rejected the defendants' denial on the grounds that "it is inconceivable that in her tender age she would make it up herself, or accuse a man although another had committed the act."[68] In a similar case involving a seven-year-old boy, the council reasoned that he was "of tender age, and hence incapable of perjuring or of accusing any other than the real perpetrator."[69] Unlike older girls, who had to prove their complaint against the system's inherent mistrust, young children's assault laid the burden of proof on the assailant. In both Esther's and Hasna's cases, the girls' guardians asked the council to reconsider their categorization as adult women and to treat them as young girls. In both cases, the council was convinced to reduce or cancel their sentence.

These cases also lend themselves to a tentative discussion of love. Historians of modern Egypt most commonly argue that companionate marriage is a twentieth-century phenomenon that stems from a European-inspired notion of national modernity.[70] Can we talk about nineteenth-century eloping couples as lovers? Did they see themselves as such? In chapter 4, I discussed two cases in which men committed murder in a brothel: one murdered a prostitute and another a client. Both claimed to have been in love and used explicit terms for love, such as *mahabba* or *ulfa*.[71] In one case, a man murdered his wife after she had left him for a man she loved. Council records again used the word *mahabba*, namely love, to describe her affection.[72] Such terms were not used in defloration cases. Hasna's and Esther's cases do imply the existence of lower-class affection, affairs, courting habits, and maybe even love. Several other cases offer examples of couples who eloped after the women's parents refused a marriage proposal. Some cases allude to long-term relationships and courting.[73]

Conclusion

This chapter examined the way social norms regarding women's virginity at marriage were incorporated into nineteenth-century Egyptian legal discourse and practice. The police station and courts became new arenas for proclaiming women's honor and for disciplining women's conduct. In these new legal arenas, narratives of coercion and consent were enacted, and girls learned how to narrate their experiences in ways that would absolve them from responsibility for their own defloration. Litigants, both women and their guardians, had an active role in the formation of premarital defloration and violation of honor as legal categories and, at the same time, in legitimizing the role of the police in community and family life.

Conclusion

Patriarchal control of women, communal and familial control of women's conduct took a different shape in 1882, on the eve of British occupation of Egypt, than they had but half a century earlier. New actors were now policing the conduct of women and girls. Policemen arrested runaway daughters and slaves—women who could not satisfactory explain their presence outdoors in unconventional hours—and brought them to the police station. Hakimas examined young women's hymens for signs of premarital defloration, allegedly producing a narrative that girls themselves were concealing or even denying. Midwives were obliged to report births, which made illegitimate babies harder to conceal. Under pressure both from above and from below, these measures were supplementing and sometimes replacing community and family mechanisms at a time when these social networks themselves were transforming. These new measures counteracted the gradual dissolution of solidarity networks following changes in land ownership, mass conscription to the army and the corvée, and rural immigration. As the urban neighborhood's social composition was changing, the city became more anonymous and therefore more difficult to control.

A social history of Khedival state formation, as outlined in this book, is a history of social transformations within and between communities. It entails asking precisely what it was about the new state that came to be felt in everyday life. Policing women, especially their mobility and visibility in public space, became one site in which modern state power was articulated. My argument throughout this volume was that the state as an abstraction became a tangible reality through interactions between policemen, hakimas, individual women, and their families. Modern state power was realized when the police station became a venue for resolving disputes, for reclaiming manumission papers, or for having an assailant punished. The "state" was not a coherent, preconceived entity that extended its gaze to new domains; instead, these new domains created this abstract, but yet very real, state power.

The different categories of women described here all had complex relationships to the normative family and community. For many women, abolition and mass manumission meant exclusion from what they had known as home and family for most of their lives. Some of them chose to remain as servants in households that previously enslaved them rather than face the uncertainties of freedom. Many others had to fend for themselves in an urban society that continued to see them as part of the domestic scene and offered little employment opportunities. Racial prejudice hampered their integration in free society, and the absence of kin and other support networks impeded their economic survival.

State handling of prostitutes epitomized social and official ambiguity toward male and female sexuality. Prostitution was neither criminalized nor regularized; it remained part of the urban landscape, yet it was required to be invisible. The police, the *shaykhs*, and neighborhood communities were concerned with suppressing and controlling the presence of prostitutes in public space: ordering them to cover themselves more when walking the streets, restricting their residence near "respectable" families, and forbidding them to solicit clients outside their doors. Policing prostitutes had a lot to do with restricting their interactions with "respectable" women. Because female sexuality was viewed as treacherous, any such interaction could easily turn the respectable mother, daughter, or wife into a prostitute. These concerns, coupled with prostitutes' own choices of residence, shaped the geography of prostitution in Egypt's urban centers.

This fear that the honorable woman would become a prostitute also affected social handling of premarital sex. The proverbial neighbor mentioned in an epigraph in chapter 4 (but one who unfortunately has two eyes), the family, the police, courts, and councils policed not only promiscuity but all "suspicious" behavior of young women who ventured into public space. Women who lost their virginity before marriage had to reclaim their respectability at the police station, councils, and courts and had to learn to narrate their bodily experiences according to legal expectations.

Finally, the hakimas were both "policed" and "policing." At the intrusive state's behest, they examined other women for violations against the female body.

At the same time, they were policed and controlled themselves, in order to make them respectable enough to become a tool in controlling morbidity, mortality, and young women's sexuality.

In the introduction, I argued that neither the "disciplined self" nor the "resisting agent" are sufficient analytical tools for understanding women's changing subjectivities in precolonial Egypt. To do that, I tried to trace the discourse of the disempowered, the kinds of options they had, the routes they chose, and life choices dictated and eliminated by socioeconomic and political transformations. Thinking about one's body, for example, could include both forensic medicine and the assumed ability to narrate a crime committed against it, as well as the notion that mental or physical illness was caused by the jinn. Abolition and mass manumission entailed new conceptualization of "family" by both former slaves and former enslavers. The desired invisibility of prostitution was related to new ways in which the urban space came to be perceived: its new orderly look, the obligation to sweep the floors and carry a lamp after dark.

I noted in the introduction that the present research has bearing on present-day dilemmas faced by women in the Middle East and beyond. Historian Geoff Eley recently proclaimed the past as a potential site of opposition as it reminds us that the present did not have to take the shape it eventually did, and the future can thus be different.[1] Historians of women and gender in the Middle East framed their discourse in the last two and a half decades around women's agency. The related concepts of agency and resistance enabled them to write post-Orientalist narratives of Middle Eastern women in which women knew more than mere oppression, gained control over their lives, and used the courts to reclaim those rights they were denied.

Without diminishing this achievement, this book demonstrates that limiting our focus to resistance or to women's capability to challenge patriarchal oppression misses the complexity of women's subjectivities. As I argued here, individual subjectivities cannot be autonomous from power relations that render meaningful even the intimacy of one's own body. Any act of resistance—a girl's choice to appeal her conviction of premarital sex or a slave's choice to escape— is embedded within a complex and sometimes ambiguous interaction between girls, private patriarchs, communities, and state representatives. Thus, to understand the complexity of women's choices in historical and present-day societies, the "romance of resistance" (to use Lila Abu-Lughod's term) offers but a partial representation of most women's lives.[2] Compliance and creative adjustment, I demonstrate here, were also part of this complex picture.

Khedival sources used in this work enable us to write such a rich history of social transformation. Historians of South Asian subaltern women found their voices very difficult to retrieve. In colonial archives, argues Kamala Visweswaran, third-person accounts of *how* subaltern women spoke are more frequent than *what* they actually said. Even when their words are reported, they are often fragmented, their speech acts ridiculed, and their political utterances are denied or depoliticized in first-person apologies they are forced to sign.[3]

Mediated as they are, police and council records enable us to reconstruct more fully the kind of life choices women were facing in nineteenth-century Egypt. The methodology I chose here, microhistory framed in its institutional and archival contexts, allowed me to demonstrate how the intimacy of individual lives was shaped by processes associated with Egypt's changing position in the world economy and vis-à-vis colonial interests. The narratives I presented here thus complement and expend feminist scholarship that delves into the complex interactions between the personal and the political. Taken together, the narratives told here demonstrate how large processes of modernity and state formations affected and were affected by the ways in which individual men and women viewed their world.

The legal system described here was short lived. In 1883, shortly after the British occupation, the Egyptian government abolished the councils of adjudication and replaced them with new ones modeled after the French legal system, and the shari'a courts were relegated exclusively to matters of personal status. These changes also affected the groups of women discussed in this book. The hakimas lost their privileged position and found themselves employed as nurses serving and assisting their male colleagues. The European-controlled Home for Freed Black Slave Women replaced the Egyptian-run manumission bureaus and police station in assisting freed slaves. Prostitution became regulated, and specific neighborhoods became official red-light districts with licensed brothels. Finally, the new penal code criminalized rape rather than defloration, ignoring prevailing social practices.

By contrast, Egypt's precolonial elite tended to operate within a conceptual framework that made sense to most Egyptians. The Khedival state-building process was shaped, in part, by their appeals and concerns. The Khedival state exerted its own modernizing, even colonizing, power over the population. Often coercive and even violent, the transformations discussed in this book nevertheless incorporated and acknowledged local customs and practices. With their inherent contradictions and tensions, these were the arenas in which modern state power was formed.

GLOSSARY

∼

NOTES

∼

BIBLIOGRAPHY

∼

INDEX

Glossary

bey. A high rank in the Ottoman administration, lower than a pasha.

daya. A traditional midwife.

effendi. An Ottoman title meaning "lord" or "master." In the nineteenth century, it was used as a form of address or reference for persons possessing a certain standard of literacy, approximate equivalent of the English mister or French monsieur. Formally, it was also used to designate functionaries in the Ottoman administration.

fatwa. Responsa; legal opinion issued by an Islamic legal scholars regarding a specific legal matter, in a response to a question addressed to them.

fiqh. Islamic jurisprudence; the science of religious law.

hadd. Punishment of acts that have been forbidden or sanctioned by punishments in the Qur'an and have thereby become crimes against religion and are liable to corporal punishment. These are unlawful intercourse *(zina),* false accusation of unlawful intercourse *(qadhf),* drinking wine, theft, and highway robbery.

hakima. A doctoress, a female medical practitioner.

Hanafi. One of the four schools of thought within Sunni Islam.

jinn. Spirits, invisible beings, either harmful or helpful, that interfere with the lives of mortals.

khedive. A Persian word meaning "ruler." Used exclusively by Egypt's rulers as the rulers' formal title after 1867, used domestically before that date as well.

mahr. The gift that the bridegroom has to give the bride when the marriage contract is made and which becomes the property of the wife.

mahr al-mithl. A *mahr* of a similar (girl); the amount of the bridal gift, which is determined through the social ranking of the male lineage to which she belongs, as well as her personal qualities.

mufti. Muslim jurist who delivers a nonbinding legal opinion known as fatwa.

pasha. A high rank in the Ottoman administration.

qadhf. A false accusation of *zina.*

qadi. A judge at the shari'a court.

qanun. A legal code issued by the ruler, which supplements the shari'a.

Shafi'i. One of the four schools of thought within Sunni Islam.

shari'a. Islamic law.

shaykh. Literally, an elderly man. In this period, a head of a tribe, a village, a neighborhood, or a guild.

siyasa. An extra-shari'a judiciary.

'ulama. Scholars specializing in Islamic law, including *qadis* and muftis.

umm walad. Literally, a child's mother. A slave who had her master's child and therefore cannot be resold and is emancipated upon her master's death.

zar. Spirit possession cult, practiced mainly by women.

zina. Illicit sexual relations.

Notes

Introduction

1. Dabtiyyat Misr, L/2/6/3, case no. 163, 8 Safar 1295 (11 Feb. 1878), 119–21.

2. Janet Abu-Lughod, *Cairo: 1001 Years of the City Victorious* (Princeton, N.J.: Princeton Univ. Press, 1971), 83–117; Khaled Fahmy, "An Olfactory Tale of Two Cities: Cairo in the Nineteenth Century," in *Historians in Cairo: Essays in Honor of George Scanlon,* ed. Jill Edwards (Cairo: American Univ. in Cairo Press, 2002), 155–89; André Raymond, *Le Caire* ([Paris]: Fayard, 1993), 297–315.

3. See, for example, Kenneth M. Cuno, *The Pasha's Peasants: Land, Society, and Economy in Lower Egypt, 1740–1858* (Cambridge, U.K.: Cambridge Univ. Press, 1992); Roger Owen, *Cotton and the Egyptian Economy, 1820–1914: A Study in Trade and Development* (Oxford: Clarendon, 1969); idem., *The Middle East in the World Economy, 1800–1914* (New York: Methuen, 1981); Ehud R. Toledano, *State and Society in Mid-Nineteenth-Century Egypt* (Cambridge, U.K.: Cambridge Univ. Press, 1990), 181–95.

4. Judith Tucker, "Decline of the Family Economy in Mid-Nineteenth-Century Egypt," *Arab Studies Quarterly* 1, no. 3 (1979): 245–47.

5. Timothy Mitchell, *Colonising Egypt* (Cambridge, U.K.: Cambridge Univ. Press, 1988), ix–xi, 41, 67–69, 79–81.

6. Mine Ener, *Managing Egypt's Poor and the Politics of Benevolence, 1800–1952* (Princeton, N.J.: Princeton Univ. Press, 2003); Khaled Fahmy, "Prostitution in Nineteenth-century Egypt," in *Outside In: On the Margins of the Modern Middle East,* ed. Eugene Rogan (London: I. B. Tauris, 2002), 77–103; Rudolph Peters, "Prisons and Marginalization in Nineteenth-Century Egypt," in *Outside In,* ed. Rogan, 31–52; 'Imad Hilal, *Al-Baghaya fi Misr: Dirasa Ta'rikhiyya Ijtima'iyya, 1834–1949* (Cairo: al-'Arabi li-l-Nashr wa-l-Tawzi', 2001); and idem, *Al-Raqiq fi Misr fi al-Qarn al-Tasi' 'Ashar* (Cairo: al-'Arabi, 1999).

7. See, for example, Toledano, *State and Society,* 19–21, 155–75; Nathan Brown, *Peasant Politics in Modern Egypt: The Struggle against the State* (Bethesda, Md.: Jahan Book, 1990), 20–21; Gabriel Baer, "Submissiveness and Revolt of the Fellah," in his *Studies in the Social History of Modern Egypt* (Chicago: Univ. of Chicago Press, 1969), 96–100; Cuno, 121–28, 147; Khaled Fahmy, "The Police and the People in Nineteenth-Century Egypt," *Die Welt des Islams* 39 (1999): 341–77; Juan Cole,

Colonialism and Revolution in the Middle East: Social and Cultural Origins of Egypt's 'Urabi Movement (Princeton, N.J.: Princeton Univ. Press, 1992), 87–89, 195–96, 202, 217.

8. John T. Chalcraft, *The Striking Cabbies of Cairo and Other Stories: Crafts and Guilds in Egypt, 1863–1914* (Albany: State Univ. of New York Press, 2005), 3.

9. See, particularly, Ranajit Guha, *Elementary Aspects of Peasant Insurgency in Colonial India* (Delhi: Oxford Univ. Press, 1983); Shahid Amin, *Event, Metaphor, Memory: Chauri Chaura, 1922–1992* (Berkeley: California Univ. Press, 1995). See also two founding essays of the subaltern studies group: Ranajit Guha, "The Prose of Counter-Insurgency," in Guha, *Subaltern Studies II: Writings on South Asian History and Society* (Delhi: Oxford Univ. Press, 1983), 1–42; and "Some Aspects of the Historiography of Colonial India," in *Selected Subaltern Studies,* eds. Ranajit Guha and Gayatri Chakravorty Spivak (New York: Oxford Univ. Press, 1988), 37–45; Gayatri Chakravorty Spivak, "Subaltern Studies: Deconstructing Historiography," in *Selected Subaltern Studies,* ed. Spivak and Ranajit Guha (New York: Oxford Univ. Press, 1988), 3–4.

10. Rosalind O'Hanlon, "Recovering the Subject: Subaltern Studies and Histories of Resistance in Colonial South Asia," *Modern Asian Studies* 22 (1988), 189–224. See also Gyan Prakash, "Subaltern Studies as Postcolonial Criticism," *American Historical Review* 99 (1994), 1475–90; See also Talal Asad's critique of the universal subject in *The Formations of the Secular: Christianity, Islam, Modernity* (Stanford, Calif.: Stanford Univ. Press, 2003), 70–74; and Jon E. Wilson, "Subjects and Agents in the History of Imperialism and Resistance," in *Powers of the Secular Modern: Talal Asad and His Interlocutors,* ed. Charles Hirschkind and David Scott (Stanford, Calif.: Stanford Univ. Press, 2006), 180–205.

11. Saba Mahmood, *Politics of Piety: The Islamic Revival and the Feminist Subject* (Princeton, N.J.: Princeton Univ. Press, 2005), 14–32.

12. Chalcraft, 64, 74, 102; Cole, 69–73, 96–97; Pascale Ghazaleh, *Masters of the Trade: Crafts and Craftspeople in Cairo, 1750–1850* (Cairo: American Univ. in Cairo Press, 1999), 1.

13. Ener, xvii, 18.

14. Mario Ruiz, "Intimate Disputes, Illicit Violence: Gender, Law, and the State in Colonial Egypt, 1849–1923" (PhD diss., Univ. of Michigan, 2004), 13–15.

15. Lisa Pollard, *Nurturing the Nation: The Family Politics of Modernizing, Colonizing and Liberating Egypt, 1805–1923* (Berkeley: California Univ. Press, 2005), 5; Beth Baron, *Egypt as a Woman: Nationalism, Gender and Politics* (Berkeley: Univ. of California Press, 2005), 32–33.

16. Elizabeth Thompson, "Public and Private in Middle Eastern Women's History," *Journal of Women's History* 15, no. 1 (Spring 2003): 52–69.

17. See, for example, Dror Ze'evi, "Changes in Legal-Sexual Discourses: Sex Crimes in the Ottoman Empire," *Continuity and Change* 16, no. 2 (2001): 219–42; Colin Imber, *Studies in Ottoman History and Law* (Istanbul: Isis, 1996); B. F. Musallam, *Sex and Society in Islam: Birth Control before the Nineteenth Century* (Cambridge, U.K.: Cambridge Univ. Press, 1983).

18. For a discussion of marginality in historical societies in North Africa see, for example, Abdelhamid Larguèche, *Les Ombres de Tunis: Pauvres, Marginaux et Minorités aux XVIIIe et XIXe*

Siècles (Paris: Arcantères, 2000); and Abdelhamid Larguèche and Dalenda Bouzgarrou-Larguèche, *Marginales en terre d'Islam* (Tunis: Cérès, 1992).

19. Ann Laura Stoler, *Race and the Education of Desire: Foucault's History of Sexuality and the Colonial Order of Things* (Durham, N.C.: Duke Univ. Press, 1997).

20. Uma Chakravarti, "Wifehood, Widowhood and Adultery: Female Sexuality, Surveillance and the State in 18th Century Maharashtra," *Contributions to Indian Sociology* 29 (1995): 3–22; Veena Poonacha, "Redefining Gender Relations: The Imprint of the Colonial State on the Coorg/Kodava Norms of Marriage and Sexuality," *Contributions to Indian Sociology* 29 (1995): 39–64; Prem Chowdhry, "Contesting Claims and Counter-claims: Questions of the Inheritance and Sexuality of Widows in a Colonial State," *Contributions to Indian Sociology* 29 (1995): 65–82. See also in the same issue Janaki Nair, "Prohibited Marriage: State Protection and the Child Wife," *Contributions to Indian Sociology* 29 (1995): 157–86; Meera Kosabi, "Gender Reform and Competing State Controls over Women: The Rakhmabai Case (1884–1888)," *Contributions to Indian Sociology* 29 (1995): 239–64.

21. Lata Mani, *Contentious Traditions: The Debate on Sati in Colonial India* (Berkeley: Univ. of California Press, 1998); Veena Das, *Life and Words: Violence and the Descent into the Ordinary* (Berkeley: Univ. of California Press, 2007).

22. See, for example, Manar Hasan, "The Politics of Honor: Patriarchy, the State and the Murder of Women in the Name of Family Honor," in *Israeli Family and Community: Women's Time,* ed. Hannah Naveh (London: Vallentine Mitchell, 2003), 1–37; Lama Abu Odeh, "Crimes of Honour and the Construction of Gender in Arab Societies" in *Feminism and Islam: Legal and Literary Perspectives,* ed. Mai Yamani (Berkshire, U.K.: Ithaca, 1996), 141–94; Lynn Welchman and Sara Hossain, eds., *"Honour": Crimes, Paradigms, and Violence against Women* (New York: Zed Books, 2005); Pınar İlkkaracan, ed., *Women and Sexuality in Muslim Societies* (Istanbul: Women for Women's Human Rights, 2000).

23. On the Huddud Ordinance in Pakistan see, for example, Asifa Quraishi, "Her Honour: An Islamic Critique of the Rape Provisions in Pakistan's Ordinance on *Zina* " *Islamic Studies* 38, no. 3 (1999): 403–31; Afiya Shehrbano Zia, "Rape in Pakistan: *Zina* Laws—Legalities and Loopholes," in *Women and Sexuality in Muslim Societies,* ed. İlkkaracan, 327–39.

24. Dipesh Chakrabarty, *Provincilizing Europe: Postcolonial Thought and Historical Difference* (Princeton, N.J.: Princeton Univ. Press, 2000).

25. Dror Ze'evi, "The Use of Ottoman Shari'a Court Records as a Source for Middle Eastern Social History: A Reappraisal," *Islamic Law and Society* 5, no. 1 (Feb. 1998): 35–57; Abraham Marcus, *The Middle East on the Eve of Modernity: Aleppo in the Eighteenth Century* (New York: Columbia Univ. Press, 1989); Ronald C. Jennings, *Studies on Ottoman Social History in the Sixteenth and Seventeenth Centuries: Women, Zimmis and Sharia Courts in Kayseri, Cyprus and Trabzon* (Istanbul: Isis, 1999); Leslie Peirce, *Morality Tales: Law and Gender in the Ottoman Court of Aintab* (Berkeley: Univ. of California Press, 2003); Iris Agmon, *Family & Court: Legal Culture and Modernity in Late Ottoman Palestine* (Syracuse, N.Y.: Syracuse Univ. Press, 2006).

26. Carlo Ginzburg, "The Inquisitor as Anthropologist," in *Clues, Myths, and the Historical Method,* trans. John Tedeschi and Anne C. Tedeschi (Baltimore: Johns Hopkins Univ. Press, 1989), 156–64; idem, *The Cheese and the Worms: The Cosmos of a Sixteenth-Century Miller,* trans. John Tedeschi and Anne C. Tedeschi (Baltimore: Johns Hopkins Univ. Press, 1980), xix–xx.

27. Guha, *Elementary Aspects of Peasant Insurgency,* 15.

1. Egyptian Legal Reform

1. Majlis al-Ahkam, S/7/10/60, case no. 318, 10 Rabi' Thani 1289 (16 June 1872), n.p.

2. See, for example, F. Robert Hunter, *Egypt Under the Khedives 1805–1879: From Household Government to Modern Bureaucracy* (Pittsburgh, Pa.: Univ. of Pittsburgh Press, 1984), 59; Peters, "Prisons and Marginalisation," 36–37, 44–45; Latifa Muhammad Salim, *Al-Nizam al-Qada'i al-Misri al-Hadith* ([Cairo]: al-Hay'a al-Misriyya al-'Amma li-l-Kitab, 2000–2001), 1:36.

3. Fahmy, "The Police and the People," 374. See also Fahmy, "The Anatomy of Justice: Forensic Medicine and Criminal Law in Nineteenth-Century Egypt," *Islamic Law and Society* 6 (1999): 252.

4. Judith Tucker, *Women in Nineteenth-Century Egypt* (Cambridge, U.K.: Cambridge Univ. Press, 1985), 13.

5. Avi Rubin, "Ottoman Modernity: The Nizamiye Courts in the Late Nineteenth Century" (PhD diss., Harvard Univ., 2006); Timothy Mitchell, "The Limits of the State: Beyond Statist Approaches and Their Critics," *The American Political Science Review* 85, no. 1 (1991), 77–96.

6. Peter Gran, "Modern Middle East History Beyond Oriental Despotism, World History Beyond Hegel: An Agenda Article," in *New Frontiers in the Social History of the Middle East,* ed. Enid Hill (Cairo: American Univ. in Cairo Press, 2002): 162–98.

7. Agmon, 236.

8. Rubin, 175–224.

9. Milen Petrov, "Everyday Forms of Compliance: Subaltern Commentaries on Ottoman Reform," *Comparative Studies in Society and History* 46 (2004): 730–59.

10. Ehud R. Toledano, "Social and Economic Change in the 'Long Nineteenth Century'," in *The Cambridge History of Egypt,* ed. Martin Daly (Cambridge, U.K.: Cambridge Univ. Press, 1998), 2:256–58.

11. Toledano, *State and Society,* 83–84.

12. F. Robert Hunter, "State-Society Relations in Nineteenth-Century Egypt: The Years of Transition, 1848–79," *Middle Eastern Studies* 36, no. 3 (July 2000): 146, 150, 156; Hilmi Ahmad Shalabi, *Al-Muwazzafun fi Misr fi 'Asr Muhammad 'Ali* ([Cairo]: al-Hay'a al-Misriyya al-'Amma li-l-Kitab, 1989), 23–27, 96; Toledano, *State and Society,* 17–18, 78–80; Hunter, *Egypt under the Khedives,* 80–92.

13. Carter Vaughn Findley, "The Tanzimat," *The Cambridge History of Turkey: Turkey in the Modern World,* ed. Reşat Kasaba (Cambridge, U.K.: Cambridge Univ. Press, 2008), 4:18; Ruth A. Miller, *Legislating Authority: Sin and Crime in the Ottoman Empire and Turkey* (New York: Routledge, 2005), 14; Butrus Abu-Manneh, "The Islamic Roots of the Gülhane Rescript," *Die Welt des Islams* 34, no. 2 (1994), 173–203; Gabriel Baer, "Tanzimat in Egypt: The Penal Code," *Bulletin of the*

School of Oriental and African Studies 26 (1963): 29–49; Donald Quataert, *The Ottoman Empire, 1700–1922* (Cambridge, U.K.: Cambridge Univ. Press, 2005), 63–64.

14. Fahmy, "The Police and the People," 349; Baer, "Tanzimat in Egypt," 35–37; Rudolph Peters, "Islamic and Secular Criminal Law in Nineteenth-Century Egypt: The Role and Function of the Qadi," *Islamic Law and Society* 4, no. 1 (1997): 72–73.

15. For more details about the different councils and their foundation, see Peters, "Islamic and Secular," 75–76; idem, "Administrators and Magistrates: The Development of a Secular Judiciary in Egypt, 1842–1871," *Die Welt des Islam* 39, no. 3 (1999): 381–89; Ahmad Fathi Zaghlul, *Al-Muhama* (Cairo: Matba'at al-Ma'arif, 1900), 182–85, 192–95, 199, 209–11; Salim, 1:28; Hunter, *Egypt under the Khedives,* 44, 50–51.

16. Peters, "Administrators and Magistrates," 392–93; idem, "Islamic and Secular," 71.

17. Fahmy, "The Police and the People," 366–67, 375.

18. Majlis Khususi, S/11/8/8, no. 28, articles 5–6, 17 Jumada Thani 1282 (5 Nov. 1865), 113–16; Amin Sami, *Taqwim al-Nil wa-Asma' man Tawwallaw Amr Misr wa-Muddat Hukmihim 'alayha wa-Mulahaza Ta'rikhiyya 'an Ahwal al-Khilafa al-'Amma wa-Shu'un Misr al-Khassa an al-Mudda al-Munhasira bayna al-Sana al-Ula wa-Sanat 1333 al-Hijriyya (622–1915 Miladiyyc),* (Cairo: al-Matba'a al-Amiriyya, 1916–36), 3:946–47; Zaghlul, 222.

19. Toledano, *State and Society,* 222–25; Fahmy, "The Police and the People," 350–51; Baer, "The Village Shaykh, 1800–1950," in *Studies in the Social History of Modern Egypt,* 38; Cuno, 166–78.

20. Nelly Hanna, "The Administration of Courts in Ottoman Egypt," in *The State and its Servants: Administration in Egypt from Ottoman Times to the Present,* ed. Nelly Hanna (Cairo: Cairo Univ. Press, 1995), 44–59; Muhammad Khalid Masud, Brinkley Messick, and David S. Powers, "Muftis, Fatwas and Islamic Legal Interpretation," in *Islamic Legal Interpretation: Muftis and their Fatwas,* ed. Masud, Messick, and Powers (Cambridge, Mass.: Harvard Univ. Press, 1996), 9–12; Brinkley Messick, *The Calligraphic State: Textual Domination and History in a Muslim Society* (Berkeley: Univ. of California, 1996), 140–41; Judith E. Tucker, "'And God Knows Best': The Fatwas as a Source for the History of Gender in the Arab World," in *Beyond the Exotic: Women's Histories in Islamic Societies,* ed. Amira El Azhary Sonbol (Syracuse, N.Y.: Syracuse Univ. Press, 2005), 165–79; Galal H. el-Nahal, *The Judicial Administration of Ottoman Egypt in the Seventeenth Century* (Minneapolis: Bibliotheca Islamica, 1979).

21. Ma'iyya Saniyya, S/1/18/2, no. 14 (muhafazat iskandriya), 96, 151, 22 Rabi' Thani 1271 (10 Jan. 1855).

22. Ma'iyya Saniyya, S/1/18/2, no. 15, 11 Jumada Awwal 1271 (29 Jan 1855), 151, 178.

23. Hunter, *Egypt under the Khedives,* 44.

24. *La'ihat majlisa aqalim bahri wa-qibli,* articles 6, 7, 9, in Zaghlul, 97–98 (of appendixes).

25. Majlis Khususi, S/11/8/6, no. 70, 3 Jumada Awwal 1280 (14 Oct. 1863), 104–5; Fahmy, "The Anatomy of Justice," 229; Peters, "Islamic and Secular," 76; Peters, "Administrators and Magistrates," 385–89; Zaghlul, 209–11.

26. Majlis Khususi, S/11/8/8, no. 28, 17 Jumada Thani 1282 (5 Nov. 1865), 113–16, articles 1–4.

27. Filib Jallad, "Dabtiyya," in his *Qamus al-Idara wa-l-Qada'* (Alexandria: al-Matba'a al-Bukhariya, 1892), 1187-88, article no. 1.

28. Rudolph Peters, "Muhammad al-'Abbasi al-Mahdi (d. 1897), Grand Mufti of Egypt, and His al-Fatawa al-Mahdiyya," *Islamic Law and Society* 1, no. 1 (1994): 74-82.

29. Sami, 3:630.

30. Peters, "Muhammad al-'Abbasi al-Mahdi," 75.

31. Sami, 3:630; Majlis Khususi, S/11/8/19, no. 194, 30 Rabi' Thani 1290 (25 June 1873), 161-62.

32. Hunter, *Egypt under the Khedives,* 39-40.

33. Majlis Khususi, S/11/8/8, no. 1, 22 Rabi' Thani 1282 (12 Sept. 1865), 1-5.

34. Majlis Khususi, S/11/8/8, no. 12, 4 Jummada Awwal 1282 (23 Sept. 1865), 42-50.

35. Majlis Khususi, S/11/8/15, no. 56, 17 Shawwal 1287 (8 Jan. 1871), 50; Majlis Khususi, S/11/8/15, no. 122, 15 Jumada Thani 1288 (31 Aug. 1871), 147-48; Majlis Khususi, S/11/8/16, no. 9, 6 Rajab 1288 (20 Sept. 1871), 5-6 (available also in Sami, 3:966-67).

36. Ann Laura Stoler, "Colonial Archives and the Art of Governance: On the Content in the Form," in *Archives, Documentation, and Institutions of Social Memory: Essays from the Sawyer Seminar,* ed. Francis Xavier Blouin and William G. Rosenberg (Ann Arbor: Univ. of Michigan Press, 2007), 272; see also idem, *Along the Archival Grain: Epistemic Anxieties and Colonial Commonsense* (Princeton, N.J.: Princeton Univ. Press, 2009).

37. Hunter, "State-Society Relations," 148-49.

38. Dror Ze'evi, "Women in Seventeenth-Century Jerusalem: Western and Indigenous Perspectives," *International Journal of Middle East Studies* 27 (May 1995): 161-62.

39. Baron, *Egypt as a Woman,* 50-51.

40. In her article on child marriage in late nineteenth-century India, Janaki Nair similarly argues that the ban was enforced, in part, by holding local priests and community leaders accountable for the marriage of underage girls. See Nair, 170.

41. Majlis al-Ahkam, S/7/10/60, case no. 318, 10 Rabi' Thani 1289 (16 June 1872), n.p.

42. Baer, "Submissiveness and Revolt of the Fellah," 96-100; Cuno, 127-28; Peter Gran, "Upper Egypt in Modern History: A 'Southern Question'?" in *Upper Egypt: Identity and Change,* ed. Nicholas Hopkins and Reem Saad (Cairo: American Univ. in Cairo Press, 2005), 85-86; Cole, 87-89, 195-96.

43. Majlis al-Ahkam, S/7/10/216, case no. 371, 17 Jumada Thani 1300 (24 Apr. 1883), n.p.

44. Majlis al-Ahkam, S/7/10/60, case no. 318, 10 Rabi' Thani 1289 (16 June 1872), n.p.

45. Majlis al-Ahkam, S/7/10/29, case no. 13, 22 Jumada Thani 1285 (7 Oct. 1868), n.p.

46. Majlis al-Ahkam, S/7/10/108, case no. 322, 8 Jumada Thani 1294 (19 June 1877), 76-77.

47. Ibid.

48. See, for example, Majlis al-Ahkam, S/7/10/216, case no. 371, 17 Jumada Thani 1300 (24 Apr. 1883), n.p.; Majlis al-Ahkam, S/7/10/108, case no. 322, 8 Jumada Thani 1294 (19 June 1877), 76-77; Majlis al-Ahkam, S/7/10/29, case no. 13, 22 Jumada Thani 1285 (7 Oct. 1868), n.p.

49. Majlis al-Ahkam, S/7/10/216, case no. 371, 17 Jumada Thani 1300 (24 Apr. 1883), n.p.

50. Majlis al-Ahkam, S/7/10/108, case no. 322, 8 Jumada Thani 1294 (19 June 1877), 76–77.

51. Hasan, 1–37.

52. Ibid.

2. Medicine, Law, and the Female Body

1. Majlis al-Ahkam, S/7/10/6, case no. 516, 11 Ramadan 1280 (2 Feb. 1864), 168–69.

2. The hakimas are called in secondary literature doctoresses, midwives, or hakimas. The term midwife is confusing here because their training and practice reached beyond that of midwifery, and should not be confused with the traditional midwife (daya). Hakima is indeed a doctoress, the female form of a hakim—a doctor. Recent scholarship prefers hakima, and I will follow.

3. A.-B. Clot Bey, Memoires de A.-B. Clot Bey (Cairo: Institut français d'archéologie orientale, 1949), 320–22. The quote is taken from 320.

4. Hibba Abugideiri, Gender and the Making of Modern Medicine in Colonial Egypt (Farnham, UK: Ashgate, 2010), 129–33. On the school of hakimas and the motivations for its establishment, see Khaled Fahmy, "Women, Medicine and Power in Nineteenth-Century Egypt," in Remaking Women: Feminism and Modernity in the Middle East, ed. Lila Abu-Lughod (Princeton, N.J.: Princeton Univ. Press, 1998), 41–51; and Fahmy, "Prostitution in Nineteenth-Century Egypt," 84.

5. I rely here on Judith Butler's discussion of sex and the body as mediated through discourse. See Judith Butler, Bodies that Matter: On the Discursive Limits of "Sex" (London: Routledge, 1993); and her Excitable Speech: A Politics of the Performative (London: Routledge, 1997).

6. John Walker, Folk Medicine in Modern Egypt: Being the Relevant Parts of the Tibb al-Rukka or Old Wives' Medicine of 'Abd al-Rahman Isma'il (London: Luzac, 1934), 7.

7. Marcia Inhorn, Quest for Conception: Gender, Infertility, and Egyptian Medical Traditions (Philadelphia: Univ. of Pennsylvania Press, 1994).

8. 'Abd al-Rahman Isma'il, Kitab Tibb al-Rukka (Cairo: al-Bahiyya, 1892), 22, 46, 49; Ahmad Amin, Qamus al-'Adat wa-l-Taqalid wa-l-Ta'abir al-'Arabiyya (Cairo: Matba'at al-Janna 1953), 116–19, 141–43, 324.

9. Ahmad Amin, 142–43.

10. 'Ali Mubarak, al-Khitat al-Tawfiqiyya al-Jadida li-Misr al-Qahira wa-Muduniha wa-Biladiha al-Qadima wa-l-Shahira (Cairo: al-Matba'a al-Kubra al-Amiriyya. 1886), 14:141.

11. Ibid., 2:30.

12. Ibid., 8:33.

13. See, for example, "al-Zar aw al-'Ifrit," al-Hilal 3, no. 13 (1.3.1895), 505–7; "al-Zar aw al-'Ifrit," al-Hilal 3, no. 14 (15.3.1895), 551; "al-Talasim," "al-Qarina," al-Hilal 2, no. 10 (15.1.1894), 304–6.

14. "al-Qarina," al-Muqtataf 28, no. 9 (Sept. 1903), 800.

15. Isma'il, 72–78.

16. Ehud R. Toledano, As If Silent and Absent: Bonds of Enslavement in the Islamic Middle East (New Haven, Conn.: Yale Univ. Press, 2007), 212–27.

17. Edward William Lane, The Manners & Customs of the Modern Egyptians (London: Dent, [1908]), 168. In one case cited in the Supreme Council records, an effendi was accused of deflowering

a midwife's daughter, whom he knew because her mother served as the midwife of his harem. See Majlis al-Ahkam, S/7/10/26, case no. 86, 22 Sha'ban 1284 (17 Dec. 1867), n.p.

18. Lane, *Manners and Customs,* 509.

19. Gorgy P. G. Sobhy, "Customs and Superstitions of the Modern Egyptians Connected with Pregnancy and Childbirth," *Records of the Egyptian Government School of Medicine* 2 (1904): 101–6.

20. Phyllis Stock-Morton, "Control and Limitation of Midwives in Modern France: The Example of Marseille," *Journal of Women's History* 8, no. 1 (Spring 1996): 60.

21. See 'Ali ibn Abi Bakr al-Marghinani, *The Hedaya, Guide: A Commentary on the Mussulman Laws,* trans. Charles Hamilton (Lahore: New Book, [1957]), 354–55; Muhammad Amin bin 'Umar Ibn 'Abidin, *Radd al-Muhtar 'ala al-Durr al-Mukhtar Sharh Tanwir al-Absar* (Beirut: Dar al-Kutub al-'Ilmiyya), 6:53.

22. Avner Giladi, "Liminal Craft, Exceptional Law: Preliminary Notes on Midwives in Medieval Islamic Writings," *International Journal of Middle East Studies* 42 (2010): 185–202; Ron Shaham, *The Expert Witness in Islamic Courts: Medicine and Crafts in the Service of Law* (Chicago: Univ. of Chicago Press, 2010): 83–100.

23. Clot Bey, *Memoires,* 321.

24. Sander L. Gilman, *Difference and Pathology: Stereotypes of Sexuality, Race and Madness* (Ithaca, N.Y.: Cornell Univ. Press, 1985), 83–89.

25. LaVerne Kuhnke, *Lives at Risk: Public Health in Nineteenth-Century Egypt* (Berkeley: Univ. of California Press, 1990), 3–4, 33–34; Amira El Azhary Sonbol, *The Creation of a Medical Profession in Egypt, 1800–1922* (Syracuse, N.Y.: Syracuse Univ. Press, 1991), 35; Daniel Panzac, "Médicine Révolutionnaire et Révolution de la Médicine dan l'Égypte de Muhammad Ali: Le Dr. Clot-Bey," *Revue des Mondes Musulmans et de la Méditerranée,* no. 52/53 (1989): 95–110.

26. Naguib Mahfouz, *The History of Medical Education in Egypt* (Cairo: Bulaq, 1935), 26.

27. Kuhnke, 34–44; Sonbol, *The Creation of a Medical Profession,* 61; Mahfouz, 27–32; Panzac, 102–5; Jamal al-Din al-Shayyal, *Ta'rikh al-Tarjama wa-l-Haraka al-Thaqafiyya fi 'Asr Muhammad 'Ali* ([Cairo]: Dar al-Fikr al-'Arabi, 1951), 105–7. For more about the missions, see Albert Hourani, *Arabic Thought in the Liberal Age, 1798–1939* (London: Oxford Univ. Press, 1970), 53–54; 'Ali Mubarak, 1:88.

28. See Michel Foucault, "Governmentality," in *The Foucault Effect: Studies in Governmentality,* ed. Graham Burchell, Colin Gordon, and Peter Miller, trans. Rosi Braidotti and revised by Colin Gordon (Chicago: Univ. of Chicago Press, 1991), 87–104; and idem, *History of Sexuality,* vol. 1, trans. Robert Hurley (New York: Pantheon Books, 1978).

29. Mervat F. Hatem, "The Professionalization of Health and the Control of Women's Bodies as Modern Governmentalities in Nineteenth-Century Egypt," *Women in the Ottoman Empire: Middle Eastern Women in the Early Modern Era,* ed. Madeline C. Zilfi (Leiden: E. J. Brill, 1997), 66–80.

30. Clot Bey, *Memoires,* 322.

31. Islamic law legitimized abortion during the first 120 days of pregnancy, provided the husband consented. More on Islamic legal handling of abortion, see Marion Katz, "The Problem of Abortion in Medieval Fiqh," in *Islamic Ethics of Life: Abortion, War, and Euthanasia,* ed. John Brockopp (Columbia: Univ. of South Carolina Press, 2003), 30–37.

32. Clot Bey, *Memoires*, 322; Ahmad al-Rashidi, *Kitab al-Wiladc* (Bulaq: Dar al-Tiba'a al-'Amira, 1842), 10; David Arnold notes similar reactions to male-dominated colonial medicine in late nineteenth-century India, which the colonial administration had a hard time overcoming. See David Arnold, "Touching the Body: Perspectives on the Indian Plague, 1896–1900," *Subaltern Studies* 5 (1987), 62.

33. Al-Rashidi, *Kitab al-Wilada*, 10.

34. Ibid., 8–9.

35. Ahmad al-Rashidi, *Bahjat al-Ru'asa' fi Amrad al-Nisa'* (Bulac: Dar al-Tiba'a al-'Amira, 1844), 285, 290, 297, 298, 301, 587–91.

36. Ibid., 583–84.

37. Ibid., 588–89; for medicalized discourse on female adolescence in nineteenth-century France, see Kathleen Alaimo, "The Authority of Experts: The Crisis of Female Adolescence in France and England, 1880–1920," in *Secret Gardens, Satanic Mills: Placing Girls in European History*, eds. Mary Jo Maynes, Birgitte Soland, and Christina Benninghaus (Bloomington: Indiana Univ. Press, 2005), 158.

38. Clot Bey, *Memoires*, 160.

39. Mahfouz, 73.

40. Ibid., 71–72; Kuhnke, 124–28; Fahmy, "Women, Medicine and Power," 47–48; Sonbol, *The Creation of a Medical Profession*, 46.

41. Fahmy, "Women, Medicine and Power," 61–63; Mahfouz, 72–74; Abugideiri, 119–20; Kuhnke, 126; Sonbol, *The Creation of a Medical Profession*, 47.

42. Abugideiri, 119.

43. Kuhnke, 123–25; Abugideiri, 121–24; Mahfouz, 73; Fahmy, "Women, Medicine and Power," 35, 48–49.

44. Kuhnke, 129.

45. Al-Rashidi, *Kitab al-Wilada*; idem, *Bahjat al-Ru'asa'*; Alfred Velpeau, *Traité élémentaire de l'art des accouchemens: ou principes de tokologie et d'embryologie* (Paris : J. B. Baillière, 1829). *Kitab al-Wilada* is clearly an adaptation of Velpeau's manual, but it includes an original introduction that refers to the specific Egyptian context. *Bahjat al-Ru'asa'*'s authorship, however, is not clear. The question of authorship of nineteenth-century Egyptian works is highly contested. Many early literary works in Arabic were dismissed as bad translations or adaptations of European literature and have received scholarly attention only recently. The question of authorship of scientific translations, as far as I know, has not been yet investigated.

46. Abugideiri, 129; Kuhnke, 129; Mahfouz, 72–73.

47. Majlis al-Ahkam, S/7/10/218, case no. 491, 8 Rajab 1300 (13 May 1883), n.p.

48. Khaled Fahmy, "Medicine and Power: Towards a Social History of Medicine in Nineteenth-Century Egypt," *Cairo Papers in Social Science* 23, no. 2, (Summer 2000): 39–46. In his work on the plague in colonial India, David Arnold argues that hospitals disconnected the sick from the support and nurture of their families and were therefore largely resisted. See Arnold, 62.

49. Majlis al-Ahkam, S/7/10/4, no. 60, 15 Rabi' Thani 1280 (15 Sept. 1863), 42–43.

50. Muhafazat Misr, L/1/20/5, case no. 24, 8 Shawwal 1277 (15 Apr. 1861), 137–38.

51. Fahmy, "Medicine and Power" 30.

52. Majlis al-Ahkam, S/7/10/8, case no. 633, 16 Shawwal 1280 (24 Mar. 1864), 40–42.

53. Majlis al-Ahkam, S/7/10/1, case no. 74, 7 Jumada Awwal 1279 (29 Oct. 1862), 29.

54. Ma'iyya Saniyya, S/1/33/1, no. 96, 8 Rajab 1281 (6 Dec. 1864), 162–163.

55. Sami, 3:167.

56. In Upper Egypt as late as March 1876, a *daya* examined the body of a murder victim to determine if she had been deflowered prior to her death, while a doctor examined her to determine the cause of death. Majlis al-Ahkam, S/7/10/98, no. 525, 13 Sha'ban 1293 (1 Sept. 1876), 122–23.

57. Thomas Rogers Forbes, *Surgeons at the Bailey: English Forensic Medicine to 1878* (New Haven, Conn.: Yale Univ. Press, 1985), 86–93; Elizabeth Kolsky, "'The Body Evidencing the Crime': Gender, Law and Medicine in Colonial India" (PhD diss., Columbia Univ., 2002), 404–5.

58. For similar rationale for child marriage in colonial and precolonial India, see Chakravarti, 10.

59. Shaham, *Expert Witness in Islamic Courts*, 87–88; Mahmud Yazbak, "Minor Marriages and *Khiyar Al-Bulugh* in Ottoman Palestine: A Note on Women's Strategies in a Patriarchal Society," *Islamic Law and Society* 9, no. 3 (2002): 395–99. See, for example, Mahkamat Misr—Murafa'at wa-Da'awa, 1/99/3/1430, 6 Jumada Thani 1287 (1 Sept. 1870), 127; for a *fiqh* reference, see Ibn 'Abidin, 4:170; Muhammad ibn Muhammad al-Mahdi al-'Abbasi, *Al-Fatawa al-Mahdiyya fi al-Waqa'i' al-Misriyya* (Cairo: al-Matba'a al-Azhariyya, 1883 or 1884–1887), 15 Safar 1269 (26 Nov. 1852) 1:45; Muhammad Kamil ibn Mustafa Tarabulusi, *Al-Fatawa al-Kamiliyya fi al-Hawadith al-Tarabulusiyya 'ala Madhhab al-Imam Abi Hanifa al-Nu'man 'alayhi Saha'ib al-Rahma wa-l-Ridwan* (Cairo: Matba'at Muhammad Afandi Mustafa, 1896), 24.

60. Al-Rashidi, *Bahjat al-Ru'asa'*, 592–93.

61. See, for example, Dabtiyyat Misr, L/2/46/4, case no. 10, 22 Rabi' Thani 1282 (12 Sept. 1865), 2; Majlis al-Ahkam, S/7/10/25, case no. 2, 27 Jumada Awwal 1284 (25 Sept. 1867), n.p.

62. Majlis al-Ahkam, S/7/10/12, case no. 1143, 15 Rabi' Awwal 1281 (17 Aug. 1864), 236–37.

63. Janaki Nair makes similar observations regarding the criminalization of child marriage in late nineteenth-century India: men proclaimed ignorance of the prohibition and contested its logic, anyway. Legal proceeding thus had a pedagogical role, serving as a warning to neighboring villages as well. See Nair, 159, 169.

64. See, for example, Marcus, *The Middle East on the Eve of Modernity,* 323–24.

65. Judith E. Tucker, *In the House of the Law: Gender and Islamic Law in Ottoman Syria and Palestine* (Berkeley: Univ. of California Press, 1998), 67–68; idem, "'And God Knows Best,'" 174.

66. Al-Marghinani, 35. See also Ibrahim ibn Muhammad ibn Ibrahim al-Halabi, *Multaqa al-Abhur* (Beirut: Mu'assasat al-Risalah, 1989), 244; Ibn 'Abidin, 4:166–67.

67. It is interesting to note that archival records from the period use the term *attiba al-siyasa,* that is, "doctors practicing *siyasa*-based medicine." In the 1890s, *tibb shar'i* became the official term for forensic medicine.

68. Velpeau, *Elementary Treatise on Midwifery,* 63; al-Rashidi, *Kitab al-Wilada,* 81; it is interesting that in the translation, al-Rashidi mentions only the possibility of punishing those who are anatomically nonvirgin and omits the possibility of acquitting the guilty.

69. Dabtiyyat Misr, L/2/51/3, case no. 327, 29 Rabi' Awwal 1285 (18 July 1868), 66–67.

70. Dabtiyyat Misr, L/2/6/2, case no. 221, 26 Dhu al-Qa'da 1294 (1 Dec. 1877), 200–201.

71. Dabtiyyat Iskandriya, L/4/18/11, case no. 750, 28 Rabi' Awwal 1297 (22 Sept 1869), 74–75.

72. Dabtiyyat Iskandriya, L/4/18/10, case no. 374, 18 Shawwal 1296 (3 Oct. 1879), n.p.

73. Dabtiyyat Iskandriya, L/4/18/9, case no. 36, 1 Jumada Awwal 1296 (22 Apr. 1879), 48.

74. Dabtiyyat Misr, L/2/6/8, case no. 533, 16 Jumada Awwal 1296 (6 May 1279), 59–60.

75. Dabtiyyat Misr, L/2/6/3, case no. 163, on 8 Safar 1295 (11 Feb. 1878), 119–21.

76. Majlis al-Ahkam, S/7/10/256, case no. 295, 16 Rabi' Awwal 1302 (2 Jan. 1885), n.p.

77. Majlis al-Ahkam, S/7/10/146, case no. 318, 5 Sha'ban 1296 (25 July 1879), n.p.; Dabtiyyat Misr, L/2/6/13, case no. 824, n.d, n.p.

78. For cases of induced abortion, see, for example Majlis al-Ahkam, S/7/10/105, case no. 177, 4 Rabi' Thani 1294 (17 Apr. 1877), 122; Majlis al-Ahkam, S/7/26/1, case no 115, 26 Rajab 1272 (1 Apr. 1856), 33; Dabtiyyat Misr, L/2/5/40, case no. 82 (*qadi* effendi), 3 Jumada Thani 1272 (9 Feb. 1858), 130; Ehud R. Toledano, *Slavery and Abolition in the Ottoman Middle East* (Seattle: Univ. of Washington Press, 1998), 60–61.

79. If the fetus carried clear signs of human organs, it was considered to be "formed," and its legal heirs were entitled to blood money. If the fetus did not yet show such signs, the heirs were entitled to lesser compensation. If premature labor ensued and caused the death of a child shortly after birth, full blood money was required. Estimating the fetus's age was therefore a routine part of the forensic procedure in miscarriage cases. Shaham, *Expert Witness in Islamic Courts,* 89–91; al-Halabi, 2:300.

80. Abu 'Ali al-Husayn bin 'Ali Ibn Sina, *Al-Qanun fi al-Tibb* (Baghdad: al-Muthanna, 1970), 2:572.

81. Al-Rashidi, *Bahjat al-Ru'asa',* 426.

82. Dabtiyyat Misr, L/2/5/41, case no. 116, 20 Rajab 1272 (27 Mar. 1856), n.p.

83. "Dabtiyya," in Jallad, 4:216.

84. Majlis al-Ahkam, S/7/10/119, case no. 328, 22 Sha'ban 1295 (20 Aug. 1878), 129.

85. Isma'il, 49. Burns were also used as a cure for rheumatism and sciatica. See Ahmad Amin, 180.

86. Majlis al-Ahkam, S/7/10/103, case no. 84, 12 Safar 1294 (25 Feb. 1877), 152.

87. Isma'il, 72–78.

3. Female Slaves, Manumission, and Abolition

1. Dabtiyyat Misr, L/2/6/2, case no. 195, 21 Dhu al-Qa'da 1294 (26 Nov. 1877), 155–68.

2. See Toledano, *As if Silent and Absent,* 24–34.

3. Gayatri Chakravorty Spivak, "Can the Subaltern Speak?" in *Marxism and the Interpretation of Culture,* ed. Cary Nelson and Larry Grossberg (Urbana: Univ. of Illinois Press, 1988), 271–313.

4. Mani, 159–60.

5. Eve Troutt Powell, "Will that Subaltern Ever Speak? Finding African Slaves in the Historiography of the Middle East," in *Middle East Historiographies: Narrating the Twentieth Century,* eds. Israel Gershoni, Amy Singer, and Y. Hakan Erdem (Seattle: Univ. of Washington Press, 2003), 243–44.

6. Dabtiyyat Misr, L/2/6/2, case no. 195, 21 Dhu al-Qa'da 1294 (26 Nov. 1877), 155–68.

7. Ibid.

8. On the status of slaves in Islamic law, see R. Brunschvig, "'Abd," *Encyclopedia of Islam* (Leiden: E. J. Brill, 1960), 1:26–29; Tucker, *Women in Nineteenth-Century Egypt,* 179; Hilal, *Al-Raqiq fi Misr,* 196–97; John Hunwick, "The Same but Different: Africans in Slavery in the Mediterranean Muslim World," in *The African Diaspora in the Mediterranean Muslim World,* ed. John Hunwick and Eve Troutt Powell (Princeton, N.J.: Markus Wiener, 2002), xv–xvi; Shaun E. Marmon, ed., *Slavery in the Islamic Middle East* (Princeton, N.J.: Markus Wiener, 1999), 5–6; Toledano, *Slavery and Abolition,* 6; Terence Walz, "Black Slavery in Egypt," in *Slaves and Slavery in Muslim Africa,* ed. John Ralph Willis (London: Frank Cass, 1985), 2:139; Joseph Schacht, *An Introduction to Islamic Law* (Oxford: Clarendon, 1966), 128.

9. Tucker, *Women in Nineteenth-Century Egypt,* 180, 189; Hilal, *Al-Raqiq fi Misr,* 211; Marmon, 15; Nelly Hanna, "Slave Women and Concubines in Ottoman Egypt," in *Beyond the Exotic,* ed. Sonbol, 125.

10. Reda Mowafi, *Slavery, Slave Trade, and Abolition Attempts in Egypt and the Sudan, 1820–1882* ([Stockholm]: Esselte Studium, 1981), 13; Gabriel Baer, "Slavery in Nineteenth-Century Egypt," *Journal of African History* 8, no. 3 (1967): 423; Toledano, *Slavery and Abolition,* 14; Diane Robinson-Dunn, *The Harem, Slavery and British Imperial Culture: Anglo-Muslim Relations in the Late Nineteenth Century* (Manchester: Manchester Univ. Press, 2006), 13–14.

11. Tucker, *Women in Nineteenth-Century Egypt,* 181–84, 187; Hilal, *Al-Raqiq fi Misr,* 196–99, 206–7; Brunschvig, 26–30.

12. Free Egyptians, on the other hand, were sometimes ethnically defined as Arabic speaking (*abna al-'arab*) or Turkish speaking (*abna al-atrak*). See Eve Troutt Powell, *A Different Shade of Colonialism: Egypt, Great Britain and the Mastery of the Sudan* (Berkeley: Univ. of California Press, 2003), 17.

13. Toledano, *Slavery and Abolition,* 53; Leslie Peirce, *The Imperial Harem* (New York: Oxford Univ. Press, 1993); Baer, "Slavery," 417–18; Ehud R. Toledano, "Slave Dealers, Pregnancy, Abortion, and the World of Women: The Story of a Circassian Slave-girl in Mid-Nineteenth-Century Cairo," *Slavery and Abolition* 2, no. 1 (1981): 53.

14. Tucker, *Women in Nineteenth-Century Egypt,* 167; Hilal, *Al-Raqiq fi Misr,* 42–44; Baer, "Slavery," 423.

15. Tucker, *Women in Nineteenth-Century Egypt,* 171; Mowafi, 12–14; Hilal, *Al-Raqiq fi Misr,* 192–95; Baer, "Slavery," 422.

16. Dabtiyyat Misr, L/2/6/2, case no. 195, 21 Dhu al-Qa'da 1294 (26 Nov. 1877), 155–68.

17. Mowafi, 15; Hilal, *Al-Raqiq fi Misr,* 200; Brunschvig, 26.

18. For details on the slave trade, see Mowafi, 29–31, 45–54; Toledano, *Slavery and Abolition,* 15–54.

19. Troutt Powell, "Will That Subaltern Ever Speak?" 245.

20. Mani, 159–90.

21. Alvan S. Southworth, *Four Thousand Miles of African Travel: A Personal Record of a Journey up the Nile and through the Soudan to the Confines of Central Africa, Embracing a Discussion of the Sources of the Nile, and an Examination of the Slave Trade* (New York: Baker, Pratt, 1875), 220–222.

22. Sophia Poole, *The Englishwoman in Egypt: Letters from Cairo Written During a Residence There in 1842–46,* ed. Azza Kararah (Cairo: American Univ. in Cairo Press, 2003), 232–33.

23. Lucie Duff-Gordon, *Letters from Egypt (1862–1869)* (London: Routledge and K. Paul, 1969), 73–74.

24. Ibid., 74.

25. Ibid., 96.

26. Lucie Duff-Gordon, *Letters from Egypt.* A "revised edition" with memoir by her daughter Janet Ross and a new introduction by George Meredith appeared in 1902 (London: R. B. Johnson); transcribed at the Gutenberg Project, http://www.gutenberg.org/files/17816/17816-h/17816-h.htm. This section does not appear in the 1969 edition.

27. Duff-Gordon, *Letters from Egypt* (1969 edition), 91.

28. Ibid., 98.

29. See, for example, Dabtiyyat Misr, L/2/5/30, case no. 412 ('Ali effendi, ra'is ta'ifat al-yasrajiyya fi al-mahrusa), 22 Sha'ban 1270 (18 May 1854), 15; Dabtiyyat Misr, L/2/5/31, case no. 737, 24 Shawwal 1270 (18 July 1854), 50; Dabtiyyat Misr, L/2/5/31, case no. 198 (Sulayman Agha Abu Dawwud ra'is al-yasrajiyya al-aswad bi-l-mahrusa), 14 Dhu al-Qa'da 1270 (8 Aug. 1854), 124; Dabtiyyat Misr, L/2/5/40, case no. 172 (sayira—da'irat sa'adat mustafa bik), 18 Jumada Thani 1272 (1 Mar. 1856), 172.

30. Majlis al-Ahkam, S/7/10/59, case no. 227, 9 Muharram 1289 (18 Mar. 1872), n.p.

31. Majlis al-Ahkam, S/7/10/12, case no. 1001, 17 Muharram 1281 (21 June 1864), 81.

32. Majlis al-Ahkam, S/7/10/14, case no. 28, 26 Rabi' al-Awwal 1281 (28 Aug. 1864), 37–38.

33. Majlis al-Ahkam, S/7/10/12, case no. 1139, 15 Rabi' al-Awwal 1281 (17 Aug. 1864), 232–33.

34. Majlis al-Ahkam, S/7/10/15, case no. 207, 27 Shawwal 1281 (24 Mar. 1865), 21–22.

35. Poole, 146.

36. Majlis al-Ahkam, S/7/57/2, case no. 44, 24 Safar 1274 (11 Oct. 1857), 67–69.

37. Majlis al-Ahkam, S/7/57/2, case no. 101, 8 Rabi' Thani 1274 (24 Nov. 1857), 151–53; for a case of a male slave beaten to death at the estate of Ilhami Pasha, Sa'id Pasha's great nephew, see Fahmy, "The Police and the People," 370–74.

38. Mahkamat Iskandriya—Da'awa, sijill no. 1, case no. 229, 12 Jumada Thani 1276 (5 Jan. 1860), 107.

39. Toledano, *As if Silent and Absent,* 70–79.

40. Majlis al-Ahkam, S/7/10/109, case no. 357, 29 Jumada Thani 1294 (9 July 1877), 34.

41. Majlis al-Ahkam, S/7/10/5, case no. 63, 15 Rabi' Thani 1280 (28 Sept. 1863), 24.

42. See, for example, Majlis al-Ahkam, S/7/57/3, case no. 98, 2 Rajab 1274 (15 Feb. 1858), 140–41; Dabtiyyat Misr, L/2/5/40, case no. 370 (wakil da'irat marhum Ibrahim basha), 20 Rajab 1272 (26 Mar. 1856), 35, 38; Majlis al-Ahkam, S/7/57/5, case no. 282, 12 Sha'ban 1274 (27 Mar. 1858), 46–47; Muhafazat Misr, L/1/20/2, case no. 18, 29 Safar 1272 (9 Nov. 1855), 3.

43. Baer, "Slavery," 437; Sami, 3:1489; Toledano, *As if Silent and Absent,* 156–65.

44. Troutt Powell, *A Different Shade of Colonialism,* 40–41; Mowafi, 7; Hilal, *Al-Raqiq fi Misr,* 25, 48, 51–52; Y. Hakan Erdem, *Slavery in the Ottoman Empire and Its Demise, 1800–1909* (New York: St. Martin's, with St. Antony's College [Oxford], 1996), 39–42; Khaled Fahmy, *All The Pasha's Men: Mehmed Ali, His Army and the Making of Modern Egypt* (Cambridge, U.K.: Cambridge Univ. Press, 1997), 86–89.

45. Erdem, 55–57; Toledano, *Slavery and Abolition,* 8.

46. Merchants trading black and white slaves were organized into two separate guilds, the former labeled the *jalaba* and the latter the *yasrajiyya*. By the 1850s, especially since the decline in white slave trade, both traded in both black and white slaves, and the terms were used interchangeably. Hilal, *Al-Raqiq fi Misr,* 70; Baer, "Slavery," 428.

47. See, for example, Dabtiyyat Misr, L/2/5/30, case no. 504 ('Ali effendi, ra'is ta'ifat al-yasrajiyya fi al-mahrusa), 13 Ramadan 1270 (8 June 1854), 90. Dabtiyyat Misr, L/2/5/30, case no. 591 ('Ali effendi, ra'is ta'ifat al-yasrajiyya fi al-mahrusa), 4 Shawwal 1270 (29 June 1854), 147.

48. Dabtiyyat Misr, L/2/5/30, case no. 402 ('Ali effendi, ra'is ta'ifat al-yasrajiyya fi al-mahrusa), 19 Sha'ban 1270 (15 May 1854), 4. In Islamic law, the purchaser has the right to cancel a transaction if a defect *('aib)* is found in the purchased goods, if it existed at the time of the sale but was discovered only after the transaction itself. Mohd. Ma'sum Billah, "Caveat Emptor versus *Khiyar al-'Aib:* A Dichotomy," *Arab Law Quarterly* 13, no. 3 (1998), 278–99.

49. See, for example, Dabtiyyat Misr, L/2/5/31, case no. 789 ('Ali efendi—ra'is al-yasrajiyya), 1 Dhu al-Qa'da 1270 (25 July 1854), 82.

50. Dabtiyyat Misr, L/2/5/30, case nos. 509, 511–12, 514–18, 520–21, 527, 530–32, 534, 536–37, 540, 544, 549, 551, 15–22 Ramadan 1270 (10–17 June 1854), 96–97, 101, 104, 108–10, 115–16.

51. This sum equaled about two weeks' work for an unskilled laborer or a week's work for a skilled one. Estimate of salaries are based on Toledano, *State and Society,* 212–13.

52. Dabtiyyat Misr, L/2/5/30, case no. 407 ('Ali effendi, ra'is ta'ifat al-yasrajiyya fi al-mahrusa), 20 Sha'ban 1270 (16 May 1854), 10; Dabtiyyat Misr, L/2/5/30, case no. 423 ('Ali effendi, ra'is ta'ifat al-yasrajiyya fi al-mahrusa), 24 Sha'ban 1270 (20 May 1854), 19, 23. Toledano does not mention this legal resort in his discussion of the Ottoman Empire, and it might have been relied on more prominently in Egypt than in other parts of the empire. See Toledano, *As if Silent and Absent,* 61.

53. Dabtiyyat Misr, L/2/5/30, case no. 949 (mir alay al-Tubjiyya) 20 Sha'ban 1270 (16 May 1270), 29; Dabtiyyat Misr, L/2/5/31, case no. 687, 15 Shawwal 1270 (19 July 1854), 23; Dabtiyyat Misr, L/2/5/31, case no. 217 (mula effendi), 7 Dhu al-Qa'da 1270 (1 Aug. 1854), 98; Majlis al-Ahkam, S/7/57/3, case no. 101, 29 Jumada Thani 1274 (13 Feb. 1858), 144–48.

54. Such cases are documented in the fatwa literature. See, for example, al-Mahdi al-'Abbasi, 29 Shawwal 1265 (16 Sept. 1849), 255, 7 Jamada al-Awwal 1283 (15 Sept. 1866), 258.

55. Hilal, *Al-Raqiq fi Misr,* 201–2; See, for example: Dabtiyyat Misr, L/2/5/31, case no. 225 (mula fadilatu effendi), 26 Dhu al-Qa'da 1270 (20 Aug. 1854), 167; Muḥafazat Misr, L/1/20/2, case no. 20, 24 Sha'ban 1272 (29 Apr. 1856), 63.

56. Dabtiyyat Misr, L/2/5/40, case no. 478 (al-sayira—min majlis bahri), 10 Jumadda Awwal 1272 (17 Jan. 1856), 82, 84.

57. Dabtiyyat Misr, L/2/5/40, case no. 591 (sayira—batrik al-rum), 3 Jumada Thani 1272 (9 Feb. 1856), 132.

58. Baer, "Slavery," 435–37.

59. Ehud R. Toledano, "Late Ottoman Concepts of Slavery (1830s–1880s)," *Poetics Today,* 14, no. 3 (1993): 477–506; Troutt Powell, introduction to *A Different Shade of Colonialism.*

60. Jallad, 2:250. Toledano notes a similar shift in Ottoman discourse. Late nineteenth-century Ottoman manumission documents note the existence of a "natural desire for freedom." See Toledano, *As if Silent and Absent,* 22–23. See also idem, "Late Ottoman Concepts of Slavery (1830s–1880s)," 477–506.

61. Robinson-Dunn, 31.

62. Tucker, *Women in Nineteenth-Century Egypt,* 174.

63. Hilal, *Al-Raqiq fi Misr,* 343–47; Mowafi, *Slavery, Slave Trade, and Abolition,* 56; Baer, "Slavery," 430–31; Ma'iyya Saniyya, S/1/1/7, case no. 91 (mudiriyyat rawdat al-bahrayn), 11 Dhu al-Qa'da 1272 (12 July 1856), 16; Robinson-Dunn, chapter 2.

64. Hilal, *Al-Raqiq fi Misr,* 51–53; Mowafi, 54–57; see, for example the dismissal of a negligent customs official in Sami, 3:292.

65. Hilal, *Al-Raqiq fi Misr,* 348–49; Troutt Powell, *A Different Shade of Colonialism,* 66–67; Mowafi, 60–80; Toledano, *Slavery and Abolition,* 205–23; Baer, "Slavery," 432.

66. Tucker, *Women in Nineteenth-Century Egypt,* 177; Hilal, *Al-Raqiq fi Misr,* 357–60; Baer, "Slavery," 433. See Jallad, 2:239–53; Sami, 3:1487–91; Mowafi, 129–30.

67. Hilal, *Al-Raqiq fi Misr,* 368.

68. Dabtiyyat Misr, L/2/5/39, case no. 39 (muhafazat Misr), 5 safar 1272 (15 Oct. 1855), 73, 84.

69. Majlis al-Ahkam, S/7/57/3, case no. 135, 14 Shawwal 1274 (29 Mar. 1858), 174–75.

70. Baer, "Slavery," 429.

71. Zaghlul, 165 (of appendix).

72. Ibid., 162 (of appendix); translated in Rudolph Peters, "The Infatuated Greek: Social and Legal Boundaries in Nineteenth-Century Egypt," *Égypte/Monde Arabe* 34 (1998): 64.

73. Majlis al-Ahkam, S/7/10/9, case no. 684, 27 Shawwal 1280 (4 Apr. 1864), 83–84.

74. Majlis al-Ahkam, S/7/10/57, case no. 175, 29 Dhu al-Qa'da 1288 (8 Feb. 1872), n.p.

75. Majlis al-Ahkam, S/7/57/3, case no. 135, 14 Shawwal 1274 (29 Mar. 1858), 174–75.

76. Sami, 3:1076.

77. Ibid., 3:1539.

78. "Dabtiyya," article 6, in Jallad, 4:216.

79. Dabtiyyat Misr, L/2/6/2, case no. 195, 21 Dhu al-Qaʻda 1294 (26 Nov. 1877), 155–68.

80. See, for example, Majlis al-Ahkam, S/7/10/9, case no. 684, 27 Shawwal 1280 (4 Apr. 1864), 83–84; Muhafazat Misr, L/1/20/3, case no. 2, 25 Safar 1277 (10 Sept. 1860), 85–86.

81. Troutt Powell, "The Silence of the Slaves," in *African Diaspora,* ed. Hunwick and Troutt Powell, xxxii.

82. A.-B. Clot Bey, *Aperçu Général sur l'Égypte* (Paris: Masson et cie, 1840), 1:275.

83. Tucker, *Women in Nineteenth-Century Egypt,* 188.

84. Baer, "Slavery," 435–37.

85. Sami, 3:1490.

86. Dabtiyyat Misr, L/2/6/2, case no. 195, 21 Dhu al-Qaʻda 1294 (26 Nov. 1877), 155–68.

87. See, for example, Eyal Ginio, "Living on the Margins of Charity: Coping with Poverty in an Ottoman Provincial City," *Poverty and Charity in Middle Eastern Contexts,* ed. Michael Bonner, Mine Ener, and Amy Singer (Albany: State Univ. of New York Press, 2003), 170–71; Mohammed Ennaji, *Serving the Master: Slavery and Society in Nineteenth-Century Morocco,* trans. Seth Graebner (New York: St. Martin's, 1999), 57–67; Toledano, *As if Silent and Absent,* 33–34, 89.

88. Baer, "Slavery," 438–39.

89. Hunwick, "Different," xix–xx; John Hunwick, "Islamic Law and Polemics over Race and Slavery in North and West Africa (16th–19th Century)," in *Slavery in the Islamic Middle East,* ed. Shaun E. Marnon (Princeton, N.J.: Markus Wiener, 1999), 43–44.

90. Troutt Powell, *A Different Shade of Colonialism,* 72–87.

91. Dabtiyyat Misr, L/2/6/2, case no. 195, 21 Dhu al-Qaʻda 1294 (26 Nov. 1877), 155–68.

92. Walz, 146–49.

93. Eve Troutt Powell, "The Tools of the Master: Slavery and Empire in Nineteenth-Century Egypt," *Occasional Papers of the School of Social Science, Institute for Advanced Study,* paper no. 13 (Sept. 2002), 3.

94. It is unclear, however, how significant were the documents themselves before the nineteenth century as the shariʻa court, at least in theory, preferred an oral testimony to a written document. Medline Zilfi, "Thoughts on Women and Slavery in the Ottoman Era and Historical Sources," in *Beyond the Exotic,* ed. Sonbol, 131.

95. Jallad, 2:240, 245; Sami, 3:1489. Manumission documents did not gain such significance in the Ottoman center. See Toledano, *As if Silent and Absent,* 116.

96. Muhafazat Misr, L/1/20/2, case no. 18, 29 Shaʻban 1272 (3 May 1856), 3; Muhafazat Misr, L/1/20/2, case no. 20, 24 Shaʻban 1272 (29 Apr. 1856), 63.

97. Dabtiyyat Misr, L/2/5/40, case no. 5 (maʻiyya khidiwiyya), 1 Jumada Awwal 1272 (8 Jan. 1856), 52, 62.

98. Such a choice was prevalent among female former slaves in other parts of the empire as well. See Toledano, *As if Silent and Absent,* 144.

99. Majlis al-Ahkam, S/7/57/3, case no. 101, 29 Jumada Thani 1274 (13 Feb. 1858), 144–48.

100. Majlis al-Ahkam, S/7/57/3, case no. 98, 2 Rajab 1274 (15 Feb. 1858), 140–41.

101. Dabtiyyat Misr, L/2/5/40, case no. 681 (sayira—mir alai al-sudan), 16 Jumada Thani 1272 (22 Feb. 1858), 168.

102. Dabtiyyat Misr, L/2/6/2, case no. 195, 21 Dhu al-Qa'da 1294 (26 Nov. 1877), 155–68.

103. Mahkamat Misr—murafa'at wa-da'awa, 1/99/3/1430, 18 Ramadan 1287 (9 Dec. 1870), 30.

104. Dabtiyyat Misr, L/2/6/2, case no. 195, 21 Dhu al-Qa'da 1294 (26 Nov. 1877), 155–68.

105. Erdem, 174–76.

106. Gabriel Baer, *Egyptian Guilds in Modern Times* (Jerusalem: Israel Oriental Society, 1964), 30–31.

107. Lane, *Manners and Customs,* 128.

108. Majlis al-Ahkam, S/7/57/3, case no. 120, 24 Rajab 1274 (9 Mar. 1858), 162–63.

109. Majlis al-Ahkam, S/7/57/3, case no. 135, 14 Sha'ban 1274 (29 Mar. 1858), 174–75.

110. Dabtiyyat Misr, L/2/6/2, case no. 195, 21 Dhu al-Qa'da 1294 (26 Nov. 1877). 155–68.

111. Hilal, *Al-Raqiq fi Misr,* 194, relying on Clot Bey, *Aperçu Général,* 1:275

112. Majlis al-Ahkam, S/7/10/103, case no. 58, 30 Muharram 1294 (13 Feb. 1877), n.p.

113. Majlis al-Ahkam, S/7/10/27 case no. 202, 26 Muharram 1285 (17 May 1868), n.p.

114. Dabtiyyat Misr, L/2/51/6, case no. 228, 28 Dhu al-Qa'da 1294 (2 Dec. 1877) 7–10.

115. See also Walz, 146.

116. "Dabtiyya," in Jallad, 2:216.

117. See, for example, Ludwig Deutsch's painting *The Nubian Dance,* 1886.

118. Isma'il, 33–34; see also Ahmad Amin, 268–69.

119. Richard Natvig, "Some Notes on the History of the *Zar* Cult in Egypt," in *Women's Medicine: The Zar-Bori Cult in Africa and Beyond,* eds. I. M. Lewis, Ahmed al-Safi, and Sayyid Hurreiz (Edinburgh: Edinburgh Univ. Press, 1991), 178–82.

120. Pamela Constantinides, "The History of *Zar* in the Sudan: Theories of Origin, Records Observation and Oral Tradition," in *Women's Medicine,* ed. Lewis, al-Safi, and Hurreiz, 83–99; See also Toledano, *As if Silent and Absent,* chapter 5.

4. Prostitutes and Other Women of Ill Repute

1. Muhafazat Misr, L/1/20/3, case no. 25, 17 Muharram 1277 (4 Aug. 1860), 44–45.

2. Majlis al-Ahkam, S/7/57/3, case no. 115, 20 Rajab 1274 (5 Mar. 1858), 158–59.

3. Hilal, *Al-Baghaya fi Misr,* 19.

4. Fahmy, "Prostitution in Nineteenth-Century Egypt," 90; idem, "Women, Medicine and Power," 45.

5. According to Edward Lane, a woman who "passed the night free" is a woman who remained virgin in her wedding night; see Lane, *"hurr," An Arabic-English Lexicon* (Beirut: Librarie du Liban, 1980), 2:538; for discussion of the legal aspects of the term see *Al-Mawsu'a al-Fiqhiyya* (Kuwait: Ministry of Religious Endowments and Islamic Affairs, 1990), 17:171.

6. John Lewis Burckhardt, *Arabic Proverbs; or, The Manners and Customs of the Modern Egyptians, Illustrated from their Proverbial Sayings Current at Cairo* (London: Curzon, [1972]),

173. Another proverb is: "The jealousy of the harlot is adultery, that of a virtuous woman—weeping" (154).

7. Burckhardt, 36.

8. Ibid., 33.

9. See article 8 of the Police Act. Jallad, 4:216–17.

10. Dabtiyyat Iskandriya, L/4/18/11, case no. 748, 27 Rabi' Awwal 1297 (8 Mar. 1880), 71–72. See also Dabtiyyat Iskandriya, L/4/18/11, case no. 727, 18 Rabi' Awwal 1297 (28 Feb. 1880), 38–40.

11. Terms such as *mumis* and *'ahira* became prevalent only with the regulation of prostitutions in 1882, as these terms were used in formal codes and regulations.

12. Literature on public performers is abundant. See, for example, John Rodenbeck, "'Awalim; or, the Persistence of Error," in *Historians in Cairo: Essays in Honor of George Scanlon,* ed. Jill Edwards (Cairo: American Univ. in Cairo Press, 2002), 107–21; Karin van Niewkerk, *A Trade Like Any Other: Female Singers and Dancers in Egypt* (Austin: Univ. of Texas Press, 1995), 21–37; A.-B. Clot Bey, *Aperçu Général,* 2:84–89; Burckhardt, 173–78; Tucker, *Women in Nineteenth-Century Egypt,* 151; 'Ali Mubarak, 11:15.

13. Dabtiyyat Misr, L/2/6/8, case no. 489, 3 Jumada Awwal 1296 (24 Apr. 1879), 22–23.

14. Dabtiyyat Iskandriya, L/4/18/11, case no. 750, 28 Rabi' Awwal 1297 (28 Feb. 1880), 74–75.

15. For literature on prostitution and the urban space in other parts of the world, see Timoty Gilfoyle, "Prostitutes in History: From Parables of Pornography to Metaphors of Modernity," *The American Historical Review* 104, no. 1 (Feb. 1999): 132–35. Most studies of prostitution focus on urban centers such us New York, Buenos Aires, Paris, and Nairobi and discuss the interaction of prostitutes with the urban community or with its law-enforcement mechanisms, the police, and the courts. See, for example, Timothy Joseph Gilfoyle, *City of Eros: New York City, Prostitution, and the Commercialization of Sex, 1790–1920* (New York: W. W. Norton, 1992); Donna J. Guy, *Sex and Danger in Buenos Aires: Prostitution, Family, and Nation in Argentina* (Lincoln: Univ. of Nebraska Press, 1991); Alain Corbin, *Women for Hire: Prostitution and Sexuality in France after 1850,* trans. Alan Sheridan (Cambridge, Mass.: Harvard Univ. Press, 1990); Luise White, *The Comforts of Home: Prostitution in Colonial Nairobi* (Chicago: Univ. of Chicago Press, 1990); Gail Hershatter, *Dangerous Pleasures: Prostitution and Modernity in Twentieth-Century Shanghai* (Berkeley: Univ. of California Press, 1997).

16. Ener, 31–37; Toledano, *State and Society,* 196–200.

17. Majlis al-Ahkam, S/7/10/103, case no. 58, 30 Muharram 1294 (13 Feb. 1877), n.p.

18. Ibid.

19. 'Ali Mubarak, 12:69–70, 73–75, 93–95; Gabriel Baer, "The Beginning of Urbanization," in his *Studies in the Social History,* 140.

20. 'Ali Mubarak, 7: 65; Michael J. Reimer, *Colonial Bridgehead: Government and Society in Alexandria, 1807–1882* (Boulder: Westview, 1997), 89–96; Baer, "The Beginning of Urbanization," 137–38.

21. 'Ali Mubarak, 1:244–45; Raymond, 297.

22. Doris Behrens-Abouseif, *Azbakiyya and Its Environs: From Azbak to Isma'il, 1476–1879* (Cairo: Institut français d'archéologie orientale, 1985), 92–93.

23. According to 'Ali Mubarak, Azbakiyya housed about 24 percent of Cairo's coffeehouses and 47 percent of its taverns (252 coffeehouses and 228 taverns), and Bulaq lagged somewhat behind with 15 percent of Cairo's coffeehouses and 10 percent of the taverns (160 coffeehouses and 50 taverns). See 'Ali Mubarak, 1:237–38.

24. 'Ali Mubarak, 3:79; Janet Abu-Lughod, 97.

25. Fahmy, "Prostitution in Nineteenth-Century Egypt," 89; Behrens-Abouseif, 81–100.

26. Janet Abu-Lughod, 90–91; Nelly Hanna, *An Urban History of Bulaq in the Mamluk and Ottoman Periods* (Cairo: Institut français d'archéologie orientale, 1983). 104; Poole, 33, 65.

27. 'Ali Mubarak, 1:236–37.

28. Dabtiyyat Iskandriya, L/4/18/11, case no. 712, 8 Rabi' Awwal 1297 (18 Feb. 1880), 14–15.

29. Majlis al-Ahkam, S/7/10/118, case no. 285, 18 Rajab 1295 (17 July 1878), 141.

30. See, for example, Dabtiyyat Iskandriya, L/4/18/10, case no. 377, 19 Shawwal 1296 (4 Oct. 1879), n.p.; Majlis al-Ahkam, S/7/10/27, case no. 202, 26 Muharram 1285 (6 May 1869), n.p.; Muhafazat Misr, L/1/20/8, case no. 5, 10 Rajab 1278 (10 Jan. 1862), 16–17.

31. See, for example, Dabtiyyat Iskandriya, L/4/18/10, case no. 377, 19 Shawwal 1296 (4 Oct. 1879), n.p.; Majlis al-Ahkam, S/7/10/119, case no. 326, 22 Sha'ban 1295 (20 Aug. 1878), 117; Majlis al-Ahkam, S/7/10/29, case no. 28, 16 Rajab 1285 (30 Oct. 1868), n.p.

32. See, for example, Dabtiyyat Iskandriya, L/4/18/10, case no. 295, 17 Dhu al-Qa'da 1296 (1 Nov. 1879), n.p.

33. Ibid.; Dabtiyyat Iskandriya, L/4/18/11, case no. 727, 18 Rabi' Awwal 1297 (28 Feb. 1880), 38–40.

34. See, for example, Muhafazat Misr, L/1/20/8, case no. 5, 10 Rajab 1278 (10 Jan. 1862), 16–17; Majlis al-Ahkam, S/7/10/45, case no. 62, n.d., n.p.

35. Majlis al-Ahkam, S/7/10/27, case no. 202, 26 Muharram 1285 (17 May 1868), n.p.

36. Elyse Semerdjian, "Sinful Professions: Illegal Occupations of Women in Ottoman Aleppo, Syria," *Hawwa* 1, no. 1 (2003): 180–87; Ralph S. Hattox, *Coffee and Coffeehouses: The Origins of a Social Beverage in the Medieval Near East* (Seattle: Univ. of Washington Press, 1985), 101–11; Bruce William Dunne, "Sexuality and the 'Civilizing Process' in Modern Egypt" (PhD diss., Georgetown Univ., 1996), 64–66; 'Ali Mubarak, 7:72. See, for example, Dabtiyyat Misr, L/2/6/13, case no. 856, 9 Sha'ban 1296 (27 July 1879), n.p.; Dabtiyyat Iskandriya, L/4/18/11, case no. 750, 28 Rabi' Awwal 1297 (9 Mar. 1880), 74–75; Dabtiyyat Iskandriya, L/4/18/10, case no. 349, 25 Ramadan 1296 (11 Sept. 1879), n.p.

37. Dabtiyyat Misr, L/2/6/9, case no. 929, 14 Shawwal 1296 (30 Sept. 1879), 184–85.

38. Dabtiyyat Iskandriya, L/4/18/10, case no. 377, 19 Shawwal 1296 (4 Oct. 1879), n.p.

39. See, for example, Majlis al-Ahkam, S/7/10/27, case no. 202 26 Muharram 1285 (17 May 1868), n.p.

40. See, for example, Dabtiyyat Iskandriya, L/4/18/11, case no. 727, 18 Rabi' Awwal 1297 (28 Feb. 1880), 38–40; Majlis al-Ahkam, S/7/10/103, case no. 96, 15 Safar 1294 (28 Feb. 1877), 210–12.

41. Dabtiyyat Iskandriya, L/4/18/11, case no. 712, 8 Rabi' Awwal 1297 (18 Feb. 1880), 14–15; Majlis al-Ahkam, S/7/10/217, case no. 420, 20 Rabi' Thani 1300 (27 Apr. 1883), n.p.

42. Burckhardt, 36.

43. Majlis al-Ahkam, S/7/10/63, case no. 42, 15 Sha'ban 1289 (16 Oct. 1872), n.p.

44. Peirce, *Morality Tales,* 89–90.

45. Dunne, 45; see Article 124 in Uriel Heyd, *Studies in Old Ottoman Criminal Law* (Oxford: Oxford Univ. Press, 1973), 130, 303–4. See also Peirce, *Morality Tales,* 178–79; Abraham Marcus, "Privacy in Eighteenth-Century Aleppo: The Limits of Cultural Ideas," *International Journal of Middle Eastern Studies* 18 (1986): 166, 177; Marcus, *The Middle East on the Eve of Modernity,* 322–23; Semerdjian, 70–72.

46. Tucker, *Women in Nineteenth-Century Egypt,* 151; Dunne, "Sexuality and the 'Civilizing Process'," 51–54.

47. Dunne, "Sexuality and the 'Civilizing Process,'" 81–85, 92; Fahmy, "Prostitution in Nineteenth-Century Egypt," 82–85; Hilal, *Al-Baghaya fi Misr,* 157–59; Tucker, *Women in Nineteenth-Century Egypt,* 151–52.

48. See, for example, Dabtiyyat Misr, L/2/5/31, case no. 1169 (mu'awin Dabtiyyat Bulaq), 22 Shawwal 1270 (16 July 1854), 40; Dabtiyyat Misr, L/2/5/31, case no. 209 (isbitaliya), 7 Dhu al-Qa'da 1270 (1 Aug. 1854), 81; Dabtiyyat Misr, L/2/5/39, case no. 2 (hukumkhane wa-isbitaliya), 14 Muharram 1272 (25 Sept. 1855), 24; Dabtiyyat Misr, L/2/5/39, case no. 38 (muhafazat Misr), 5 Safar 1272 (15 Oct. 1855), 73.

49. Fahmy, "Prostitution in Nineteenth-Century Egypt," 94–98; Hilal, *Al-Baghaya fi Misr,* 160.

50. Fahmy, "An Olfactory Tale of Two Cities," 164, 181; Raymond, 308–13; Janet Abu-Lughod, 95–97, 103–17.

51. Fahmy, "An Olfactory Tale of Two Cities," 172–75; Janet Abu-Lughod, 91–95.

52. Fahmy, "The Police and the People," 1–38; Janet Abu-Lughod, 88.

53. Those could be monkey trainers and bear trainers, singers, and dancers as well as immigrants from Upper Egypt and Sudanese freed slaves. "Dabtiyya," in Jallad, 4: 215–21.

54. "Dabtiyya," in Jallad, 4:215–21. For more about the management of the poor, see Ener.

55. "Dabtiyya," Jallad, 4:217, 221.

56. Ibid., 4:216–17.

57. 'Ali Mubarak, 1:216.

58. Majlis al-Ahkam, S/7/10/63, case no. 71, 27 Ramadan 1289 (28 Nov. 1872), n.p.

59. Ibid.; Majlis al-Ahkam, S/7/10/63, case no. 42, 15 Sha'ban 1289 (16 Oct. 1872), n.p.

60. Majlis al-Ahkam, S/7/10/63, case no. 71, 27 Ramadan 1289 (28 Nov. 1872), n.p.

61. Majlis al-Ahkam, S/7/10/8, case no. 605, 13 Shawwal 1280 (21 Mar. 1864), 19–20.

62. Majlis al-Ahkam, S/7/10/21, case no. 191, 13 Rabi' Awwal 1284 (13 July 1867), 74–99.

63. Majlis al-Ahkam, S/7/10/63, case no. 71, 27 Ramadan 1289 (28 Nov. 1872), n.p.; Majlis al-Ahkam, S/7/10/63, case no. 42, 15 Sha'ban 1289 (16 Oct. 1872), n.p.

64. Majlis al-Ahkam, S/7/10/26, case no. 86, 22 Sha'ban 1284 (17 Dec. 1867), n.p.

65. Dabtiyyat Iskandriya, L/4/18/11, case no. 727, 18 Rabi' Awwal 1297 (28 Feb. 1880), 38–40.

66. Dabtiyyat Misr, L/2/6/8, case no. 659, 20 Jumada Thani 1296 (10 June 1879), 32–33; Dabtiyyat Iskandriya, L/4/18/11, case no. 750, 28 Rabi' Awwal 1297 (9 Mar. 1830), 74–75.

67. Hilal, *Al-Baghaya fi Misr,* 52–53, 64.

68. Dabtiyyat Misr, L/2/51/6, case no. 228, 28 Dhu al-Qa'da 1294 (2 Dec. 1877), 7–10; and Majlis al-Ahkam, S/7/10/115, case no. 114, 27 Rabi' Awwal 1295 (31 Mar. 1878), 78–79.

69. Dabtiyyat Misr, L/2/51/6, case no. 228, 28 Dhu al-Qa'da 1294 (2 Dec. 1877), 7–10.

70. Clot Bey, *Aperçu Général,* 1:275, 336.

71. Dunne, "Sexuality and the 'Civilizing Process'," 98–99; Tucker, *Women in Nineteenth-Century Egypt,* 155; Fahmy, "Prostitution in Nineteenth-Century Egypt," 84.

72. Toledano, *State and Society,* 197.

73. Majlis al-Ahkam, S/7/10/103, case no. 58, 30 Muharram 1294 (13 Feb. 1877), n.p.

74. Majlis al-Ahkam, S/7/10/27, case no. 202, 26 Muharram 1285 (17 May 1868), n.p.

75. See, for example, Dabtiyyat Misr, L/2/6/1, case no. 24, 25 Rajab 1294 (4 Aug. 1877), 36–44; Dabtiyyat Iskandriya, L/4/18/10, case no. 349, 25 Ramadan 1296 (11 Sept. 1879), n.p.; Majlis al-Ahkam, S/7/10/29, case no. 28, 16 Rabi' Awwal 1285 (5 July 1868), n.p. On lower-class European in nineteenth-century Egypt, see Will Hanley, "Second-Rate Foreigners: Algerians and Maltese in Alexandria, 1880–1914" (Middle Eastern Studies Association Annual Meeting, Washington, D.C., 2005); idem, "Foreignness and Localness in Alexandria, 1880—1914," (PhD diss., Princeton Univ., 2007); Khaled Fahmy, "Toward a Social History of Modern Alexandria," in *Alexandria, Real and Imagined,* ed. Anthony Hirst and Michael Silk (Burlington, Vt.: Ashgate, 2004), 290–96.

76. Hilal, *Al-Baghaya fi Misr,* 71–72.

77. Ibid., 131.

78. Majlis al-Ahkam, S/7/10/103, case no. 58, 30 Muharram 1294 (13 Feb. 1877), n.p.

79. Dabtiyyat Misr, L/2/6/13, case no. 856, 9 Sha'ban 1296 (27 July 1879), n.p.

80. Muhafazat Misr, L/1/20/8, case no. 5, 10 Rajab 1278 (10 Jan. 1862), 16–17.

81. Tucker, *Women in Nineteenth-Century Egypt,* 155.

82. Mahkamat Misr—murafa'at wa-da'awa, 1/99/3/1430, 21 Ramadan 1287 (12 Dec. 1870), 61.

83. Dabtiyyat Iskandriya, L/4/18/11, case no. 748, 27 Rabi' Awwal 1297 (8 Mar. 1880), 71–72.

5. Virginity, Honor, and Premarital Defloration

1. Majlis al-Ahkam, S/7/10/10, case no. 940, 8 Dhu al-Hijja 1280 (12 May 1864), 185–89.

2. See, for example, Joseph Ginat, *Blood Revenge: Family Honor, Mediation and Outcasting* (Brighton, England: Sussex Academic Press, 1997), 129–30; Raphael Patai, *The Arab Mind* (New York: Scribner, 1976), 120; Gideon M. Kressel, "Shame and Gender," *Anthropological Quarterly* 65, no. 1 (1992): 34–46.

3. For notions of honor and their role in contemporary and historical legal systems, see Purna Sen, "Honour, Culture and Alliances," in *Honour: Crimes, Paradigms and Violence against Women,* ed. Lynn Welchman and Sara Hossain (London: Zed Books, 2005), 45; Pat O'Malley, "From Feudal Honour to Bourgeois Reputation: Ideology, Law and the Rise of Industrial Capitalism," *Sociology* 15

(1981): 81–87; Sandra Gayol, "'Honor Moderno': The Significance of Honor in Fin-de-Siècle Argentina," *Hispanic American Historical Review* 84, no. 3 (2004): 483; Jane Burbank, *Russian Peasants Go to Court: Legal Culture in the Countryside, 1905–1917* (Bloomington: Indiana Univ. Press, 2004), 147–71. For cross-cultural analysis of honor, see Frank Stewart, *Honor* (Chicago: Chicago Univ. Press, 1994).

4. Amira El Azhary Sonbol, "Rape and Law in Ottoman and Modern Egypt," in *Women in the Ottoman Empire: Middle Eastern Women in the Early Modern Era,* ed. Madeline C. Zilfi (Leiden: E. J. Brill, 1997), 217.

5. Peirce, *Morality Tales,* 133–34, 179.

6. Zaghlul, 160–61 (of appendix); Peters, "The Infatuated Greek," 64. The translation relies on Peters's, with few modifications. Whereas Peters translates the word shariʿa sometimes as "law" and sometimes as "shariʿa," I use only "shariʿa".

7. Majlis al-Ahkam, S/7/10/4, case no. 234, 13 Jumada Thani 1280 (24 Nov. 1863), 169–70.

8. Muhafazat Misr, L/1/20/3, case no. 36, 6 Safar 1272 (16 Oct. 1855), 59–60.

9. Majlis al-Ahkam, S/7/10/62, case no. 422, 6 Rajab 1289 (8 Sept. 1872), n.p.

10. Majlis al-Ahkam, S/7/10/12, case no. 979, 7 Muharram 1281 (11 June 1864), 53–54.

11. Majlis al-Ahkam, S/7/10/216, case no. 371, 17 Jumada Thani 1300 (24 Apr. 1883), n.p.

12. Majlis al-Ahkam, S/7/10/108, case no. 322, 8 Jumada Thani 1294 (19 June 1877), 76–77.

13. Majlis al-Ahkam, S/7/10/200, case no. 579, 16 Shawwal 1299 (29 Aug. 1881), n.p.

14. Maglis al-Ahkam, S/7/10/65, case no. 127, 27 Dhu al-Qaʿda 1289 (26 Jan. 1863), n.p.

15. Majlis al-Ahkam, S/7/10/108, case no. 307, 27 Jumada Awwal 1294 (9 June 1877), 26–27.

16. Majlis al-Ahkam, S/7/10/120, case no. 357, 19 Ramadan 1295 (16 Sept. 1878), 29–30.

17. Mahkamat Iskandriya—daʿawa, sijill no. 3, case no. 87, 13 Rabiʿ Thani 1286 (21 July 1869), 82.

18. The Arabic root *b.k.r.* is associated with the beginning and freshness of the firstborn, the first fruit to mature, the first rain of the season, and the first part of the day, whereas the word *thayyib* generally applies to unmarried women who are not virgins, or to use Lane's nineteenth-century dictionary definition, "a woman to whom a man has gone in." According to Lane, this word can be seen as a derivation of the root *th.w.b.,* meaning "return" to a place that has already been visited. Archival records often used the term *mustaʿmala,* literally, "used" or "secondhand." These terms referred mainly to women and only rarely, if at all, to men. A man's sexual experience had no bearing on his family's reputation and was therefore socially irrelevant. See *"Thayyib,"* in Lane, *Arabic-English Lexicon,* 1:363; *"Bikr,"* ibid., 1:240; and b.k.r, ibid., 1:239–41; and *"hurma,"* ibid., 1:555. See also *"hurma,"* Martin Hinds and el-Said al-Badawi, *A Dictionary of Egyptian Arabic* (Beirut: Librarie du Liban, 1986), 261; and *"Bint,"* ibid., 104. Similar usage of "girl" and "woman" is prevalent in present-day Lebanon, Turkey, and Palestine as well. See Nadera Shalhoub-Kevorkian, "Towards a Cultural Definition of Rape: Dilemmas in Dealing with Rape Victims in Palestinian Society," *Women's Studies International Forum* 22, no. 2 (1999): 163; Ayşe Parla, "The Honor of the State: Virginity Examinations in Turkey," *Feminist Studies* 27, no. 1 (Spring 2001): 79; Samantha Wehbi, "Women with Nothing to Lose—Marriageability and Women's Perceptions of Rape and Consent in Contemporary Beirut," *Women's Studies International Forum* 25, no. 2 (2002): 298n5.

19. Al-Marghinani, 35; See also Ron Shaham, *Family and the Courts in Modern Egypt: A Study Based on Decisions by the Shari'a Courts 1900–1955* (Leiden: E. J. Brill, 1997), 28. Al-Halabi, 243–44; Ibn 'Abidin, 1:252–53, 4:164–65.

20. See, for example, Parla, 65–88; Fatima Mernissi, "Virginity and Patriarchy," *Women's Studies International Forum,* no. 5 (1982), 183–91; Nawwal al-Sa'dawi, *The Hidden Face of Eve,* trans. by Sherif Hetata (London: Zed Books, 2007), 38–49; Abu Odeh, 141–94.

21. Burckhardt, 140.

22. Clot Bey, *Aperçu General,* 2:43–44.

23. 'Ali Mubarak, 11:15.

24. Ibid., 10:67.

25. Majlis al-Ahkam, S/7/10/65, case no. 127, 27 Dhu al-Qa'da 1289 (26 Jan. 1873), n.p. Scholars have noted the prevalence of a similar custom in present-day Middle Eastern societies as well. See, for example, Dilek Cindoğlu, "Virginity Tests and Artificial Virginity in Modern Turkish Medicine," *Women's Studies International Forum* 20, no. 2 (1997): 253–61.

26. Marcus, *The Middle East on the Eve of Modernity,* 323–24.

27. Ruiz; Fahmy, "Women, Medicine and Power." On social control of adolescent girls and historical and contemporary societies, see Parla, "The Honor of the State," 66; Mary E. Odem, *Delinquent Daughters: Protecting and Policing Adolescent Female Sexuality in the United States, 1885–1920* (Chapel Hill: Univ. of North Carolina Press, 1995), 2–6; Sueann Caulfield and Martha de Abreu Esteves, "50 Years of Virginity in Rio de Janeiro: Sexual Politics and Gender Roles in Juridical and Popular Discourse, 1890–1940," *Luso-Brazilian Review* 30 (1993): 55–56; Joan Sangster, *Regulating Girls and Women: Sexuality, Family and the Law in Ontario, 1920–1960* (Ontario: Oxford Univ. Press, 2001), 123–26.

28. Majlis al-Ahkam, S/7/10/256, case no. 295, 16 Rabi' Awwal 1302 (2 Jan. 1885), n.p.

29. Sonbol, "Rape and Law," 217. *Hadd* is the legal term for the punishment of acts that are forbidden or sanctioned by punishment in the Qur'an and have thereby become crimes against religion. See B. Carra de Vaux, J. Schacht, and A. M. Goichon, *"Hadd,"* *Encyclopedia of Islam,* 2nd ed., 3:20a.

30. Ibn 'Abidin, 6:26, 43; al-Marghinani, 187. For a discussion of the concept of duress in Islamic law, see Khaled Abou el Fadl, "The Common and Islamic Law of Duress," *Arab Law Quarterly* 6, part 2 (1991): 121–59; for discussion of *zina,* see ibid., 147–48.

31. Imber, 177–82, 280; Tucker, *In the House of the Law,* 160–62; Leslie P. Peirce, "Le Dilemme de Fatma: Crime Sexuel et Culture Juridique dans une Cour Ottomane au Début des Temps Modernes," *Annales* 53 (1998): 298–99; Sonbol, "Rape and Law," 219–22; for legal texts, see al-Halabi, 1:333–36; Ibn 'Abidin, 6: 43–48.

32. The court rejected a woman's complaint if she claimed, for example, that she was drugged, was unconscious during the act, or did not witness the offense and therefore could not be certain that the defendant was indeed the offender: see, for example, Mahkamat Iskandriya—da'awa, sijill no. 3, case no. 43, 5 Dhu al-Hijja 1285 (18 Mar. 1869), 51; Mahkamat Iskandriya—da'awa, sijill no.

2, case no. 269, 12 Rabi' Awwal 1284 (12 July 1867), 286. On the status of *zina* in Ottoman law see Imber, 183–85.

33. Tucker, *In the House of the Law,* 161–62; Sonbol, "Rape and Law," 216–21; Shaham, *Family and the Courts in Modern Egypt,* 27–28; Lane, *Manners and Customs,* 164.

34. See, for example, Dabtiyyat Misr, L/2/6/4, case no. 719, 15 Jumada Thani 1295 (15 June 1878), n.p.; Dabtiyyat Misr, L/2/6/11, case no. 1061, 20 Dhu al-Qa'da 1296 (4 Nov. 1879), 63–64; Majlis al-Ahkam, S/7/26/2, case no. 133, 20 Jumada Awwal 1274 (6 Nov. 1857), 88.

35. Zaghlul, 161 (of appendix).

36. Ibid., 162 (of appendix).

37. Susan Estrich, *Real Rape* (Cambridge, Mass.: Harvard Univ. Press, 1987).

38. Majlis al-Ahkam—I'lamat, S/7/33/3, case no. 7, 24 Muharram 1279 (20 July 1862), n.p.; Majlis al-Ahkam, S/7/10/146, case no. 308, 19 Jumada Thani 1285 (4 Oct. 1868), n.p.; Dabtiyyat Misr, L/2/6/2, case no. 130, 23 Shawwal 1294 (28 Oct. 1877), 45–46.

39. Dabtiyyat Misr, L/2/6/4, case no. 549, 11 Jumada Awwal 1295 (12 May 1878), n.p.; Dabtiyyat Misr, L/2/6/11, case no. 1061, 20 Dhu al-Qa'da 1296 (4 Nov. 1879), 63–64.

40. Majlis al-Ahkam, S/7/10/136, case no. 308, 19 Jumada Thani 1285 (6 Oct. 1868), n.p.

41. Dabtiyyat Misr, L/2/6/8, case no. 533, 16 Jumada Awwal 1296 (6 May 1879), 59–60.

42. Majlis al-Ahkam, S/7/10/105, case no. 177, 4 Rabi' Thani 1294 (17 Apr. 1877), 122.

43. Majlis al-Ahkam, S/7/10/4, case no. 234, 13 Jumada Thani 1280 (24 Nov. 1863), 169–70; Majlis al-Ahkam, S/7/10/146, case no. 308, 19 Jumada Thani 1285 (4 Oct. 1868), n.p.

44. Majlis al-Ahkam, S/7/10/105, case no. 177, 4 Rabi' Thani 1294 (17 Apr. 1877), 122. In this particular case, the Appellate Council overruled Asyut Council's verdict and chose to accept a woman's claim that she was intimidated by the defendant, who deterred her from complaining.

45. Majlis al-Ahkam, S/7/10/5, case no. 279, 28 Jumada Thani 1280 (8 Dec. 1863), 183–84; Dabtiyyat Misr, L/2/51/7, case no. 337, 20 Rabi' Awwal 1295 (24 Mar. 1878), 54–55.

46. Dabtiyyat Misr, L/2/6/8, case no. 1061, 20 Dhu al-Qa'da 1296 (5 Nov. 1879), 63–64.

47. See, for example, Dabtiyyat Misr, L/2/6/8, no. 727, 9 Rajab 1296 (31 Jan. 1279), 182–83; Dabtiyyat Iskandriya, L/4/18/11, no. 748, 27 Rabi' Awwal 1297 (8 Mar. 1880), 71–72; Mahkamat Misr al-Shar'iyya—I'lamat, 9 (1297–1298), no. 204, 27 June 1880, 114.

48. Thompson, 56; Ruiz, 107.

49. Dabtiyyat Misr, L/2/6/8, case no. 727, 9 Rajab 1296 (28 June 1879), 182–83.

50. Judith E. Tucker, "Problems in the Historiography of Women in the Middle East: The Case of Nineteenth-Century Egypt," *International Journal of Middle Eastern Studies* 15 (1983): 331; see, for example, Mahkamat Iskandriya—da'awa, Sijill no. 3, case no. 167, 9 Safar 1286 (19 May 1869), 143; Majlis al-Ahkam, S/7/10/15, case no. 277, 27 Dhu al-Hijja 1281 (21 May 1865), 77; Majlis al-Ahkam, S/7/10/15, case no. 313, 20 Muharram 1282 (13 June 1865), 116.

51. Dabtiyyat Misr, L/2/51/3, case no. 327, 29 Rabi' Awwal 1285 (18 July 1868), 66–67.

52. Dabtiyyat Misr, L/2/6/8, case no. 533, 16 Jumada Awwal 1296 (6 May 1879), 59–60.

53. Dabtiyyat Iskandriya, L/4/20/9, case no. 183, 27 Safar 1281 (1 Aug. 1864), 971–73.

54. See, for example, Majlis al-Ahkam, S/7/10/98, case no. 525, 13 Sha'ban 1293 (1 Sept. 1876), 122–23; Majlis al-Ahkam, S/7/10/109, case no. 398, 4 Sha'ban 1294 (13 Aug. 1877), 230–31.

55. See, for example, Majlis al-Ahkam, S/7/10/66, case no. 169, 14 Muharram 1290 (13 Mar. 1873), n.p.; Majlis al-Ahkam, S/7/10/66, case no. 169, 14 Muharram 1290 (13 Mar. 1873), n.p.; Dabtiyyat Misr, L/2/51/6, case no. 284, 21 Jumada Thani 1294 (1 July 1877), 123–25; Dabtiyyat Misr, L/2/51/7, case no. 441, 14 Rabi' Thani 1295 (16 Apr. 1878), 131–32.

56. Muhafazat Misr, L/1/20/3, case no. 47, 23 Safar 1277 (8 Sept. 1850), 69–70.

57. Mahkamat Iskandriya, L/4/21/3, case no. 14, 30 Jumada Thani 1285 (15 Oct. 1868), 74–76.

58. Majlis al-Ahkam, S/7/10/26, case no. 86, 22 Sha'ban 1284. (17 Dec. 1864), n.p.

59. Majlis al-Ahkam, S/7/10/5, case no. 279, 28 Jumada Thani 1280 (8 Dec. 1863), 183–84.

60. Majlis al-Ahkam, S/7/10/6, case no. 516, 11 Ramadan 1280 (18 Feb. 1864), 168–69; Dabtiyyat Misr, L/2/6/10, case no. 1009, 20 Dhu al-Qa'da 1296 (4 Nov. 1879), 32–33.

61. Dabtiyyat Misr, L/2/51/7, case no. 441, 14 Rabi' Thani 1295 (16 Apr. 1878), 131–32.

62. Ginio, 173–76; Marcus, *The Middle East on the Eve of Modernity*, 158; Suraiya Faroqhi, *Towns and Townsmen of Ottoman Anatolia: Trade, Crafts, and Food Production in an Urban Setting, 1520–1650* (Cambridge, U.K.: Cambridge Univ. Press, 1984), 278–79; Tucker, *Women in Nineteenth-Century Egypt*, 92–93; Madeline C. Zilfi, "Servants, Slaves, and the Domestic Order in the Ottoman Middle East," *Hawwa* 2/1 (2004): 1–33.

63. See, for example, Dabtiyyat Misr, L/2/51/7, case no. 441, 14 Rabi' Thani 1295 (16 Apr. 1878), 131–32; Majlis al-Ahkam, S/7/10/5, case no. 279, 28 Jumada Thani 1280 (8 Dec. 1863), 183–84; Majlis al-Ahkam, S/7/10/6, case no. 516, 11 Ramadan 1280 (18 Feb. 1864), 168–69; Dabtiyyat Misr, L/2/6/10, case no. 1009, 20 Dhu al-Qa'da 1296 (4 Nov. 1879), 32–33; Majlis al-Ahkam, S/7/10/247, case no. 440, 8 Dhu al-Hijja 1301 (27 Sept. 1884), n.p.; Majlis al-Ahkam, S/7/10/1, case no. 218, 14 Rajab 1279 (4 Jan. 1863), 91.

64. Majlis al-Ahkam, S/7/10/25, case no. 65, 7 Sha'ban 1284 (2 Dec. 1867), n.p.

65. Majlis al-Ahkam, S/7/10/5, case no. 31, 7 Rabi' Thani 1280 (20 Sept. 1863), 15–17; Dabtiyyat Misr, L/2/6/8, case no. 489, 3 Jumada Awwal 1296 (24 Apr. 1879), 22–23

66. Majlis al-Ahkam, S/7/10/120, case no. 357, 19 Ramadan 1295 (16 Sept. 1878), 29–30.

67. Majlis al-Ahkam, S/7/10/108, case no. 307, 27 Jumada Awwal 1294 (9 June 1877), 26–27.

68. Majlis al-Ahkam, S/7/10/218, case no. 491, 8 Rajab 1300 (15 May 1883), n.p.

69. Majlis al-Ahkam, S/7/10/217, case no. 425, 15 Jumada Thani 1300 (23 Apr. 1883), n.p.

70. Beth Baron, "The Making and Breaking of Marital Bonds in Modern Egypt," in *Women in Middle Eastern History*, ed. Nikki Keddie and Beth Baron (New Haven, Conn.: Yale Univ. Press, 1991), 275–91.

71. Dabtiyyat Misr, L/2/51/6, case no. 228, 28 Dhu al-Qa'da 1294 (2 Dec. 1877), 7–10; Majlis al-Ahkam, S/7/10/103, case no. 58, 30 Muharram 1294 (13 Feb. 1877), n.p.

72. Majlis al-Ahkam, S/7/10/25, case no. 14, 2 Jummada Thani 1284 (29 Sept. 1867), n.p.

73. See, for example, Majlis al-Ahkam, S/7/10/62, case no. 422, 5 Rajab 1289 (8 Sept. 1872), n.p.; Majlis al-Ahkam, S/7/10/4, case no. 12, 2 Rabi' Thani 1280 (15 Sept. 1863), 5–6; Dabtiyyat Misr, L/2/6/8, case no. 659, 20 Jumada Thani 1296 (10 June 1879), 132–33.

Conclusion

1. Geoff Eley, *Crooked Line: From Cultural History to the History of Society* (Ann Arbor: Univ. of Michigan Press, 2005), 190.

2. Lila Abu-Lughod, "The Romance of Resistance," *American Ethnologist* 17, no. 1 (1990): 41–55.

3. Kamala Visweswaran, "Small Speeches, Subaltern Gender: Nationalist Ideology and its Historiography," *Subaltern Studies* 9 (1996): 83–125.

Bibliography

Archival Sources: Egyptian National Archives *(Dar al-Watha'iq al-Qawmiyya)*

Police Records

Dabtiyyat Misr (Cairo's police headquarters)
    Sadir Qalam Da'awa L/2/6
    Jurnalat Warid Athman L/2/39
    Qayd al-Qararat L/2/51
    Qayd Jurnalat L/2/33
    Sadir Dawawin bi-Qalam Da'awa L/2/5
    Warid Isbitaliya L/2/46
Dabtiyyat Iskandriya (Alexandria's police headquarters)
Qayd Nata'ij, L/4/18
Qayd Qararat bi-Majlis Iskandriya L/4/20
Qayd Qararat Sadira, L/4/21
Cairo Province records *(Muhafazat Misr)*
Qayyid al-Qararat al-Sadira min Majlis Diwan Muhafazat Misr, L/1/20

Supreme Council of Adjudication *(Majlis al-Ahkam)*

al-Madabit al-Sadira, S/7/10
Qayd al-I'lamat S/7/31
Sadir wa-Warid Qalam 'Ulama S/7/26
Qayyid Khalasat al-Dawawin, S/7/57

Shari'a court records

Mahkamat Misr: Sijill al-I'lamat, Mazbatat Murafa'at
Mahkamt Iskandriya: Da'awa
Mahkamat Bulaq: Da'awa wa-Murafa'at

Cabinet records

Majlis Khususi (Privy Council)
    al-Qararat wa-l-Lawa'ih al-Sadira S/11/8
Ma'iyya Saniyya—'Arabi
Qayd al-Awamir wa-l-Qararat, S/1/33
al-Awamir al-'Uliyya al-Sadira li-l-Mudiriyyat, S/1/1
Sadir al-Awamir al-'Uliyya li-l-Dawawin, S/1/18

Books and Articles

Abou el Fadl, Khaled. "The Common and Islamic Law of Duress." *Arab Law Quarterly* 6, part 2 (1991): 121–59.

Abu-Lughod, Janet. *Cairo: 1001 Years of the City Victorious.* Princeton, N.J.: Princeton Univ. Press, 1971.

Abu-Lughod, Lila. "The Romance of Resistance." *American Ethnologist* 17, no. 1 (1990): 41–55.

Abu-Manneh, Butrus. "The Islamic Roots of the Gülhane Rescript." *Die Welt des Islams* 34, no. 2 (1994): 173–203.

Abu Odeh, Lama. "Crimes of Honour and the Construction of Gender in Arab Societies." In *Feminism and Islam: Legal and Literary Perspectives,* edited by Mai Yamani, 141–94. Berkshire, U.K.: Ithaca, 1996.

Abugideiri, Hibba. *Gender and the Making of Modern Medicine in Colonial Egypt.* Farnham, U.K.: Ashgate, 2010.

Agmon, Iris. *Family & Court: Legal Culture and Modernity in Late Ottoman Palestine.* Syracuse, N.Y.: Syracuse Univ. Press, 2006.

Alaimo, Kathleen. "The Authority of Experts: The Crisis of Female Adolescence in France and England, 1880–1920." In *Secret Gardens, Satanic Mills: Placing Girls in European History,* edited by Mary Jo Maynes, Birgitte Soland, and Christina Benninghaus, 164–78. Bloomington: Indiana Univ. Press, 2005.

Amin, Ahmad. *Qamus al-'Adat wa-l-Taqalid wa-l-Ta'abir al-'Arabiyya.* Cairo: Matba'at al-Janna, 1953.

Amin, Shahid. *Event, Metaphor, Memory: Chauri Chaura, 1922–1992.* Berkeley: California Univ. Press, 1995.

Arnold, David. "Touching the Body: Perspectives on the Indian Plague, 1896–1900." *Subaltern Studies* 5 (1987): 55–90.

Asad, Talal. *The Formations of the Secular: Christianity, Islam, Modernity.* Stanford, Calif.: Stanford Univ. Press, 2003.

Baer, Gabriel. *Egyptian Guilds in Modern Times.* Jerusalem: Israel Oriental Society, 1964.

———. "Slavery in Nineteenth-Century Egypt." *Journal of African History* 8, no. 3 (1967): 417–41.

———. *Studies in the Social History of Modern Egypt.* Chicago: Univ. of Chicago Press, 1969.

———. "Tanzimat in Egypt: The Penal Code." *Bulletin of the School of Oriental and African Studies* 26 (1963): 29–49.

Baron, Beth. *Egypt as a Woman: Nationalism, Gender and Politics.* Berkeley: Univ. of California Press, 2005.

———. "The Making and Breaking of Marital Bonds in Modern Egypt " In *Women in Middle Eastern History,* edited by Nikki Keddie and Beth Baron, 275–91. New Haven, Conn.: Yale Univ. Press, 1991.

Behrens-Abouseif, Doris. *Azbakiyya and Its Environs: From Azbak to Isma'il, 1476–1879.* Cairo: Institut français d'archéologie orientale, 1985.

Billah, Mohd. Ma'sum. "Caveat Emptor versus Khiyar al-'Aib: A Dichotomy." *Arab Law Quarterly* 13, no. 3 (1998): 278–99.

Brown, Nathan. *Peasant Politics in Modern Egypt: The Struggle against the State.* Bethesda, Md.: Jahan Book, 1990.

Brunschvig, R. "'Abd." *Encyclopedia of Islam.* Vol. 1, 26–29. Leiden: E. J. Brill, 1960.

Burchell, Graham, Colin Gordon, and Peter Miller, eds. *The Foucault Effect: Studies in Governmentality.* Chicago: Chicago Univ. Press, 1991.

Burbank, Jane. *Russian Peasants Go to Court: Legal Culture in the Countryside, 1905–1917.* Bloomington: Indiana Univ. Press, 2004.

Burckhardt, John Lewis. *Arabic Proverbs; or, The Manners and Customs of the Modern Egyptians, Illustrated from Their Proverbial Sayings Current at Cairo.* London: Curzon, [1972].

Butler, Judith. *Bodies that Matter: On the Discursive Limits of "Sex".* London: Routledge, 1993.

———. *Excitable Speech: A Politics of the Performative.* London: Routledge, 1997.

Caulfield, Sueann, and Martha de Abreu Esteves. "50 Years of Virginity in Rio de Janeiro: Sexual Politics and Gender Roles in Juridical and Popular Discourse, 1890–1940." *Luso-Brazilian Review* 30 (1993): 47–74.

Chakrabarty, Dipesh. *Provincilizing Europe: Postcolonial Thought and Historical Difference.* Princeton, N.J.: Princeton Univ. Press, 2000.

Chakravarti, Uma. "Wifehood, Widowhood and Adultery: Female Sexuality, Surveillance and the State in 18th Century Maharashtra." *Contributions to Indian Sociology* 29 (1995): 3–22.

Chalcraft, John T. *The Striking Cabbies of Cairo and Other Stories: Crafts and Guilds in Egypt, 1863–1914*. Albany: State Univ. of New York Press, 2005.

Chowdhry, Prem. "Contesting Claims and Counter-claims: Questions of the Inheritance and Sexuality of Widows in a Colonial State." *Contributions to Indian Sociology* 29 (1995): 65–82.

Cindoğlu, Dilek. "Virginity Tests and Artificial Virginity in Modern Turkish Medicine." *Women's Studies International Forum* 20, no. 2 (1997): 253–61.

Clot Bey, A.-B. *Aperçu Général sur l'Égypte*. Paris: Masson et cie, 1840.

———. *Memoires de A.-B. Clot Bey*. Cairo: Institut français d'archéologie orientale, 1949.

Cole, Juan. *Colonialism and Revolution in the Middle East: Social and Cultural Origins of Egypt's 'Urabi Movement*. Princeton, N.J.: Princeton Univ. Press, 1992.

Constantinides, Pamela. "The History of *Zar* in the Sudan: Theories of Origin, Records Observation and Oral Tradition." In *Women's Medicine: The Zar-Bori Cult in Africa and Beyond*, edited by I. M. Lewis, Ahmed al-Safi, and Sayyid Hurreiz, 83–99. Edinburgh: Edinburgh Univ. Press, 1991.

Corbin, Alain. *Women for Hire: Prostitution and Sexuality in France after 1850*. Translated by Alan Sheridan. Cambridge, Mass.: Harvard Univ. Press, 1990.

Cuno, Kenneth M. *The Pasha's Peasants: Land, Society, and Economy in Lower Egypt, 1740–1858*. Cambridge, U.K.: Cambridge Univ. Press, 1992.

Das, Veena. *Life and Words: Violence and the Descent into the Ordinary*. Berkeley: Univ. of California Press, 2007.

Duff-Gordon, Lucie. *Letters from Egypt (1862–1869)*. London: Routledge and K. Paul, 1969. A "revised edition" with a memoir by her daughter Janet Ross and a new introduction by George Meredith was published in 1902 in London by R. B. Johnson. Transcribed at the Gutenberg Project, http://www.gutenberg.org/files/17816/17816-h/17816-h.htm.

Dunne, Bruce William. "Sexuality and the 'Civilizing Process' in Modern Egypt." PhD diss., Georgetown Univ., 1996.

Eley, Geoff. *Crooked Line: From Cultural History to the History of Society*. Ann Arbor: Univ. of Michigan Press, 2005.

Ener, Mine. *Managing Egypt's Poor and the Politics of Benevolence, 1800–1952*. Princeton, N.J.: Princeton Univ. Press, 2003.

Ennaji, Mohammed. *Serving the Master: Slavery and Society in Nineteenth-Century Morocco*. Translated by Seth Graebner. New York: St. Martin's, 1999.

Erdem, Y. Hakan. *Slavery in the Ottoman Empire and Its Demise, 1800–1909*. New York: St. Martin's, with St. Antony's College (Oxford), 1996.

Estrich, Susan. *Real Rape.* Cambridge, Mass.: Harvard Univ. Press, 1987.

Fahmy, Khaled. *All The Pasha's Men: Mehmed Ali, His Army and the Making of Modern Egypt.* Cambridge, U.K.: Cambridge Univ. Press, 1997.

———. "The Anatomy of Justice: Forensic Medicine and Criminal Law in Nineteenth-Century Egypt." *Islamic Law and Society* 6 (1999): 224–71.

———. "Medicine and Power: Towards a Social History of Medicine in Nineteenth-Century Egypt." *Cairo Papers in Social Science* 23, no. 2 (Summer 2000): 15–62.

———. "An Olfactory Tale of Two Cities: Cairo in the Nineteenth Century." In *Historians in Cairo: Essays in Honor of George Scanlon,* edited by Jill Edwards, 155–89. Cairo: American Univ. in Cairo Press, 2002.

———. "The Police and the People in Nineteenth-Century Egypt." *Die Welt des Islams* 39 (1999): 341–77.

———. "Prostitution in Nineteenth-Century Egypt." In *Outside In: On the Margins of the Modern Middle East,* edited by Eugene Rogan, 77–103. London: I. B. Tauris, 2001.

———. "Toward a Social History of Modern Alexandria." In *Alexandria, Real and Imagined,* edited by Anthony Hirst and Michael Silk, 281–305. Burlington, Vt.: Ashgate, 2004.

———. "Women, Medicine and Power in Nineteenth-Century Egypt." In *Remaking Women: Feminism and Modernity in the Middle East,* edited by Lila Abu-Lughod, 35–72. Princeton, N.J.: Princeton Univ. Press, 1998.

Faroqhi, Suraiya. *Towns and Townsmen of Ottoman Anatolia: Trade, Crafts, and Food Production in an Urban Setting, 1520–1650.* Cambridge, U.K.: Cambridge Univ. Press, 1984.

Findley, Carter Vaughn. "The Tanzimat." In *The Cambridge History of Turkey: Turkey in the Modern World,* edited by Reşat Kasaba, vol. 4, 11–37. Cambridge, U.K.: Cambridge Univ. Press, 2008.

Forbes, Thomas Rogers. *Surgeons at the Bailey: English Forensic Medicine to 1878.* New Haven, Conn.: Yale Univ. Press, 1985.

Foucault, Michel. *History of Sexuality.* Vol. 1. Translated by Robert Hurley. New York: Pantheon Books, 1978.

———. "Governmentality." In *The Foucault Effect: Studies in Governmentality,* edited by Graham Burchell, Colin Gordon, and Peter Miller, 87–104. Translated by Rosi Braidotti and revised by Colin Gordon. Chicago: Univ. of Chicago Press, 1991.

Gayol, Sandra. "'Honor Moderno': The Significance of Honor in Fin-de-Siècle Argentina." *Hispanic American Historical Review* 84, no. 3 (2004): 475–98.

Ghazaleh, Pascale. *Masters of the Trade: Crafts and Craftspeople in Cairo, 1750–1850.* Cairo: American Univ. in Cairo Press, 1999.

Giladi, Avner. "Liminal Craft, Exceptional Law: Preliminary Notes on Midwives in Medieval Islamic Writings." *International Journal of Middle Easte Studies* 42 (2010): 185–202.

Gilfoyle, Timoty. *City of Eros: New York City, Prostitution, and the Commercialization of Sex, 1790–1920.* New York: W. W. Norton, 1992.

————. "Prostitutes in History: From Parables of Pornography to Metaphors of Modernity." *The American Historical Review* 104, no. 1 (Feb. 1999): 117–41.

Gilman, Sander L. *Difference and Pathology: Stereotypes of Sexuality, Race and Madness.* Ithaca, N.Y.: Cornell Univ. Press, 1985.

Ginat, Joseph. *Blood Revenge: Family Honor, Mediation, and Outcasting.* Brighton, England: Sussex Academic Press, 1997.

Ginio, Eyal. "Living on the Margins of Charity: Coping with Poverty in an Ottoman Provincial City." In *Poverty and Charity in Middle Eastern Contexts,* edited by Michael Bonner, Mine Ener and Amy Singer, 165–84. Albany: State Univ. of New York Press, 2003.

Ginzburg, Carlo. *The Cheese and the Worms: The Cosmos of a Sixteenth-Century Miller.* Translated by John Tedeschi and Anne C. Tedeschi. Baltimore: Johns Hopkins Univ. Press, 1980.

————. *Clues, Myths, and the Historical Method.* Translated by John Tedeschi and Anne C. Tedeschi. Baltimore: Johns Hopkins Univ. Press, 1989.

Gran, Peter. "Modern Middle East History beyond Oriental Despotism, World History beyond Hegel: An Agenda Article." In *New Frontiers in the Social History of the Middle East,* edited by Enid Hill, 162–98. Cairo: American Univ. in Cairo Press, 2002.

————. "Upper Egypt in Modern History: A 'Southern Question'?" In *Upper Egypt: Identity and Change,* edited by Nicholas Hopkins and Reem Saad, 79–96. Cairo: American Univ. in Cairo Press, 2005.

Guha, Ranajit. *Elementary Aspects of Peasant Insurgency in Colonial India.* Delhi: Oxford Univ. Press, 1983.

————. "The Prose of Counter-Insurgency." In *Subaltern Studies II: Writings on South Asian History and Society,* 1–42. Delhi: Oxford Univ. Press, 1983.

————. "Some Aspects of the Historiography of Colonial India." In *Selected Subaltern Studies,* edited by Ranajit Guha and Gayatri Chakravorty Spivak, 37–45. New York: Oxford Univ. Press, 1988.

Guy, Donna J. *Sex and Danger in Buenos Aires: Prostitution, Family, and Nation in Argentina.* Lincoln: Univ. of Nebraska Press, 1991.

Al-Halabi, Ibrahim ibn Muhammad ibn Ibrahim. *Multaqa al-Abhur.* Beirut: Mu'assasat al-Risalah, 1989.

Hanley, Will. "Foreignness and Localness in Alexandria, 1880–1914." PhD diss., Princeton Univ., 2007.

———. "Second-Rate Foreigners: Algerians and Maltese in Alexandria, 1880–1914." Middle Eastern Studies Association Annual Meeting, Washington, D.C., 2005.

Hanna, Nelly. "The Administration of Courts in Ottoman Egypt." In *The State and its Servants: Administration in Egypt from Ottoman Times to the Present,* edited by Nelly Hanna, 44–59. Cairo: Cairo Univ. Press, 1995.

———. "Slave Women and Concubines in Ottoman Egypt." In *Beyond the Exotic: Women's Histories in Islamic Societies,* edited by Amira El Azhary Sonbol, 119–30. Syracuse, N.Y.: Syracuse Univ. Press, 2005.

———. *An Urban History of Bulaq in the Mamluk and Ottoman Periods.* Cairo: Institut français d'archéologie orientale, 1983.

Hasan, Manar. "The Politics of Honor: Patriarchy, the State and the Murder of Women in the Name of Family Honor." In *Israeli Family and Community: Women's Time,* edited by Hannah Naveh, 1–37. London: Vallentine Mitchell, 2003.

Hatem, Mervat F. "The Professionalization of Health and the Control of Women's Bodies as Modern Governmentalities in Nineteenth-Century Egypt." In *Women in the Ottoman Empire: Middle Eastern Women in the Early Modern Era,* edited by Madeline C. Zilfi, 66–80. Leiden: E. J. Brill, 1997.

Hattox, Ralph S. *Coffee and Coffeehouses: The Origins of a Social Beverage in the Medieval Near East.* Seattle: Univ. of Washington Press, 1985.

Hershatter, Gail. *Dangerous Pleasures: Prostitution and Modernity in Twentieth-Century Shanghai.* Berkeley: Univ. of California Press, 1997.

Heyd, Uriel. *Studies in Old Ottoman Criminal Law.* Oxford: Oxford Univ. Press, 1973.

Hilal, 'Imad. *Al-Baghaya fi Misr: Dirasa Ta'rikhiyya Ijtima'iyya, 1834–1949.* Cairo: al-'Arabi li-l-Nashr wa-l-Tawzi', 2001.

———. *Al-Raqiq fi Misr fi al-Qarn al-Tasi' 'Ashar.* Cairo: al-'Arabi, 1999.

Hinds, Martin, and el-Said al-Badawi. *A Dictionary of Egyptian Arabic.* Beirut: Librarie du Liban, 1986.

Hourani, Albert. *Arabic Thought in the Liberal Age, 1798–1939.* London: Oxford Univ. Press, 1970.

Hunwick, John. "Islamic Law and Polemics over Race and Slavery in North and West Africa (16th–19th Century)." In *Slavery in the Islamic Middle East,* edited by Shaun E. Marmon, 43–68. Princeton, N.J.: Markus Wiener, 1999.

———. "The Same but Different: Africans in Slavery in the Mediterranean Muslim World." In *The African Diaspora in the Mediterranean Muslim World,* edited by

John Hunwick and Eve Troutt Powell, ix–xxiv. Princeton, N.J.: Markus Wiener, 2002.

Hunwick, John, and Eve Troutt Powell, eds. *The African Diaspora in the Mediterranean Muslim World.* Princeton, N.J.: Markus Wiener, 2002.

Hunter, F. Robert. *Egypt Under the Khedives 1805–1879: From Household Government to Modern Bureaucracy.* Pittsburgh, Pa.: Univ. of Pittsburgh Press, 1984.

———. "State-Society Relations in Nineteenth-Century Egypt: The Years of Transition, 1848–79." *Middle Eastern Studies* 36, no. 3 (July 2000): 145–59.

Ibn 'Abidin, Muhammad Amin bin 'Umar. *Radd al-Muhtar 'ala al-Durr al-Mukhtar Sharh Tanwir al-Absar.* Beirut: Dar al-Kutub al-'Ilmiyya.

Ibn Sina, Abu 'Ali al-Husayn bin 'Ali. *Al-Qanun fi al-Tibb.* Baghdad: al-Muthanna, 1970.

İlkkaracan, Pınar, ed. *Women and Sexuality in Muslim Societies.* Istanbul: Women for Women's Human Rights, 2000.

Imber, Colin. *Studies in Ottoman History and Law.* Istanbul: Isis, 1996.

Inhorn, Marcia. *Quest for Conception: Gender, Infertility, and Egyptian Medical Traditions.* Philadelphia: Univ. of Pennsylvania Press, 1994.

Isma'il, 'Abd al-Rahman. *Kitab Tibb al-Rukka.* Cairo: al-Bahiyya, 1892.

Jallad, Filib. *Qamus al-Idara wa-l-Qada'.* Alexandria: al-Matba'a al-Bukhariya, 1892.

Jennings, Ronald C. *Studies on Ottoman Social History in the Sixteenth and Seventeenth Centuries: Women, Zimmis and Sharia Courts in Kayseri, Cyprus and Trabzon.* Istanbul: Isis, 1999.

Katz, Marion. "The Problem of Abortion in Medieval Fiqh." In *Islamic Ethics of Life: Abortion, War, and Euthanasia,* edited by John Brockopp, 25–50. Columbia: Univ. of South Carolina Press, 2003.

Kolsky, Elizabeth. "'The Body Evidencing the Crime': Gender, Law and Medicine in Colonial India." PhD diss., Columbia Univ., 2002.

Kosabi, Meera. "Gender Reform and Competing State Controls over Women: The Rakhmabai Case (1884–1888)." *Contributions to Indian Sociology* 29 (1995): 239–64.

Kozma, Liat. "Negotiating Virginity: Narratives of Defloration from Late Nineteenth-Century Egypt." *Comparative Studies of South Asia, Africa and the Middle East* 24, no. 1 (2004): 55–65.

Kressel, Gideon M. "Shame and Gender." *Anthropological Quarterly* 65, no. 1 (1992): 34–46.

Kuhnke, LaVerne. *Lives at Risk: Public Health in Nineteenth-Century Egypt.* Berkeley: Univ. of California Press, 1990.

Lane, Edward William. *An Arabic-English Lexicon.* Beirut: Librarie du Liban, 1980.

———. *The Manners & Customs of the Modern Egyptians.* London: J. M. Dent, [1908].

Larguèche, Abdelhamid. *Les Ombres de Tunis: Pauvres, Marginaux et Minorités aux XVIIIe et XIXe Siècles*. Paris: Arcantères, 2000.

Larguèche, Abdelhamid, and Dalenda Bouzgarrou-Larguèche. *Marginales en Terre d'Islam*. Tunis: Cérès, 1992.

Lewis, I. M., Ahmed al-Safi, and Sayyid Hurreiz, eds. *Women's Medicine: The Zar-Bori Cult in Africa and Beyond*. Edinburgh: Edinburgh Univ. Press, 1991.

al-Mahdi, Muhammad ibn Muhammad al-'Abbasi. *Al-Fatawa al-Mahdiyya fi al-Waqa'i' al-Misriyya*. Cairo: al-Matba'a al-Azhariyya, 1883 or 1884–87.

Mahfouz, Naguib. *The History of Medical Education in Egypt*. Cairo: Bulaq, 1935.

Mahmood, Saba. *Politics of Piety: The Islamic Revival and the Feminist Subject*. Princeton, N.J.: Princeton Univ. Press, 2005.

Mani, Lata. *Contentious Traditions: The Debate on Sati in Colonial India*. Berkeley: Univ. of California Press, 1998.

Marcus, Abraham. "Privacy in Eighteenth-Century Aleppo: The Limits of Cultural Ideas." *International Journal of Middle Eastern Studies* 18 (1986): 165–83.

———. *The Middle East on the Eve of Modernity: Aleppo in the Eighteenth Century*. New York: Columbia Univ. Press, 1989.

al-Marghinani, 'Ali ibn Abi Bakr. *The Hedaya, Guide: A Commentary on the Mussulman Laws*. Translated by Charles Hamilton. Lahore: New Book, [1957].

Marmon, Shaun E., ed. *Slavery in the Islamic Middle East*. Princeton, N.J.: Markus Wiener, 1999.

Masud, Muhammad Khalid, Brinkley Messick, and David S. Powers, eds. *Islamic Legal Interpretation: Muftis and their Fatwas*. Cambridge, Mass.: Harvard Univ. Press, 1996.

Al-Mawsu'a al-Fiqhiyya. Kuwait: Ministry of Religious Endowments and Islamic Affairs, 1990.

Mernissi, Fatima. "Virginity and Patriarchy." *Women's Studies International Forum* 5, no. 2 (1982): 183–94.

Messick, Brinkley. *The Calligraphic State: Textual Domination and History in a Muslim Society*. Berkeley: Univ. of California, 1996.

Miller, Ruth A. *Legislating Authority: Sin and Crime in the Ottoman Empire and Turkey*. New York: Routledge, 2005.

Mitchell, Timothy. *Colonising Egypt*. Cambridge, U.K.: Cambridge Univ. Press, 1988.

———. "The Limits of the State: Beyond Statist Approaches and their Critics." *The American Political Science Review* 85, no. 1 (Mar. 1991): 77–96.

Mowafi, Reda. *Slavery, Slave Trade, and Abolition Attempts in Egypt and the Sudan, 1820–1882*. [Stockholm]: Esselte Studium, 1981.

Mubarak, ʿAli. *al-Khitat al-Tawfiqiyya al-Jadida li-Misr al-Qahira wa-Muduniha wa-Biladiha al-Qadima wa-l-Shahira.* Bulaq Misr: al-Matbaʿa al-Kubrʿ al-Amiriyya, (1304–6) 1886–89.

Musallam, B. F. *Sex and Society in Islam: Birth Control before the Nineteenth Century.* Cambridge, U.K.: Cambridge Univ. Press, 1983.

el-Nahal, Galal H. *The Judicial Administration of Ottoman Egypt in the Seventeenth Century.* Minneapolis: Bibliotheca Islamica, 1979.

Nair, Janaki. "Prohibited Marriage: State Protection and the Child Wife." *Contributions to Indian Sociology* 29 (1995): 157–86.

Natvig, Richard. "Some Notes on the History of the *Zar* Cult in Egypt." In *Women's Medicine: The Zar-Bori Cult in Africa and Beyond,* edited by I. M. Lewis, Ahmed al-Safi, and Sayyid Hurreiz, 178–88. Edinburgh: Edinburgh Univ. Press, 1991.

Odem, Mary E. *Delinquent Daughters: Protecting and Policing Adolescent Female Sexuality in the United States, 1885–1920.* Chapel Hill: Univ. of North Carolina Press, 1995.

O'Hanlon, Rosalind. "Recovering the Subject: Subaltern Studies and Histories of Resistance in Colonial South Asia." *Modern Asian Studies* 22 (1988): 189–224.

O'Malley, Pat. "From Feudal Honour to Bourgeois Reputation: Ideology, Law and the Rise of Industrial Capitalism." *Sociology* 15 (1981): 79–93.

Owen, Roger. *Cotton and the Egyptian Economy, 1820–1914: A Study in Trade and Development.* Oxford: Clarendon, 1969.

———. *The Middle East in the World Economy, 1800–1914.* New York: Methuen, 1981.

Panzac, Daniel. "Médecine Révolutionnaire et Révolution de la Médecine dan l'Égypte de Muhammad Ali: Le Dr. Clot-Bey.» *Revue des Mondes Musulmans et de la Méditerranée,* no. 52/53 (1989): 95–110.

Petrov, Milen. "Everyday Forms of Compliance: Subaltern Commentaries on Ottoman Reform." *Comparative Studies in Society and History* 46 (2004): 730–59.

Parla, Ayşe. "The Honor of the State: Virginity Examinations in Turkey." *Feminist Studies* 27, no. 1 (Spring 2001): 65–88.

Patai, Raphael. *The Arab Mind.* New York: Scribner, 1976.

Peirce, Leslie. "Le Dilemme de Fatma: Crime Sexuel et Culture Juridique dans une Cour Ottomane au Début des Temps Modernes." *Annales* 53 (1998): 291–319.

———. *The Imperial Harem.* New York: Oxford Univ. Press, 1993.

———. *Morality Tales: Law and Gender in the Ottoman Court of Aintab.* Berkeley: Univ. of California Press, 2003.

Peters, Rudolph. "Administrators and Magistrates: The Development of a Secular Judiciary in Egypt, 1842–1871." *Die Welt des Islam* 39, no. 3 (1999): 378–97.

————. "The Infatuated Greek: Social and Legal Boundaries in Nineteenth-Century Egypt." *Égypte/Monde Arabe* 34 (1998): 53–65.

————. "Islamic and Secular Criminal Law in Nineteenth-Century Egypt: The Role and Function of the Qadi." *Islamic Law and Society* 4, no. 1 (1997): 70–90.

————. "Muhammad al-'Abbasi al-Mahdi (d. 1897), Grand Mufti of Egypt, and His al-Fatawa al-Mahdiyya." *Islamic Law and Society* 1 (1994): 66–82.

————. "Prisons and Marginalisation in Nineteenth-Century Egypt." In *Outside In: On the Margins of the Modern Middle East,* edited by Eugene Rogan, 31–52. London: I. B. Tauris, 2002.

Pollard, Lisa. *Nurturing the Nation: The Family Politics of Modernizing, Colonizing and Liberating Egypt, 1805–1923.* Berkeley: California Univ. Press, 2005.

Poole, Sophia. *The Englishwoman in Egypt: Letters from Cairo Written During a Residence There in 1842–46.* Edited by Azza Kararah. Cairo: American Univ. in Cairo Press, 2003.

Poonacha, Veena. "Redefining Gender Relations: The Imprint of the Colonial State on the Coorg/Kodava Norms of Marriage and Sexuality." *Contributions to Indian Sociology* 29 (1995): 39–64.

Prakash, Gyan. "Subaltern Studies as Postcolonial Criticism." *American Historical Review* 99 (1994): 1475–90.

Quataert, Donald. *The Ottoman Empire, 1700–1922.* Cambridge, U.K.: Cambridge Univ. Press, 2005.

Quraishi, Asifa. "Her Honour: An Islamic Critique of the Rape Provisions in Pakistan's Ordinance on *Zina.*" *Islamic Studies* 38, no. 3 (1999): 403–31.

al-Rashidi, Ahmad. *Bahjat al-Ru'asa' fi Amrad al-Nisa'.* Bulaq: Dar al-Tiba'a al-'Amira, 1844.

————. *Kitab al-Wilada.* Bulaq: Dar al-Tiba'a al-'Amira, 1842.

Raymond, André. *Le Caire.* [Paris]: Fayard, 1993.

Reimer, Michael J. *Colonial Bridgehead: Government and Society in Alexandria, 1807–1882.* Boulder: Westview, 1997.

Robinson-Dunn, Diane. *The Harem, Slavery and British Imperial Culture: Anglo-Muslim Relations in the Late Nineteenth Century.* Manchester: Manchester Univ. Press, 2006.

Rodenbeck, John. "'Awalim; or, the Persistence of Error." In *Historians in Cairo: Essays in Honor of George Scanlon,* edited by Jill Edwards, 107–21. Cairo: American Univ. in Cairo Press, 2002.

Rogan, Eugene, ed. *Outside In: On the Margins of the Modern Middle East.* London: I. B. Tauris, 2001.

Rubin, Avi. "Ottoman Modernity: The Nizamiye Courts in the Late Nineteenth Century." PhD diss., Harvard Univ., 2006.

Ruiz, Mario. "Intimate Disputes, Illicit Violence: Gender, Law, and The State in Colonial Egypt, 1849–1923." PhD diss., Univ. of Michigan, 2004.

al-Sa'dawi, Nawwal. *The Hidden Face of Eve*. Translated by Sherif Hetata. London: Zed Books, 2007.

Salim, Latifa Muhammad. *Al-Nizam al-Qada'i al-Misri al-Hadith*. [Cairo]: al-Hay'a al-Misriyya al-'Amma li-l-Kitab, 2000–2001.

Sami, Amin. *Taqwim al-Nil wa-Asma' man Tawwallaw Amr Misr wa-Muddat Hukmihim 'alayha wa-Mulahaza Ta'rikhiyya 'an Ahwal al-Khilafa al-'Amma wa-Shu'un Misr al-Khassa 'an al-Mudda al-Munhasira bayna al-Sana al-Ula wa-Sanat 1333 al-Hijriyya (622–1915 Miladiyya)*. Cairo: al-Matba'a al-Amiriyya, 1916–36.

Sangster, Joan. *Regulating Girls and Women: Sexuality, Family and the Law in Ontario, 1920–1960*. Ontario: Oxford Univ. Press, 2001.

Schacht, Joseph. *An Introduction to Islamic Law*. Oxford: Clarendon, 1966.

Semerdjian, Vivian Elyse. "Sinful Professions: Illegal Occupations of Women in Ottoman Aleppo, Syria." *Hawwa* 1, no. 1 (2003): 60–85.

Sen, Purna. "Honour, Culture and Alliances." *Honour: Crimes, Paradigms and Violence against Women*, edited by Lynn Welchman and Sara Hossain, 42–63. London: Zed Books, 2005.

Shaham, Ron. *The Expert Witness in Islamic Courts: Medicine and Crafts in the Service of Law*. Chicago: Univ. of Chicago Press, 2010.

———. *Family and the Courts in Modern Egypt: A Study Based on Decisions by the Shari'a Courts 1900–1955*. Leiden: E. J. Brill, 1997.

Shalabi, Hilmi Ahmad. *Al-Muwazzafun fi Misr fi 'Asr Muhammad 'Ali*. [Cairo]: al-Hay'a al-Misriyya al-'Amma li-l-Kitab, 1989.

Shalhoub-Kevorkian, Nadera. "Towards a Cultural Definition of Rape: Dilemmas in Dealing with Rape Victims in Palestinian Society." *Women's Studies International Forum* 22, no. 2 (1999): 157–73.

al-Shayyal, Jamal al-Din. *Ta'rikh al-Tarjama wa-l-Haraka al-Thaqafiyya fi 'Asr Muhammad 'Ali*. [Cairo]: Dar al-Fikr al-'Arabi, 1951.

Sobhy, Gorgy P. G. "Customs and Superstitions of the Modern Egyptians Connected with Pregnancy and Childbirth." *Records of the Egyptian Government School of Medicine* 2 (1904): 101–6.

Sonbol, Amira El Azhary, ed. *Beyond the Exotic: Women's Histories in Islamic Societies*. Syracuse, N.Y.: Syracuse Univ. Press, 2005.

———. *The Creation of a Medical Profession in Egypt, 1800–1922*. Syracuse, N.Y.: Syracuse Univ. Press, 1991.

———. "Rape and Law in Ottoman and Modern Egypt." In *Women in the Ottoman Empire: Middle Eastern Women in the Early Modern Era,* edited by Madeline C. Zilfi, 214–31. Leiden: E. J. Brill, 1997.

Southworth, Alvan S. *Four Thousand Miles of African Travel: A Personal Record of a Journey up the Nile and through the Soudan to the Confines of Central Africa, Embracing a Discussion of the Sources of the Nile, and an Examination of the Slave Trade.* New York: Baker, Pratt, 1875.

Spivak, Gayatri Chakravorty. "Can the Subaltern Speak?" In *Marxism and the Interpretation of Culture,* edited by Cary Nelson and Larry Grossberg, 271–313. Urbana: Univ. of Illinois Press, 1988.

———. "Subaltern Studies: Deconstructing Historiography." In *Selected Subaltern Studies,* edited by Gayatri Chakravorty Spivak and Ranajit Guha, 1–32. New York: Oxford Univ. Press, 1988.

Stewart, Frank. *Honor.* Chicago: Chicago Univ. Press, 1994.

Stock-Morton, Phyllis. "Control and Limitation of Midwives in Modern France: The Example of Marseille." *Journal of Women's History* 8, no. 1 (Spring 1996): 60–94.

Stoler, Ann Laura. *Along the Archival Grain: Epistemic Anxieties and Colonial Commonsense.* Princeton: Princeton Univ. Press, 2009.

———. *Race and the Education of Desire: Foucault's History of Sexuality and the Colonial Order of Things.* Durham, N.C.: Duke Univ. Press, 1997.

———. "Colonial Archives and the Art of Governance: On the Content in the Form." In *Archives, Documentation, and Institutions of Social Memory: Essays from the Sawyer Seminar,* edited by Francis Xavier Blouin and William G. Rosenberg, 269–79. Ann Arbor: Univ. of Michigan Press, 2007.

Tarabulusi, Muhammad Kamil ibn Mustafa. *Al-Fatawa al-Kamiliyya fi al-Hawadith al-Tarabulusiyya ʿala Madhhab al-Imam Abi Hanifa al-Nuʿman ʿalayhi Saha'ib al-Rahma wa-al-Ridwan.* Cairo: Matbaʿat Muhammad Afandi Mustafa, 1896.

Thompson, Elizabeth. "Public and Private in Middle Eastern Women's History." *Journal of Women's History* 15, no. 1 (Spring 2003): 52–69.

Toledano, Ehud R. *As if Silent and Absent: Bonds of Enslavement in the Islamic Middle East.* New Haven, Conn.: Yale Univ. Press, 2007.

———. "Late Ottoman Concepts of Slavery (1830s–1880s)." *Poetics Today* 14, no. 3 (Fall 1993): 477–506.

———. "Slave Dealers, Pregnancy, Abortion, and the World of Women: The Story of a Circassian Slave-girl in Mid-Nineteenth-Century Cairo." *Slavery and Abolition* 2, no. 1 (1981): 53–68.

————. *Slavery and Abolition in the Ottoman Middle East.* Seattle: Univ. of Washington Press, 1998.

————. "Social and Economic Change in the 'Long Nineteenth Century.'" In *The Cambridge History of Egypt,* edited by Martin Daly, vol. 2, 252–84. Cambridge, U.K.: Cambridge Univ. Press, 1998.

————. *State and Society in Mid-Nineteenth-Century Egypt.* Cambridge, U.K.: Cambridge Univ. Press, 1990.

Troutt Powell, Eve. *A Different Shade of Colonialism: Egypt, Great Britain and the Mastery of the Sudan.* Berkeley: Univ. of California Press, 2003.

————. "The Tools of the Master: Slavery and Empire in Nineteenth-Century Egypt." *Occasional Papers of the School of Social Science, Institute for Advanced Study.* Sept. 2002, paper no. 13.

————. "Will that Subaltern Ever Speak? Finding African Slaves in the Historiography of the Middle East." In *Middle East Historiographies: Narrating the Twentieth Century,* edited by Israel Gershoni, Amy Singer, and Y. Hakan Erdem, 242–61. Seattle: Univ. of Washington Press, 2006.

Tucker, Judith E. "And God Knows Best: The Fatwa as a Source for the History of Gender in the Arab World." In *Beyond the Exotic: Women's Histories in Islamic Societies,* edited by Amira El Azhary Sonbol, 165–79. Syracuse: Syracuse Univ. Press, 2005.

————. "Decline of the Family Economy in Mid-Nineteenth-Century Egypt." *Arab Studies Quarterly* 1, no. 3 (1979): 245–71.

————. *In the House of the Law: Gender and Islamic Law in Ottoman Syria and Palestine.* Berkeley: Univ. of California Press, 1998.

————. "Problems in the Historiography of Women in the Middle East: The Case of Nineteenth-Century Egypt." *International Journal of Middle Eastern Studies* 15 (1983): 321–36.

————. *Women in Nineteenth-Century Egypt.* Cambridge, U.K.: Cambridge Univ. Press, 1985.

Van Niewkerk, Karin. *A Trade Like Any Other: Female Singers and Dancers in Egypt.* Austin: Univ. of Texas Press, 1995.

Vaux, B. Carra de, J. Schacht, and A. M. Goichon. *"Hadd." Encyclopedia of Islam.* Vol. 3, 20a. 2nd ed. Leiden: Brill, 1971.

Velpeau, Alfred. *Traité élémentaire de l'art des accouchemens: ou principes de tokologie et d'embryologie.* Paris: J. B. Baillière, 1829. Translated by Charles D. Meigs as *An Elementary Treatise on Midwifery; or, Principles of Tokology and Embryology.* Philadelphia: Lindsay and Blakiston, 1845.

Visweswaran, Kamala. "Small Speeches, Subaltern Gender: Nationalist Ideology and its Historiography." *Subaltern Studies* 9 (1996): 83–125.

Walker, John. *Folk Medicine in Modern Egypt: Being the Relevant Parts of the Tibb al-Rukka or Old Wives' Medicine of 'Abd al-Rahman Isma'il.* London: Luzac, 1934.

Walkowitz, Judith R. *Prostitution and Victorian Society: Women, Class, and the State.* Cambridge, U.K.: Cambridge Univ. Press, 1982.

Walz, Terence. "Black Slavery in Egypt." In *Slaves and Slavery in Muslim Africa,* edited by John Ralph Willis, vol. 2, 137–60. London: Frank Cass, 1985.

Wehbi, Samantha. "Women with Nothing to Lose—Marriageability and Women's Perceptions of Rape and Consent in Contemporary Beirut." *Women's Studies International Forum* 25, no. 2 (2002): 287–300.

Welchman, Lynn, and Sara Hossain, eds. *"Honour": Crimes, Paradigms, and Violence against Women.* New York: Zed Books, 2005.

White, Luise. *The Comforts of Home: Prostitution in Colonial Nairobi.* Chicago: Univ. of Chicago Press, 1990.

Wilson, Jon E. "Subjects and Agents in the History of Imperialism and Resistance." In *Powers of the Secular Modern: Talal Asad and His Interlocutors,* edited by Charles Hirschkind and David Scott, 180–205. Stanford, Calif.: Stanford Univ. Press, 2006.

Yazbak, Mahmud. "Minor Marriages and *Khiyar Al-Bulugh* in Ottoman Palestine: A Note on Women's Strategies in a Patriarchal Society." *Islamic Law and Society* 9, no. 3 (2002): 386–409.

Zaghlul, Ahmad Fathi. *Al-Muhama.* Cairo: Matba'at al-Ma'arif 1900.

Ze'evi, Dror. "Changes in Legal-Sexual Discourses: Sex Crimes in the Ottoman Empire." *Continuity and Change* 16, no. 2 (2001): 219–42.

———. "The Use of Ottoman Shari'a Court Records as a Source for Middle Eastern Social History: A Reappraisal." *Islamic Law and Society* 5, no. 1 (Feb. 1998): 35–57.

———. "Women in Seventeenth-Century Jerusalem: Western and Indigenous Perspectives." *International Journal of Middle East Studies* 27 (May 1995): 157–73.

Zia, Afiya Shehrbano. "Rape in Pakistan: *Zina* Laws—Legalities and Loopholes." In *Women and Sexuality in Muslim Societies,* edited by Pınar İlkkaracan, 327–39. Istanbul: Women for Women's Human Rights, 2000.

Zilfi, Medline. "Servants, Slaves, and the Domestic Order in the Ottoman Middle East." *Hawwa* 2/1 (2004): 1–33.

———. "Thoughts on Women and Slavery in the Ottoman Era and Historical Sources." In *Beyond the Exotic: Women's Histories in Islamic Societies,* edited by Amira El Azhary Sonbol, 131–38. Syracuse: Syracuse Univ. Press, 2005.

Index